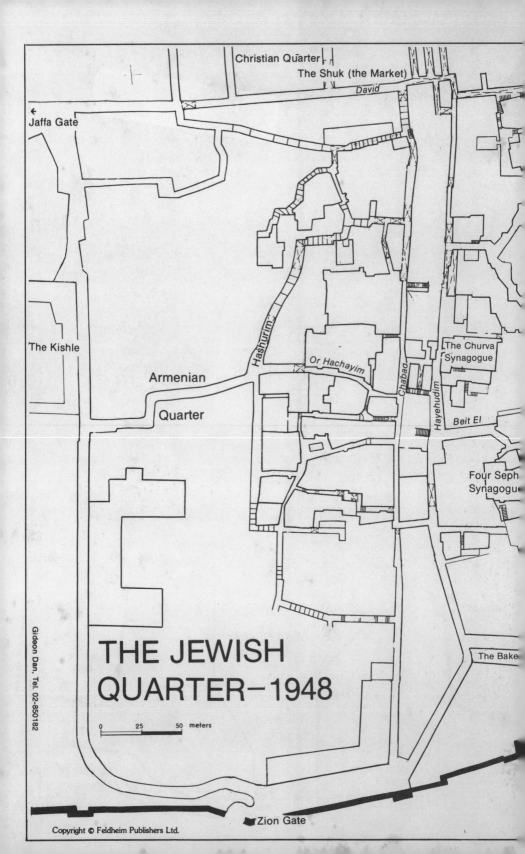

Christian Quarter

The Shuk (the Market)

David

← Jaffa Gate

The Kishle

Armenian

Quarter

Hashurim

Or Hachayim

Chabad

Hayehudim

The Churva Synagogue

Beit El

Four Seph. Synagogue

The Bake

THE JEWISH QUARTER – 1948

0   25   50   meters

Gideon Dan, Tel. 02-850182

◄ Zion Gate

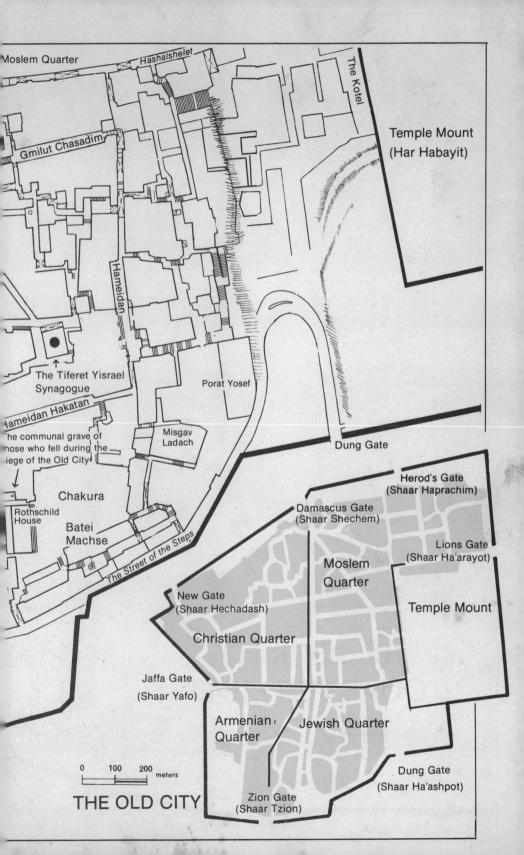

Moslem Quarter

Hashalshelet

The Kotel

Temple Mount
(Har Habayit)

Gmilut Chasadim

Hameidan

The Tiferet Yisrael
Synagogue

Porat Yosef

Hameidan Hakatan

The communal grave of
those who fell during the
siege of the Old City

Misgav
Ladach

Dung Gate

Chakura

Herod's Gate
(Shaar Haprachim)

Rothschild
House

Damascus Gate
(Shaar Shechem)

Batei
Machse

Lions Gate
(Shaar Ha'arayot)

Moslem
Quarter

The Street of the Steps

New Gate
(Shaar Hechadash)

Temple Mount

Christian Quarter

Jaffa Gate
(Shaar Yafo)

Armenian
Quarter

Jewish Quarter

0   100   200
                   meters

Dung Gate
(Shaar Ha'ashpot)

THE OLD CITY

Zion Gate
(Shaar Tzion)

FOREVER MY
JERUSALEM

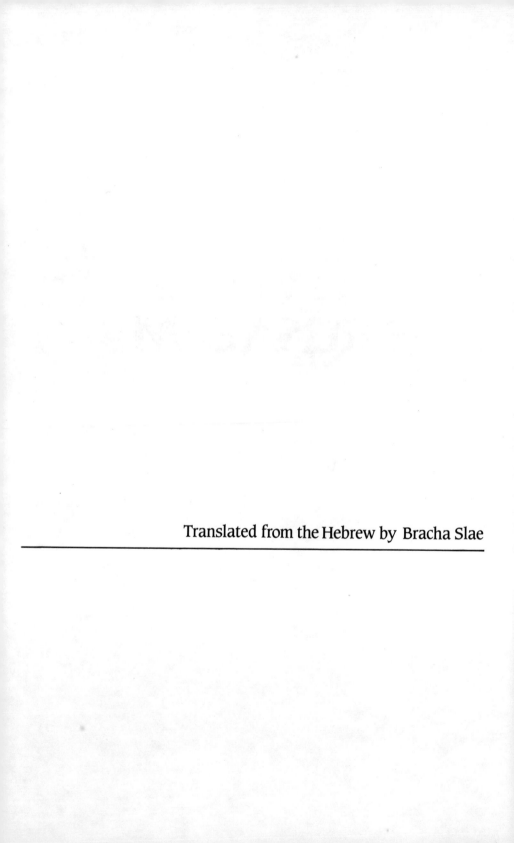

Translated from the Hebrew by Bracha Slae

Puah Shteiner

FOREVER MY
JERUSALEM

a personal account
of the siege and surrender of
Jerusalem's Old City in 1948

Feldheim Publishers   *Jerusalem / New York*

A glossary of Hebrew and Yiddish words appears at the back of the book.

First Published 1987
Second printing 1988

Hardcover edition: ISBN 0-87306-394-5
Paperback edition: ISBN 0-87306-469-0

Philipp Feldheim, Inc. Feldheim Publishers, Ltd.
200 Airport Executive Park POB 6525 / Jerusalem, Israel
Spring Valley, NY 10977

Printed in Israel

History of the Period:
The British Mandate
1917-1948

In 1917-18, towards the end of World War I, Eretz Yisrael (Palestine) was conquered by the British, bringing to an end four hundred years of Ottoman-Turkish rule. In 1920, British sovereignty over Palestine was officially recognized in the form of a mandate granted to Great Britain by the League of Nations. Britain would manage the country's affairs until such time as the native inhabitants — Jews and Arabs — reached political maturity and were able to govern themselves independently.

This British Mandate was to have been based on the spirit and principles of the Balfour Declaration of November 1917, which advocated "the establishment in Palestine of a national home for the Jewish people." The Arabs of Palestine and of the neighboring countries, however, emphatically opposed the Balfour Declaration. Not only did they use all the conventional political means at their disposal to protest the turn of events, they also resorted to unrestrained violence. They attacked every new Jewish settlement that arose and organized bloody riots in cities with large Jewish populations, such as Jerusalem, Hebron, Safed and Tiberias, during the years 1920, 1921, 1929, and from 1936 to 1939. During these attacks, many of which caught the local Jewish communities totally unprepared, Jewish homes and institutions were pillaged and set afire;

5

women and children were brutally attacked; and dozens of Jews were slaughtered.

Torn between their conflicting promises to the Jews and to the Arabs, the British finally succumbed to Arab pressure and did all they could to prevent the Jewish population from becoming a majority in the country. A series of "white papers" was issued, and laws limiting the rights of Jews to buy land or to immigrate to Eretz Yisrael were enacted — this despite the Nazi threat to European Jewry. The white paper of 1939, just before the outbreak of World War II, restricted the total number of Jews allowed to enter Eretz Yisrael to fifteen thousand annually!

Since this was completely unacceptable to the Jewish community, Aliya Bet — the illegal immigration — was organized, and boatloads of blockade runners reached the coasts of Eretz Yisrael under cover of darkness. While the high hopes aroused by the Balfour Declaration remained unfulfilled, the Jewish population of Eretz Yisrael nevertheless grew from fifty-six thousand to six hundred thousand during the thirty years of British Mandatory government.

THE RESISTANCE MOVEMENTS

To protect Jewish settlements during this time, three different resistance movements arose. The largest, the Hagana (including the Palmach), followed the Jewish leadership's policy at that time — to work for independence by using political pressure and military restraint. In 1931, several revisionist leaders seceded from the Hagana and founded Etzel — the Irgun Tzvai Leumi — whose motto was "Fight terror with terror!"

Both the Hagana and Etzel discontinued their war with the British at the outbreak of World War II. However, a subgroup of Etzel refused to abide by this truce and set up their own movement — Lochamei Herut Israel — Lechi.

After World War II, the Hagana attempted to bring the two "seceding" movements back into the fold. In 1945 the three underground movements united in the framework of the Hebrew Resistance Movement. Even then, Etzel and Lechi still occasionally carried out independent actions of their own, such as the explosion at the King David Hotel. This eventually led to the dissolution of the united resistance movement.

Throughout this period, the British fought the underground movements with all the means at their disposal — from searches and confiscation of weapons to arrest, exile and the death sentence.

THE PARTITION PLAN

Following the Arab riots of 1936, after almost twenty years of prolonged struggle, a British royal commission under Lord Peel was appointed to investigate the situation in Palestine. The solution proposed — partition of Palestine into a Jewish and an Arab state — envisioned the creation of a Jewish state occupying only a small portion of the western bank of the Jordan River. Nevertheless, the partition plan was categorically rejected by all Arab factions, whereas the Jewish Agency saw in it a basis for negotiations. Almost ten years later, on November 29, 1947, the famous United Nations vote on the fate of Palestine took place, adopting the proposal for partition of Palestine and the establishment of a Jewish state.

THE WAR OF INDEPENDENCE
AND EVENTS LEADING UP TO IT

All over the country, Jewish settlements and main roads were attacked by Arab gangs the very day after the U.N. vote. For five and a half months, until the last British soldier left the country on May 15, 1948, the country suffered from bloody riots and upheavals. Following the declaration of its independence on May 14, the newborn State of Israel was attacked by seven Arab states bent on wiping it out and pushing its 600,000 Jewish inhabitants "into the sea."

A fierce battle for control of the roads — especially the road from Tel Aviv to Jerusalem — was waged. The entire Jewish population of Jerusalem, at that time almost twenty percent of the total population of the country, came under siege. From April 1948 until the opening of the Burma Road and the first cease-fire on June 11, the only food to reach Jerusalem arrived by armed convoy.

Inside the Old City of Jerusalem, the situation was even more serious. Since December 1947 (immediately after the U.N. resolution on Palestine), the Jewish Quarter, which was the only section of the Old City still populated by Jews after the riots of 1936, had been under siege, cut off from all contact with the rest of the country. Only armed convoys, traveling under British military protection, were able to bring food, medicines and clandestine arms supplies to the besieged Jewish Quarter. These convoys also afforded the only means of transportation between the "old" and "new" city, and a last opportunity for many residents to leave their homes in the Jewish Quarter before it was completely cut off on May 15.

By May 15, when the British left the country and war officially broke out, less than two thousand residents were left in the Jewish Quarter, including a large percentage of aged and children, together with some two hundred young Jewish soldiers, most of whom had been "imported" from outside. They had only a minimal amount of arms with which to defend the besieged Quarter against the thirty-three thousand Arab inhabitants of the Old City. Two or three days after war broke out, Arab gangs attacked the quarter, threatening to slaughter each and every Jew there, but the residents and soldiers miraculously succeeded in repelling the attack.

After destroying the Etzion Bloc on May 14, the Arab Legion

headed for the Mount of Olives. On May 19, they arrived and promptly aimed their artillery at the Jewish Quarter, bombarding it day and night. For ten days the besieged Quarter held out, but on May 28, 1948, its defenders surrendered to the Arab Legion. All the males (residents and soldiers, including some of the wounded) and two women were taken to Trans-Jordan as prisoners of war. All weapons were confiscated. Women, children, the aged and the wounded were evacuated to Katamon, a newly captured suburb in southwest Jerusalem.

Whatever had been left of the Jewish Quarter after the two weeks of intensive bombardment was now ravished and plundered by the victorious Arabs. They destroyed most of the remaining buildings, in particular venting their wrath on what was left of the once magnificent synagogues.

For nineteen years, the Jewish Quarter remained under Jordanian jurisdiction. In flagrant violation of the armistice agreement, no Jew was allowed to visit any of the holy sites in the Old City, and certainly not the Kotel Hamaaravi — the Wailing Wall. Only after the miraculous Six Day War were these sites restored to the Jewish people. On June 9, 1967, the entire Old City of Jerusalem and the Temple Mount, including the Wall, were, with the help of God, liberated by the Israeli Defense Forces.

May we live to see the Holy Temple rebuilt speedily in our days. Amen.

Part I

In the
Shadow of
the British
Mandate

1 A New Home in an Old Neighborhood

"You from America?" asked the Arab driver in a heavy, Middle Eastern accent. He was sitting behind the steering wheel of the van as our furniture was loaded onto his truck.

For a moment, a strange expression crossed his face. I shuddered. Where had I seen it before? Suddenly, I was back in those days of long ago.

"You from America," he said again. This time it was a statement of fact, not a question. I looked straight into his eyes.

"No, we're not from America," I answered, my own accent similar to his. "We are from Jerusalem — from the Old City."

The Arab looked from me to my husband Chaim and back again, disbelieving.

"We are from the Old City," I repeated, emphasizing each word. He lowered his eyes and was silent. As we drove down busy Jaffa Road, no one spoke.

Then, a few moments later, he renewed the conversation. "Does your house have stairs?" His face betrayed no emotion; his voice was friendly.

"Not too many."

"Not too many... that's very good," he answered pleasantly, as though nothing had transpired.

We reached Zahal Square, near the Municipality. The Old

City wall towered before us in all its glory, and the driver slowed down, waiting for instructions.

"Doesn't he know where to go?" I wondered.

"Turn left," directed Chaim, and the van passed slowly through Jaffa Gate. My heart began to pound. Ten years after the Six Day War and the liberation of the Old City of Jerusalem, we were finally returning home, to the Jewish Quarter.

* * *

For ten years, we had avidly followed the progress of the restoration of the Old City. Every street, every house that was rebuilt gave us great joy. Nevertheless, I myself had not yet been ready to live there. The memories were too overpowering. As time passed, they dimmed, but then bureaucratic difficulties cropped up. But all that was over now, and we were on the way to our new home.

After winding its way through the narrow streets, the van parked before a paved lane. I got out to open the gate while Chaim helped unload.

It was almost dark, but the children had not yet come. I went up to the top floor of our apartment where, from a tiny window in the hall, one could see part of the main road leading into town. I looked through the window, hoping to catch sight of them.

The road was empty, but I stood there, staring at the extraordinary view. The rooftops and rounded domes of the surrounding houses stretched out before me, and in the dwindling light, I could just make out a small section of the Old City wall adjoining the Zion Gate.

Perhaps it was the twilight hour which awakened my memories. My eyes were glued to the road. It was the same road we had taken then, on that bitter day on the 19th of Iyar, 5708 (May 28th, 1948), but then we had gone in the opposite direction.

14

Then we had left the Jewish Quarter, engulfed in flames, behind us. We — the old men, the women and the children — had reached the blockaded Zion Gate at twilight, the exact same hour as now. My lips whispered a prayer, "Please God, let there be no more wars..."

Just then I spotted a car down the road at the foot of the wall. I shook myself and hurriedly wiped away the tears which had wet my cheeks. The children were coming home.

Amidst much confusion, we set up beds for the two youngest ones. After I dressed them in their pajamas, I picked them up in my arms and carried them both upstairs to the tiny window. Outside, the street lights were shining.

"Do you see the wall out there?" I asked, pointing. "Over there, to the right, is Zion Gate."

"Zion Gate," they repeated after me.

"You, my precious ones, will, please God, never have to flee from there."

"Of course not," answered the eldest of the two.

"You, too, Imma; you won't flee either, will you?" added the younger, watching me and wondering what had moved me so. They hung on to my neck as I led them back downstairs. I sat on the bed and recited the Shema with them, just as my father did when I was their age.

By the time I left their room, the furniture had all been brought in. The living room was full of boxes and crates, and the movers had just gone out. As we walked downstairs to lock the gate after them, one of the men came back. It was the driver. The same strange expression covered his face again as his hand rested on the gate. "When I was a boy," he started in broken Hebrew, "this was my house!" His face was filled with hate.

"And when I was a girl, *my* house was down there!" I said quietly, pointing towards the narrow lane opposite us.

But he only repeated his words, gesturing towards our new house.

I looked at him, trying to estimate his age. He was not a youngster. "He must know what happened here," I thought.

For nineteen years, the Jewish Quarter had lain in ruins. After the liberation of the Old City in 1967, I myself had seen the wanton destruction and desolation in the Quarter, wrought by Arab hands and hatred.

The site where our new house now stood had been a pile of rubble. It was only two or three years since the ruins had been cleared away and foundations for a new building dug. We had followed its construction from the very beginning. I looked around at the stone-paved patio, at the wooden shutters, at the graceful balconies. The house was brand new, although the style was old.

This man, standing here and claiming ownership of this house, must be even more familiar with the facts than I. He was free to come here any time during those nineteen years, while we Jews were completely cut off.

"If this is your house," I wanted to say, "why did you let your people destroy it? And why didn't you rebuild it during those nineteen years?"

The Arab driver stood beside the gate, still waiting for an answer. "When I was a child," I said, emphasizing my words with gestures, "I lived here. This is the *Jewish* Quarter."

"You destroyed it; we rebuilt it," added Chaim. The driver let go of the gate.

"Shalom," he finally said, but this time there was no friendship in his voice.

"Shalom," we answered.

When he left, we did not lock the gate. It was unnecessary. We were filled with a feeling of security and belonging. We had come home.

2 The Old City

It was a lovely summer day. I was sitting on a fence in the large, newly paved Batei Machse Square gazing at the old house I had lived in as a child. From the first floor of the building I could hear the pleasant sing-song of yeshiva students studying Gemara together.

A group of teenagers was sitting on the stairs of the Rothschild building opposite, listening to a short summary of the 1948 War of Independence. I listened too; a few facts, a few numbers, one sentence about the fall of the Jewish Quarter in 1948, and another about its liberation in 1967. The boys and girls got up and continued their tour.

I walked among the children playing in the square. Smiling and full of energy, they ran all around me, holding on to each other until they had formed a long chain. Someone kicked a tin can, and the children began to race for hiding places. At the other end of the square some girls were jumping rope. I looked at them closely. Did they know what had happened here? I moved to a side and stood there for a long time, leaning on the fence, listening to their voices.

"Greetings, Your Majesty!" I heard a little boy call out.

"One, two, three . . . red herring!" yelled a girl from the other side of the square.

These were the very same games we had played here years ago. For a minute I closed my eyes, and instead of Yifat and Shirat, Orly and Dorit, I saw Chana and Rachel, Frieda and Yaffale, Lea, Chava and Batya. Today they must all have children of their own, just as I do. Who knows where they are now?

It is interesting how children's games pass from one generation to the next. There was one game, however, which is no longer played — a game which belonged specifically to our childhood. It incorporated all the features of the headlines of those days: *Maapilim* (illegal Jewish immigrants), the British, members of the Hagana, detention camps . . . I tried to recall the rules, but without much success.

A group of tourists passed by. Smiles flashed; cameras clicked. The guide gave his presentation in English. Once, upon hearing that language, we would have burst out into a loud song:

Aliya should be free!
A state for the Jew;
Shame on the British;
Our flag is white and blue.

In those days, the only people who spoke English were the British soldiers and policemen who made our lives so difficult, and so dangerous. We felt very courageous, singing that song in front of them. Chana used to egg us on.

"Let them burst with anger!" she would say. But they never did. So she would command us to sing louder the next time; maybe someday, all of those soldiers and policemen would really explode and disappear!

* * *

When we first came to the Old City I was only four. We lived there until I was seven and we were forced to evacuate in May 1948, when the Jewish Quarter fell during the War of Independence. Those were difficult years for the entire Jewish population of Palestine, and they left a lasting impression on me.

As I tried to coordinate the dates, I found it hard to believe. Could I be mistaken? Could it really be that so much happened in such a short period? But every time I count, I arrive at the same conclusion. It all took place within three years, between 1945 and 1948. For me, this was a crucial chapter in my life.

It is not quite accurate to say that we first came to live in the Old City in 1945. Both my mother and my father, like their parents and grandparents before them, had been born there.

My father was a fifth-generation Jerusalemite. He was a descendant of Rabbi Eliezer Bergman, one of the first Ashkenazi Jews to settle in the city (in the 1800's). Rabbi Bergman was also a founder of the Kollel Holland Deutschland Landsman-schaft, an organization which built Batei Machse, the first modern housing development within the walls of the Old City. In the difficult days before and after World War I, a time of dire poverty and Arab riots, part of our family left the Old City to search for a livelihood elsewhere. When my parents returned in 1945, not only was my Savta still there, but many of the inhabitants and neighbors in the Jewish Quarter were relatives, descendants of Rabbi Bergman.

The apartment we rented in Batei Machse consisted of a spacious living room and a tiny, three-by-six foot kitchen. Primitive outhouses were at the end of the courtyard and were shared by all the residents in the building. I had never seen a bathtub. We bathed standing up in the laundry tub, with water we had heated in a pail on our *primus* — the simple kerosene stoves then in use in the Middle East. Few people live in one-room apartments today, but in those days, many families did, and it seems to me that people were no less happy than they are now. Perhaps they were even more so...

Our apartment contained all the furniture we needed: a large table and chairs; a varnished, wooden clothes closet; and two high-rise beds, covered by a green spread, which doubled as a sofa in the daytime. Six-year-old Naomi and I slept on folding cots, and Yehudit, our baby, slept in her carriage. Our most precious piece of furniture was Abba's bookcase, filled to capacity with holy books. Imma's good china dishes stood on one shelf of the bookcase, together with her silver candlesticks and Abba's *kiddush* cup. On top of the bookcase stood a handsome clock which my parents had received as a wedding present.

Nothing was lacking, and it never entered my mind that we might be cramped for space. On the contrary, when I would lie down in my folding bed at night, just a little above the uneven stone floor, our domed ceiling seemed high enough for my dreams to fly up to the very heavens!

In the mornings, I woke to the pleasant tune of my father learning Gemara. From sunrise on, he sat at the table, a large Gemara open before him. When it was time for prayers, he would close his books, take his *tallit* and *tefillin*, and hurry to the synagogue. Then I would quietly open the front door and go out into the bustling courtyard until the rest of the family woke up. Even at those early hours, children and adults, members of the ten families living on our floor, were coming and going. I loved to stand at the railing and watch the activity.

At that time, running water was a modern invention that had not yet been introduced in the Old City, and the arrival of Abu Ali, the water drawer, began our day. Chattering housewives dressed in flowered housecoats, with kerchiefs on their heads and aprons at their waists, clustered around the cisterns in the courtyard, holding their empty water pails and waiting for Abu Ali. There were always noisy disputes about who was first in line until the loud cry "Maya, Maya" was heard. Accompanied by the clanging of cymbals, Abu Ali arrived. All at once a long orderly line was formed.

Abu Ali would lower the yoke and pails from his shoulder, roll up his long, faded robes, and tuck the ends into the wide belt around his waist. Then he would remove the bolt and heavy iron cover from the water cistern. He would pick up one of his pails, and with the long rope tied to the handle, lower it into the cistern. He would wait a moment, then begin to tug rhythmically on the rope, alternating right and left hands, until a pailful of clean, pure water emerged. With one deft movement he would pour the water from his pail into the container held by the first person in line. The small coin he received as payment would disappear quickly into one of the many folds in his robe, and in no time at all, the line of people was gone.

Imma and Savta would each carry a pail of water up to the top floor, and Abba, on his way home from morning prayers, would bring up a third pail. On washdays, however, when large quantities of water were needed, Abu Ali would carry all the water up to our doorstep. I never ceased to wonder at his skill. How could he walk down the length of the courtyard and up all those stairs without spilling a single drop from the heavy pails hanging down his shoulders! He walked as though the pails were empty!

Since water was scarce, women in the Old City kept their houses sparkling clean while using very little water, and whatever they had was recycled all the time. Water used to bathe the babies was later used to wash their clothes, and finally, reused once more to wash the floors.

A huge clay jug stood in one corner of the kitchen. It held our drinking water and kept it cool. Abba would strain the water through a clean white cloth tied to the mouth of the jug. During the hot summer days two smaller jugs stood on the window sill, always full of cold, refreshing water.

Sometimes, while watching Abu Ali draw the water, my imagination would run free. Holding my breath, I waited for him to pull up the rope, wondering what he might find in his pail. Perhaps a fish? Or a frog? Perhaps some long lost treasure?

Abu Ali would tug with his right hand, and then his left, again and again until once more he would be holding a pail, overflowing with water. But it was always only...water!

"What did you expect to find in a water cistern?" my grandmother once asked me, noticing the disappointed look on my face.

"Uh...," I stammered, "maybe something that was once

lost ... maybe a ... a treasure ..."

She laughed. "Water is the greatest treasure there is," she said, carefully balancing her full pail, not spilling a drop.

I only realized the truth of Savta's words during the war, when this treasure became very scarce.

3 The Wailing Wall

There was a large, latticed window in the southern wall of our house. Because this outer wall was over three feet thick, the window sill was wonderfully wide, a miniature balcony for children. In the evening, tired from playing outside, we loved to sit on the sill and look down through the lattice outside. On the small hill opposite, Salim the shepherd would gather in his goats. We could see the baby goats with their curled ears, and the little black kids coming out to greet the herd returning from pasture. Lower down, just outside the City walls, lay the Arab village of Silwan, the Biblical Shiloach, its tin roofs gleaming gold in the setting sun.

On Shabbat and holidays, throngs of people crowded down the narrow road between our house and the Old City wall on their way to the Kotel Hamaaravi — the Western Wall, the last remnant of our destroyed Temple. But at night, no one went to the Wall. It was too dangerous. Even the small area designated for Jewish prayer was unsafe, for the Arabs did as they pleased while the British guards, appointed by the Mandatory government supposedly to keep order, would look the other way if there was ever any trouble.

Today, when there is so much room in the big plaza in front of the Kotel and tens of thousands come to pray, people may find it hard to imagine how small and feeble the Jewish presence was then.

22

How many insults and degradations we suffered, unable to protest! Arab houses were built up against the Wall, leaving only a small section open for prayer. Because British law did not permit the placement of a *mechitza*, the divider between the men's and women's sections, the men clustered together at one end of the narrow area and the women at the other. We had to pray standing up, since the British did not allow us to bring chairs or benches to the area. On Simchat Torah we were not allowed to dance in the vicinity, and of course, it was against the law to blow the *shofar* at any time.

If anyone — even a sick or aged person — dared to bring a chair to the Wall, a British soldier immediately appeared and commanded him to remove the "public nuisance" at once. I remember one attempt to celebrate Simchat Torah at the Wall. Rabbi Orenstein, the rabbi of the Kotel, was promptly summoned and told to put an end to the dancing at once.

We walked to the Kotel during the daytime, but not nearly so often as we do now. We would walk in a group down the street with its many steps and past the cactus field to the Wall. Our visits were short, to keep the insults and degradations to a minimum. We would stand on one side and recite a few chapters of Tehillim, tears in our eyes, our heads bowed.

More than once, an Arab riding a donkey would push us to the side as we stood absorbed in prayer. He would gallop through the crowd, behaving as if he were in his own backyard, crying "He-ya, he-ya."

And often, as we were absorbed in a chapter of Psalms, dirty water would suddenly stream by our feet. We retreated quickly, before our shoes were covered with mud. The source of this "river" was a house built onto the Wall. The Arab woman who lived there used to take her straw broom and flick dirty water onto the worshipers whenever she washed her staircase. But none of this was considered a breach of the peace by the British policemen.

23

The Jewish women at the Kotel always cried. Our eyes, too, would fill with tears. It was impossible not to cry, for then, the Western Wall was truly the Wailing Wall. The terrible destruction was so real, and the feeling of exile so vivid. Even the doves flying overhead would mourn sadly in sympathy. Standing with our heads pressed to the huge stones of the Wall, we could hear a wailing sound — as if the very stones were sobbing. Perhaps it was the voice of the *Shechina*, the Divine Presence, ever present at the Kotel.

4 Friday Night in the Churva

It was Friday night and Imma had just finished reciting the blessing over the candles. She kissed Naomi and me as we waited impatiently to go to the synagogue with Abba. Dressed in his dark Shabbat suit, he took our *siddurim* from the bookshelf and we left the house together. I was wearing my new navy blue jumper with the gold buttons, and my hair was tied with a big, white, silk bow. Naomi, too, was dressed in her Shabbat best, and we walked on either side of Abba, our small hands firmly tucked into his large, warm ones.

From all directions people flocked to the Churva Synagogue holding their *siddurim*. The lofty, round dome of the building dominated the entire quarter. It was growing dark, but inside the synagogue, all was brightly lit. As soon as we took our places on the carved wooden benches, I tried to count the chandeliers hanging from the ceiling, but without much success. How big and beautiful they were, the pieces of crystal glass glittering amidst the great light.

My father liked to come to the synagogue early. He would open a book and begin to learn while I looked around me. I never tired of seeing the beautiful Churva. Here, no one ever caused us trouble. There were no British soldiers to sound the alarm if we started to sing. There were no Arabs to humiliate us or drive us away. The Churva was ours alone.

I would sit beside my father, lost in thought. There was so much to look at: the lights; the shiny, white marble floor; the splendid *bima* in the center of the hall; the tall walls with their stained-glass windows, the upper set portraying the symbols of the twelve tribes of Israel. But my favorite sight was always the *aron kodesh* on the eastern wall, overlaid with gold and covered with a beautiful, embroidered *parochet.*

From there, my eyes wandered to the high domed ceiling, painted sky blue and strewn with golden stars. Over and over I would ask myself, "Can this really be the ceiling of the synagogue? Perhaps it is the sky itself over my head?!"

The *gabbai,* to whom I usually directed this question, would laugh good-naturedly and answer that it was indeed the sky. But Abba and Naomi would look at me and smile, making me feel very young and confused.

"It must be the dome of the synagogue," I would tell myself. But the very next week, fresh doubts would once again find their way into my mind.

The synagogue was always filled to capacity with worshipers in Sabbath dress, their faces aglow with the light of Shabbat. They bore not the slightest resemblance to their weekday selves, to those ordinary people beset with financial and other worries. On Shabbat, they all looked like princes!

Deep in thought, I would suddenly notice that the whole congregation had stood up to sing. I, too, stood up and joined in. "Come my beloved to greet the bride; let us welcome the Sabbath." After the service was over, I didn't move, unwilling as I was to leave this wonderful place. But as everyone left, Abba would take my hand and lead me to the door.

It was always dark outside as we went home, but the stories Abba told were so fascinating that the darkness failed to frighten us. Abba was an accomplished storyteller and whatever he told us seemed to take place before our very eyes.

"Abba," I once asked him, "I have a question before we go inside."

"What do you want to ask, my little one?"

"Abba, tell me, when the Beit Hamikdash is rebuilt, will it be as beautiful as the Churva?"

Abba didn't answer. He simply smiled a wide smile and opened the door to the house.

5 The Batrak Market

It was still peacetime when we moved into the Old City — not real peace, but not yet war. Daily relations with our Arab neighbors were normal. Every morning Abu Ali would come to our courtyard to draw water, and an Arab peddler regularly made the rounds of the Jewish Quarter, crying "Baladi, baladi," selling live chickens from a basket on his shoulders and fresh eggs from a pail in his hands.

The Jewish Quarter had its own small marketplace, the Meydan, as well as a large variety of stores on Jewish Quarter Street. But the real *shuk* was the Arab marketplace, the Batrak. Even the name had a certain magic for me, conjuring up visions of a gigantic, teeming square. It was also a bit threatening — not because of the Arab shopkeepers with whom we were then on friendly terms, but because of the dark roofs covering many of the *shuk*'s alleyways.

How well I remember my first visit to the Batrak! It was the day my eldest sister Naomi began first grade and my father began his new teaching job in town. I should have started kindergarten that day, but seeing how reluctant I was, my mother decided not to insist.

"Today, we'll go to the *shuk*," said Imma, after Abba and Naomi had left that morning. I jumped with joy. We waited until the baby fell asleep in her carriage and then we brought her to Savta. Imma picked up her two big shopping baskets, giving me my own small one. We left our courtyard and began to walk through the narrow lanes of the Jewish Quarter.

I strode beside Imma, clutching my bag and feeling very, very grown up, despite the fact that it was Naomi who had just begun first grade and not I. Imma offered to take me on a tour of the *shuk* before buying the vegetables on condition that I begin kindergarten the following week like all the other children! But I merely shrugged my shoulders stubbornly. Had she offered me the chance to go to school, it would have been a different story.

Imma walked quickly and I took large steps, skipping and running and trying not to fall behind. All of a sudden we were in the *shuk*. Noisy throngs of people were walking and talking. It was almost impossible to stand still because of the pushing crowd. I was entranced with the Arab women in long embroidered dresses, balancing huge baskets of fruit on their heads.

"Make way! Make way!" someone shouted. Everyone pressed to the side as a boy pushing a large cart full of *pittot*, round oriental breads, passed by.

As I grew more accustomed to the noise and the pushing crowds, I began to look at the stores more carefully. Souvenir and jewelry shops were on both sides of the street. The storefront windows were full of caravans of olivewood camels, small dolls perched on stands, shining bronze pitchers, and metal plates engraved in intricate designs. Hanging in the doorways were necklaces made of colored glass beads or precious stones. I stopped to look at a lovely necklace of sea shells.

"Adesh?" (How much?), Imma asked the old Arab merchant who stood in the entrance, his head wrapped in the traditional white kafiya — headdress — and tied with a black akal — a

27

braided rope.

"One shilling," he answered.

Imma began to bargain, and after what seemed to me an interminably long time, she put a coin in his hand as he took down two beautiful shell necklaces — one bright pink and the other indigo blue. Imma put them in her basket and we continued on our way.

"Here is the potters' lane," she said. The narrow sidewalks on both sides of the lane were stacked with pottery of all kinds — large and small, wide and narrow, simple and fancy — overflowing from the stores. We turned left and we were surrounded by towers of colorful, mouth-watering sweets: filled cakes, coconut rolls, fruity squares topped with powdered sugar, sticky sweet sesame squares, tiny red sugared apples on thin sticks arranged in a circle, varicolored candy sticks, fragrant cookies...it was like a fairy tale.

We turned again. The "candy palaces" disappeared and we found ourselves back on a dark street where the pungent smell of fresh dill and parsley mixed with the odor of rotten tomatoes.

"Bandura, bandura," called the tomato sellers.

"Chiyara, chiyara," the cucumber peddlers called out.

At first the sudden darkness frightened me, but soon I was able to see that ragged curtains and old potato sacks had been hung overhead to shade the vegetables from the hot sun. I tried to grab Imma's hand, afraid I would get lost in the throngs of buyers and sellers, but her hands were busy picking out tomatoes. "Help me pick, little one," she said. "Choose tomatoes that are neither too hard nor too soft — not too red and not too green."

I found a beautiful red tomato and put it into the yellow brass bowl together with the rest of Imma's tomatoes. The dark-eyed Arab vendor weighed them with a strange scale hanging from a rope. Imma paid him and we proceeded on our way. Slowly our baskets filled up: squash, eggplant, onions, garlic, tomatoes and cucumbers, grape leaves and all kinds of fruit. In my tiny basket I held the delicious grapes we bought from an old Arab woman, her face covered by a veil. She was sitting cross-legged on the ground and weighing her merchandise on a big flat plate.

Carrying all we could, we pushed our way through the bustling crowd. Finally we emerged from the vegetable market onto a fairly quiet street where the sun's rays reached us once again. On one side of the street, stairs led down to a small café slightly below street level. A few men were sitting on stools around small tables, sipping steaming hot Turkish coffee from tiny china cups. Others were playing shesh-besh. Oriental music burst from an old phonograph powered by a dark-haired youth turning its handle non-stop. In the doorway sat a stout Arab, his head wrapped in a red turban, slowly fingering a string of yellow beads. Two old Arabs were concentrating on smoking their nargilehs. We passed the coffeehouse and turned into a side street.

"Well, what did you think of the *shuk*?" asked Imma.

I knew that another question would soon follow: "Are you ready to go to kindergarten now?"

I did not answer, but then I remembered the presents deep in Imma's shopping basket.

"The *shuk* is wonderful," I said, not quite sure if I was committing myself to kindergarten or not.

We were tired when we finally reached home, and Naomi was already back from school. I ran to pull the beads out of Imma's basket.

"I want the pink necklace!"

"No, I want the pink one!" I grabbed the necklace and tried it on. It was beautiful. I turned it around and pulled on it a little, when suddenly — oops!

A shower of beads and shells fell to the ground. The string of my pink shell necklace had broken!

29

6 Our Lot

There was a large open plot of land known as the Deutsche Platz between Batei Machse, where we lived, and the Rothschild building. To us children it was simply "the lot." This lot of ours bore absolutely no resemblance to the paved square which today occupies the same area. Our lot was all dirt and rock, making it quite easy to find the little square stones we needed for our popular game of "Five Stones." The lot was full of small hills and fenced-off areas, wonderful hiding places for "Hide and Seek." There was also an abundance of old cans for "Tin Can Tag" and sticks for "Giant Steps."

Every afternoon the lot was filled with crowds of children. We used to play together in large groups of all ages. Usually the boys spent the afternoon learning in *cheder* so that we girls were free to run and jump, undisturbed. It never occurred to any of the neighbors to scold us for making too much noise or to limit our outdoor play during the daylight hours, and we therefore felt that we were the rightful owners of "our" lot.

The girls in the lot knew everything. They knew, for instance, how to distinguish a British soldier from a policeman. They also knew who those strange soldiers were, the ones who occasionally marched down the Deutsche Platz in plaid skirts, their berets tilted at an angle. When I first ventured a guess that these were women soldiers, everyone laughed.

"Those are Scottish soldiers!" Rachel whispered into my ear. "Men soldiers, you hear?"

The girls on the lot were also experts in all the Mandatory laws and restrictions. They knew, for example, that no adult was permitted to walk outdoors without his identity card, and they would add in a whisper that people such as illegal immigrants who had no identity cards could have such cards "made." The girls told me that illegal possession of weapons was strictly forbidden, although they also reassured me that

there were nevertheless those who managed to procure
weapons secretly in order to defend the Jewish population
"when the time came." Our daily conversations often centered
around the news, and I was initiated into many military secrets
at an early age. The older girls explained to the younger ones
like me that the wicked British would soon be driven out of the
country. Exactly how this was to come about was the subject of
many arguments and discussions, just as it was among the
adults. There were girls who claimed that the official Jewish
military force, the Hagana, by discussing and negotiating and
using political pressure, would soon make the British depart.
But other girls fervently held to the opinion that only Etzel, an
independent and more extreme military group, could make the
British leave. "We have been patient long enough," they
claimed. "Now it is time to use force."

Still others were partial to Lechi, an even more extremist
movement. At that point in the discussion spirits would run
high and the girls would split into two, or even three, factions.
At such times I would stand on the sidelines, bewildered,
unable to decide which side to join. Chana, one of the oldest of
the group, objected to my vacillations, saying that it was high
time I made up my mind where I belonged: to the Hagana, to the
Etzel, or even to Lechi if I so desired!

Chana had a strange habit. Although she was already in
third or fourth grade she still sucked her thumb constantly —
and not just one thumb but both at once! Nevertheless her
opinion carried a lot of weight, perhaps because she was a head
taller than all the other girls.

One night I lay in bed, unable to fall asleep. Which side
should I take? Etzel had a wonderful theme song, "Two sides to
the Jordan; both are ours..." On the other hand, many Etzel
members had been arrested by the British. A few had even been
hanged, as Rachel had told us. How awful that was! "No," I
thought. "That's too scary." But the Etzel girls said that the

Hagana was "a bunch of cowards." Whom, then, should I choose?

"Why are you sitting on the bed instead of going to sleep?" my father scolded me as he walked into the house. Abba was busy signing men up for the National Guard and would sometimes not return home until I had gone to sleep. I would ask Abba's advice, I thought. I sat up and described my problem. Naomi heard and immediately took the Hagana's side. Abba said that he had been a member of the Hagana in his youth, and that he still supported them.

"But do you really believe that just talking will make the British leave?" I asked.

"How else?" exclaimed Naomi, jumping out of bed. "Will a few miserable Etzel bombs make them go?"

"Etzel's bombs are not miserable at all," I objected. "But sometimes the people who set off the bombs are caught and then ... then their end is miserable indeed."

Abba sat down beside me and took my hand in his own. "Most of the country is organized within the Hagana," he said. "The Hagana is a large, important body. I believe that political acts do have great value. If we succeed in convincing the British that we are capable of independent government, and if a majority in the United Nations vote on our behalf, then we will become an independent nation. This is something which cannot be achieved through acts of terror and violence."

That night, Abba convinced me, but, when the hand of the British was very heavy upon us and the negotiations seemed endless, it sometimes seemed to me that, perhaps, Etzel was right after all.

7 Identity Cards

"Stop, stop!"

A tall English policeman suddenly appeared just as we were coming out of the Anglo-Palestine Bank. That morning Abba had a free day, and he had taken me with him to town to settle some business matters and to do some errands for Imma. Now a policeman was blocking our path.

"Identity card, please," he demanded sternly.

Abba put his briefcase down on the sidewalk and began searching through his coat pockets. I stood close beside him.

"What will happen if he can't find his card?" I wondered fearfully.

I looked at the road. All along the street, policemen were stopping pedestrians and demanding to see their identity cards. Everyone was busy searching his purse or pockets. Finally Abba found his card.

"Thank God Abba is so organized," I thought. "He always carries his card with him." Just opposite us someone without a card was being put into a police van parked nearby. Our policeman examined Abba's card very carefully.

"What can he be thinking?" I thought angrily. "That my father is a forger?"

Finally, he returned the card and we were allowed to continue. As we were crossing the street, Abba heard someone calling his name. The voice was coming from the police van. It was full of people whose only sin was that they had forgotten their identity cards at home. Now they would be hauled off to a police station and...

In the van we caught sight of Binyamin, a distant relative who also lived in the Jewish Quarter. Abba promised to bring his identity card to the station, but to which one? No one knew.

Abba turned to the British policeman who was sitting behind the steering wheel and smoking a cigarette with obvious enjoyment. He looked very smug and satisfied with his day's work. He and his companions had caught many fish in their net!

Abba asked politely and in English where everyone would be taken, but the driver shook his head and refused to answer. Instead, he blew smoke rings. All around was a great tumult — a medley of people and voices, inside and outside, yelling and arguing in Hebrew and English, all to no avail. Soon more vans appeared — all filled with men and women. The policemen began to cordon off the area and drive off the bystanders. We too were forced to leave.

In those days it was not unusual to be imprisoned for not carrying an identity card, but the number of arrests that day shocked us. Abba decided to forgo the rest of his business and shopping and to hurry home. We turned towards the 2/a bus stop, just off Zion Square. A long line had already formed — a line of angry people. It was then that we finally discovered the reason for the British raid on the city streets. Last night a new boatload of illegal immigrants had reached the shores of Tel Aviv. Hundreds of the city's residents had come to the shore to welcome them, and before the British knew what was happening, the illegal immigrants had merged with the crowd so that it was impossible to identify them. Today all of Tel Aviv was under curfew, but many of the immigrants had already managed to flee to other parts of the country. Now the British were combing the entire country for illegal immigrants. Anyone who could not produce an identity card was liable to be banished to Cyprus.

"We must get Binyamin out as quickly as possible," said Abba when we were finally seated on the bus.

As soon as we arrived in the Old City, Abba hurried to Binyamin's house. Then he deposited me safely at home and set out again, Binyamin's identity card in his pocket. Late that night Abba returned home, tense and tired. It had taken him hours of chasing back and forth between the Kishle police station at Jaffa Gate and the Russian Compound police headquarters in town before he finally succeeded in locating Binyamin. But in spite of all Abba's efforts, Binyamin was not released until the following day.

That day none of the girls played outside. The mass arrests upset us no end. We stood beside the fence and discussed what had happened. All agreed that the British had gone too far. The Etzelniks among us shouted and fumed. "We must show the British that we will not allow such things to continue!" they declared. Frieda burst out in tears, and Chana and Rachel called mockingly to the Hagana supporters, "How long will you stand for this? How long?"

8 Ruthie

As time passed, my mother came to accept the fact that I was not going to go to kindergarten. Instead, she gave me a little brown writing kit, an empty notebook, an old pencil box, and some used pencils and crayons, so that I could prepare myself for school — my greatest desire. Every morning, while Naomi was in school, I would sit and do my homework. My own "school hours" began in the afternoon, when Naomi came home. I don't remember which of us first thought of the idea, and to this day I don't know who enjoyed it more, me, who learned, or Naomi, who taught. In any case, our "school" was a serious business, and I really did learn to read and write. Only five years old, I would sit outside and read Naomi's first-grade reader over and over again, backwards and forwards, until I knew it by heart. Naomi found a little blackboard and hung it outside on the wall. Our chalk was limestone from the lot.

When the rainy winter arrived, we moved indoors. I recall one cold winter day when Naomi, soaked to the skin, walked in

35

the door after school and heard me announce, "Today we can learn before lunch. Abba and Imma have gone away!"

"Where did they go?"

"They didn't say."

Naomi changed into dry clothes and we set up our schoolroom. Little Yehudit, who had woken up in the meantime, was also given a seat in our classroom, plus a piece of paper and a big, thick crayon for scribbling. It was pouring outside. Naomi was hungry and in no mood to teach arithmetic, so she decided to tell me a Bible story.

Suddenly Abba walked in, dripping rain. "Mazal tov!" he announced, beaming with joy. "We have a new baby girl!"

"A girl? A baby! Mazal tov!" I exclaimed.

Naomi burst into tears.

"What's wrong?" asked Abba, but Naomi was crying too hard to answer. Abba stroked her head and asked again, "What's wrong, Naomi?"

Finally she answered through her tears, "Why a girl?! I wanted a boy so badly, and now we have another girl!"

Abba smiled. "I," he said, "wanted a girl so badly — another lovely little girl like you and your sisters. When I first saw her I recited the blessing *Shehecheyanu*. It is the women who build the world. If no girls were born, the world would cease to exist."

"That's true," agreed Naomi, "but why do all the girls have to be born in our family?"

Abba burst out laughing. His hearty laughter was contagious, but Naomi still frowned.

I tried to comfort her. "Do you know," I said, "I'm happy we have a baby girl and not a boy. Rachel told me that the British hang our best boys, but no such terrible thing ever happens to a girl."

My words made her smile, but when she finally spoke, all she said was that I was talking nonsense and that she hoped the new baby would turn out to be smarter than me.

"Nevertheless," she continued, "the baby will not be all that marvelous anyway, so we have nothing to worry about."

"How do you know?" I asked.

"That's the way it always is. No babies are 'good.' It doesn't matter if they're boys or girls; they all cry day and night."

After a few days in Hadassah Hospital on Mount Scopus, Imma came home with a little baby wrapped in a brand-new, pink blanket. Just a few minutes after Imma put her in the carriage, she did indeed begin to scream, and she went on crying for weeks, just as Naomi had predicted.

During the long morning hours that followed, while Abba and Naomi were away at school and Imma was busy with the baby Ruthie, I took care of Yehudit. She was a beautiful child, with dark skin; long, black, silky curls; and dreamy, big, black eyes framed by delicate, long eyelashes. I called her the "Queen of the Babies" and she in turn adored me. I loved to sit and sing to her, or tell her stories that she could not yet understand. I did my best to prove to Imma that she had been wise not to send me to kindergarten, and I tried to help as much as I could in the house. I fed Yehudit and sometimes even put her to sleep on the folding bed that Abba brought from Aunt Rivka's house.

I also washed the breakfast dishes in our tiny kitchen each morning. Since we had neither sink nor faucet, Imma would place two deep metal bowls in front of me on a high stool — one with soapy water and one with clear, rinse water. I would carefully go to work — just as I had been taught — without wasting a drop.

In honor of Ruthie's arrival, my father introduced a modern invention into our home — electricity. All the neighbors came to see the wonder, and some then followed in our footsteps. The electric lights made life much easier, especially during the long winter nights.

Abba soon brought a new electric wonder — a radio. Every

37

day he would listen to the "Voice of Jerusalem" news broadcast, and when something special happened, the neighbors would come over to listen too. They would look at us children and comment to one another, "A new generation has come into the world, a generation which is growing up with new and modern inventions. Ah, the world is changing..."

9 Shalom, First Grade

Time passed, until one day I was finally on the way to first grade, carrying a real school bag on my back. I was five-and-a-half years old and today...today I would finally join the ranks of the big children in school.

I walked hurriedly beside Naomi and Abba on our way to hustling, bustling Jaffa Gate. People of all races and nationalities thronged around the open square between Jaffa Gate and the *shuk*. A medley of tongues filled the air. Somewhere a bus honked loudly. Several Arabs were sitting on the curb, ready for business, their bright copper shoeshine boxes gleaming in the sun. Another Arab, wearing a turban on his head, was beating a cymbal and loudly advertising, "Sus, sus, Indian dates!"

"What's that?" I asked, holding tightly to Abba's hand so as not to get lost in the crowd.

"It's a cold drink. I'll buy you one some other time. Now we're in a rush. Here's your bus."

Soon I found myself in a large classroom, sitting on a bench in the last row. Dozens of little girls were crowded together on the other benches, all of them strangers. My eyes roamed over the classroom, searching for the red-headed girl I had met last summer, but I couldn't find her.

The teacher looked very serious. She asked my name and I tried to answer, but no sound came out of my mouth. Tears blurred my vision and I felt as though I were choking. What was happening to me? Was this the day I had so eagerly looked forward to?

After the morning prayers, the teacher wrote three words on the board: Shalom First Grade. Was that all we were going to learn today? But I already knew how to read that. I knew many words. I could read the entire first-grade reader. My sister Naomi had already taught me all of this!

Later in the morning, when the teacher told us stories from the Tanach, my mood improved, but then a loud bell rang. All the girls jumped up and ran out into the schoolyard.

"What's your name?" asked the teacher again. I noticed that I was the only one left in the classroom. I shrugged my shoulders.

"Where do you live?" she persisted.

"In the Old City."

"Why are you sitting inside at recess time? Go out and play with the other girls."

I went outside. The yard was crowded and noisy. It seemed to me that thousands of girls were jumping rope, playing ball or running and playing tag. I squeezed myself into a corner near the fence and remained alone.

The day finally ended and I was again at Abba's side, much relieved. A tall Negro in a broad-rimmed straw hat was standing near the 2/a bus stop, advertising his wares in a catchy tune. "Hot peanuts! Hot peanuts!" He stirred his roasted peanuts with a long stick, inside a big tin pan set on hot coals.

"Come," said Abba. "In honor of your first day at school!" He handed me a large two-mil coin. "And this is for you, my second grader," he said to Naomi. We took the coins from Abba and turned to the vendor. He tore out a page from an old magazine and deftly folded it into a cone. Then he poured two cupfuls of hot peanuts — one for each of us.

Sitting in the bus on our way home, we told each other of our morning's adventures. Abba was teaching in the Ohel Moshe school, Naomi was now in second grade, and I was in first. Despite my lonely day at school, a wave of happiness swept over me. From now on, I, too, would get up early and rush to leave the house with the "big people." I, too, had a school bag, books, and a pencil case — all brand new. I, too, would now learn all the secrets of school. No longer would I be the baby.

Just then Naomi piped up, "Abba, I just can't believe it. Little Puah is already in first grade!" Her tone emphasized the difference in our ages and, as my older sister, how serious were her responsibilities towards me. One would think she was my mother!

10 The Search

The bell rang, bringing another lesson to a close. The girls packed their school bags and hurried home. Only I remained alone in the classroom. I had a full hour to wait for my sister Naomi, for the higher classes finished school later than the first graders.

I sat in the empty classroom, wondering what to buy with the precious coin I had tucked away in my school bag. The day before, a friend of Abba's had given it to me for a present. He sat at our table talking to Abba for a long time, discussing all the important issues of the day — British policy, Arab maneuvers, the need to prepare the Jewish population for the future. The word "war" could be heard now and then, but Abba, seeing the expression of anxiety on my face, quickly changed the subject. As the man was leaving, he gave each of us a half-shilling coin. That was a lot of money in those days, and I excitedly weighed the possibilities such wealth afforded me.

"I won't buy Turmos beans today," I thought, although,

looking through the window, I could see the little old lady who sold them sitting on the schoolyard fence, a white scarf on her head and a big bowl of shiny yellow Turmos in her lap.

"No, I will not buy Turmos today." I repeated my decision as if to give it more weight. All I needed to buy Turmos was one mil; that sort of pittance was mine every day.

"I won't buy peanuts either," I thought. Today I would buy something really special. Before I had finished deciding exactly what, I heard the loud clamor of the bell, and the older girls began streaming into the schoolyard. The girls who lived in the Old City gathered into a group and left the school together. Every day, we would walk home leisurely, taking time to gaze at all the shop windows on the city streets. One window had an almost magical attraction for us. It was a storefront full of chocolates of every size and shape imaginable. Every other day we could only look, but today we had a sizeable sum of money in our pockets...

"That's the store we want!" I whispered to Naomi, who nodded her head in agreement. The girls waited outside, gazing longingly at the sweets. Chana alone was allowed to enter the store to advise us, but on the express condition that she keep both of her thumbs far away from her mouth. Each of us chose a gigantic chocolate bar filled with nuts, and with the change, we bought a big bag of chocolate-coated candies. I hid the chocolate bar in my school bag, but I treated all the girls to candies from the paper bag. Naomi called me stingy, and, just to make me angry, she broke off one row after another of her chocolate bar and treated all her friends.

"You see, I still have enough left for myself," she said, putting what was left of the bar into her bag. In my defense, I claimed that I was saving the bar for Shabbat. But her rebuke hit home, and I walked silently with the chattering group, holding on to the two-mil coin for bus fare in my pocket. Once at home I hurriedly hid my precious chocolate bar in the clothes closet, planning to save it for Shabbat. But something happened which ruined my plans completely.

The next day, on our way home from school, there were loud cries of "Searches, searches!" Breaking into a mad run for home, we reached the open courtyard on the second floor of our house just in time to see two British soldiers beating on one of our neighbors' doors with the butts of their rifles and shouting at the top of their lungs, "Searches, searches!"

We burst into the house as Imma ran out of the kitchen and to the clothes cabinet, pulling her diamond ring out of one of the drawers. This was her one precious piece of jewelry — the ring my father had given her as an engagement gift. Hurriedly, she stuffed a few other pieces of jewelry into her pockets.

"Imma," I was shocked, "why?"

Imma didn't answer my question. Instead she ordered me to stop standing there like a piece of wood and to help her look for the money.

"But why?" I couldn't help asking.

"Because of those thieves out there," answered Naomi.

"Thieves?" I still didn't understand.

Before my question could be answered, the door was kicked open, and the two British soldiers strode into the room. Seeing the open closet, they immediately began rummaging through it, messing up all the neat piles of clothing on the shelves and throwing them on the floor. Shaking with fear, I moved closer to Imma, but she paid no attention to me.

"Where is your husband?" one of the soldiers asked.

"At work," she replied.

In my fright I called Naomi, and she hurried to my side and put her arms around me. Was it only my imagination, or were her hands also trembling?

Just then one of the British soldiers pulled a wad of money out of the closet and stuck it in his pocket, ignoring Imma's fervent protests. Then he made another discovery, my great big, nut-filled chocolate bar! Before I could grasp what was happening, he tore open the colorful wrapper, broke the bar in two and began to devour my chocolate!

"My chocolate!" I cried, almost choking.

The soldier laughed. "Your chocolate? Here it is!" He handed it to me, but the minute I reached out to take it, he stuck almost the whole bar into his mouth at once. Not believing my eyes, I watched him eat with obvious enjoyment, sharing the other half with his partner. Meanwhile, the other soldier had been running his rifle through the beds and searching under all the blankets.

"What is he looking for?" I whispered to Naomi.

"Illegal weapons."

"Wh...what?"

"Sh..."

When he finished turning the beds upside down, he took out our school bags and turned them upside down too, spilling all their contents on the floor.

"Do little girls keep illegal weapons in their school bags?" I thought in anger.

The arrogant soldier continued to throw our things around while Imma stood beside the closet, biting her lips.

"Where is your husband?" they asked again, as though they had not asked her already.

"I said he was at work," she repeated.

"No, that's not what we mean," they said. "Where is he, in the Hagana or Etzel?"

"My father is in..." I volunteered.

Naomi pinched me. "No one asked you!" she said sharply.

"Well, lady, tell us where he belongs," the soldier who had stolen my chocolate repeated.

"He doesn't belong anywhere," Imma answered.

"Never mind. We already know," they said, continuing their rummaging. At long last, they left. Our apartment looked like the upheaval of Sodom and Gomorrah.

We let out a long breath of relief, but Imma clapped her hands in grief. "His whole salary they took, those thieves, Abba's whole salary!" She was furious, but what could she do? Only sigh over and over again, "Oy, oy, oy! As if we were back in the days of the pogroms!"

Our apartment really did look like it had gone through a pogrom. Imma didn't even know where to start cleaning. Naomi was the first one to pull herself together and begin to work. She began to gather up her notebooks and put them back into her empty school bag. Suddenly she picked up the stub of her chocolate bar. "Here's my chocolate!" she called out in joy. I thought of my stolen chocolate and I was suddenly furious.

"Why did you let them eat my chocolate?" I yelled at Imma.

"What could I do?" Imma sighed. "They are the rulers here. Who are we to oppose them?"

Naomi came closer to me. "That is the result of your stinginess," she whispered. I burst into tears, but as soon as she saw me cry, she broke the remains of her chocolate bar into little pieces and tried to comfort both Imma and me with it. But the sweet taste of the chocolate couldn't erase the bitterness of the tears which welled up in my throat and ran down my cheeks.

11 Curfew

Another day of school was over. As I closed my notebook I suddenly caught sight of Abba in the classroom doorway.

"What happened?" I asked in surprise. "Why are you here?"

"Put your things away as fast as you can and let's go!"

"But..."

"Hurry up! The curfew will begin shortly, and if we don't

hurry we won't make it home in time."

I ran to put my things together, and we went out into the schoolyard. Naomi was already standing there, her school bag on her back. On David Yellin Street we turned towards the stop for the No. 1 bus, but the bus was no longer running.

"When does the curfew begin?" we asked worriedly.

"Soon," Abba answered tersely. He walked faster and we half-ran, half-walked beside him, reaching Zion Square at a run. A few people were still on the street, rushing just like we were. Several peddlers were gathering up their wares which had been spread out for display on the sidewalk. Most of the stores were already closed, and the last shopkeepers were rolling up their awnings and locking the bars on their windows. We finally reached the 2/a bus stop, but there was no bus there either. Instead, we found our grandmother waiting there.

"Savta is waiting for the bus!" I called out happily.

She walked toward us and announced, "We must walk the rest of the way, fast!"

The four of us walked together quickly. By the time we reached the shopping center on Sham'a Street, not far from Jaffa Gate, no one was on the street. Not a Jew, not an Arab, and thank God, not a single Englishman. Puffing and panting, I began to lag behind. Abba grabbed my arm and pulled me along. A few more minutes and we were at Jaffa Gate where we found a blockade in front of the menacing Kishle police station! A high barbed wire fence was stretched the length of the street, barring entrance to the Jewish Quarter.

"What rotten luck!" muttered Abba, his face grave.

A tall British soldier with a steel helmet was pacing back and forth in front of the blockade. Abba spoke to him in English.

"Sir, we live here, in the Jewish Quarter. Please let us go home."

The British soldier continued to pace back and forth, as though no one had spoken. Abba pointed to Savta and to us and spoke again in English. I guessed that he was saying that his aged mother and young children absolutely had to get home, or some similar thing that would soften the heart of anyone but a British soldier, but Abba's pleas fell on deaf ears. The soldier stopped pacing and, leaning on his gun, stood there motionless. He didn't blink an eye; not a muscle in his cold, hard face twitched.

At first we were at a complete loss. But then Savta pulled Abba to the side and whispered something in his ear. Abba nodded, and before I knew what was happening, Savta and Naomi had disappeared. Without a word, Abba pulled me backwards after him. Beside the church opposite the Kishle police station, we darted into a small side street where we found Savta and Naomi. Savta walked, and we followed, into the heart of the Armenian Quarter, through narrow streets paved with smooth square stones. The tall walls of the houses and churches filled me with terror. It seemed as if the very walls could hear my heart beating. Not a soul was on the silent streets, and nothing but the echoes of our footsteps could be heard as we strode down the hard stone pavements.

"Curfew..." I held onto Abba's large hand with all my might, my eyes fixed on Savta, our guide, who walked in front, quickly and confidently. She knew every path in the Old City. Had she not walked these streets every day of her life? But every time we turned a corner, I held my breath and my heart stopped beating, fearful that a British soldier might suddenly appear and arrest us.

We were walking down a shaded, dark street when Savta turned right and, suddenly, the hot noontime sun flooded the now open street. To our great surprise, we found ourselves in our own Jewish Quarter! With renewed spirit, we skipped down the familiar streets, keeping close to the wall so we would not be noticed.

Whoever said that stones have no power to move themselves? The white stone steps to our house seemed to jump up to meet us as soon as we caught sight of them. I was not aware of my feet moving; nevertheless I soon found myself on the stairs to our house, while Abba urged me to hurry inside before a policeman appeared.

12 The Partition Proposal

Our baby Ruth was growing up, and the bigger she got, the prettier she was. Curly black hair crowned her head and two colors fought for control of her eyes. Sometimes they were green like Abba's, and sometimes brown like Imma's.

"You little chameleon!" I would tease her. "How do you manage to change colors?"

She would look at me, give a hearty laugh and crawl from one corner of the room to another. How different she was from quiet, serious Yehudit. This little mischief-maker could squeeze herself into any corner and hide under all the furniture. When we found her, she would burst into peals of laughter.

"The whole country is on the verge of collapse and you sit and laugh!" Naomi scolded, and then she and I would burst out laughing too. It was impossible to remain indifferent to Ruthie's infectious laughter. "She has a *lev same'ach* — a happy heart," Savta would say when she fed her.

Sometimes we would take her out for a walk in her carriage, along with Yehudit, for a breath of fresh air. But the air was full of gun smoke and the atmosphere full of strife. Both the Etzel and the Hagana were holding military exercises under the very noses of the British, who indeed had begun to feel that the ground was burning under their feet.

Was it the terrorist activity of Etzel and Lechi or the political pressure of the Hagana that had brought all this about? One

47

way or the other, a turning point had finally been reached, and the British government had decided that the United Nations should determine the future of Eretz Yisrael. A U.N. inquiry committee had therefore arrived in Palestine to investigate the problem and to suggest possible solutions.

One proposal, which set the whole country astir, came unexpectedly from the Jewish Agency: partition of Eretz Yisrael between the Jews and the Arabs.

"Partition." The very word commanded attention. Everyone, everywhere, talked about the Partition Plan — even the children on the way to school, in school, and on the bus home. In the afternoon, groups of people could be seen in the streets, in the Batei Machse square, outside the synagogue and on every corner, arguing loudly. Some supported the idea of partition while others rejected it completely.

Of course the girls in the lot were also busy weighing the pros and cons. Frieda said she didn't care what happened as long as the British left the country. Other girls hoped that the U.N. committee would accept the Jewish Agency's suggestion and divide Eretz Yisrael into an Arab and a Jewish state.

"That's the only way to finally have a state of our own," they said, "for they will never give us the entire country."

The Etzelniks, of course, would not stand for that. "What? Divide our own Eretz Yisrael in two? Never!" they cried, almost ready to come to blows with their opponents.

"The Arabs have seven large countries already. Isn't that enough?" explained Chana heatedly.

"Let them go to the Arab countries and reclaim the deserts there!" her sister Rachel added.

But the moderate faction was not to be outdone either.

"A bird in the hand is worth two in the bush," quoted Chava, as Yaffale explained what she meant: the Jewish Agency had only suggested partition because they knew that any solution which did not take the Arab population into consideration would not be acceptable to the U.N. committee.

Spirits ran high. One group of girls chanted loudly, "Partition will take place — The Jewish State will be born." The others would answer, just as loudly, "Eretz Yisrael is indivisible! There are two banks to the Jordan; both are ours!"

All night long, the opinions I had heard during the day would go round and round in my head. "Partition...partition... partition," my feverish brain repeated. "Two banks to the Jordan; both are ours," the song reverberated. And above all else, one thought stood out, overshadowing the rest: *Independence.*

Perhaps a miracle would occur; perhaps our dream would come true. Perhaps...perhaps the committee would decide that there should be an independent Jewish state. After two thousand years, we would have an independent state! Even if it were just a small state, including just a part of the total area of Eretz Yisrael, it would be ours, ours alone!

13 Enmity

As the work of the U.N. inquiry committee progressed and world opinion seemed more and more in favor of granting the Jewish people an independent homeland, no matter how small, Arab-Jewish tension grew. Jews were weighing the pros and cons of the partition plan, but Arab consensus was unanimous: NO! No Jewish state. Not ever!

I remember walking beside Imma in the Batrak *shuk.* Carrying our bags, we passed the Arab women sitting on the ground with their baskets of fruit for sale before them. The vendors no longer greeted us as they used to. One Arab, who used to sell us potatoes and onions with a smile, now scowled and glanced at his neighbors out of the corner of his eye. When

49

no one was looking, he hurriedly weighed a few pounds of potatoes and threw them into my basket.

A partially blind Arab stopped his cart, laden with fresh *pittot*, just long enough to shake his fist at us. Imma bought hastily, not taking time to pick and choose as she normally did. Our baskets filled up, and I held on tightly to Imma's dress, staying close to her side.

We left the vegetable market and turned into a dark, narrow alleyway. Everywhere, we saw black eyes glittering with hatred. As we passed, the vendors fell silent and the little Arab boys stopped to point at us and run their fingers across their throats. The meaning was clear: Just you wait . . . soon we will slaughter you!

We walked a few more steps, and I held on to Imma so tightly that I couldn't even tremble. If only we were home! Imma walked faster, dragging me along. Why, why did we ever go to the *shuk*? From inside the shops and from both sides of the street all eyes were turned on us . . . fiery eyes, burning with hatred. Finally, we were out of their sight. We reached Jewish Quarter Street. Slowly, my fear abated, and I was able to speak again.

"Imma, how could such a thing happen? How is it possible? We always used to buy from them, and they were always so nice. How can everything have changed so suddenly? How did all these friendly people become so hateful?"

"They were never really our friends," Imma gestured with her hand as if to wave them away. "They have always hated us, but until now their hatred was hidden behind their smiles. Now they think that circumstances are in their favor. The British support them, and so their hidden hatred has risen to the surface."

"Imma, promise me that you will never go to the Arab *shuk* again," I pleaded. "Promise, please, Imma!"

"I promise."

"I was so scared," I said, my relief now evident. "Do you know who I felt like?"

"Who, my darling?"

"Like Little Red Riding Hood when the wolf was about to swallow her. Did you see their eyes? They were staring at us from every corner. Not just the eyes of one wolf, like in the story. Many, many wolves were lying in wait for us, waiting for their prey."

14 Preparing for the Future

"Left, right! Left, right!" Fourteen young soldiers and their commander marched towards the lot one afternoon while we were playing hide and seek.

"Children, move to the side," Yossi, their commander, called to us. We retreated from the lot and stationed ourselves at a convenient point in the yard of the Rothschild building, where we could see everything that was going on.

The young men spread out across the lot and began drilling. "Attention, stand! About face!" Yossi ordered. The boys followed the commands with ease and then progressed to more difficult exercises.

They practiced climbing on the low rooftops, from one rounded roof to the next. They disappeared, suddenly reappearing unexpectedly on an opposite rooftop. Yossi instructed them in a loud voice.

"Look! You turn around with your back facing outwards and then you let your legs down. Watch this!" He turned around, lowered his legs and dropped his whole body until he was hanging free, only his hands grasping the roof of the building.

"Can you all see?" he asked. His feet were only about three feet above ground level.

"And now — hup!" he cried and jumped to the ground.

"Forward, David, you're next."

David approached the edge of the roof and jumped.

"Aaron! Your turn!"

We watched everything with great interest. When everyone had a turn jumping, Yossi said, "Now we will practice shooting at a target."

One of the boys was sent out of the lot. A few minutes later he returned, presenting his commander with a rifle. A real rifle!

Yossi lay down behind a small mound of dirt and explained, "This mound is our post, and that is the target." He pointed to the building from which they had just jumped. "Do you see the small window on the left? I am going to shoot at it!"

Yossi cocked his rifle and a loud bang filled the air. The bullet had hit its target.

David was the first to approach the mound. Yossi again demonstrated how to cock the rifle and how to pull the trigger. David took hold of the rifle and lay down behind the mound. He cocked the rifle. We all waited tensely. A shot was heard. He had hit the target!

Another boy approached the post and repeated the exercise, but he missed. One after another, all the boys tried their luck. Some succeeded, some did not.

"Aiy!" A cry of pain was heard. Tzion fell to the ground, blood oozing from his knee. He had shot a bullet from the rifle and hit his knee! Yossi checked the wound and decided that it was nothing ... really nothing, just a scratch.

Two boys picked up Tzion and carried him to the other side of the fence, near us. Tzion groaned, but Yossi said, "It's not so bad, mate. You will have to suffer worse wounds than that."

Yossi's words were indeed a prophecy of the future. Long after that, in the last days of the Jewish Quarter, Tzion was wounded very seriously.

We watched the boys continue their drilling. We were at

once fascinated and fearful. All of a sudden, in the middle of an exercise, the boys and their commander jumped up and scattered, disappearing from sight as quickly as if the earth had swallowed them up. We stood there, dumbfounded.

English soldiers appeared at the edge of the lot! Chava, who was the first to catch sight of them, called to us — "Hurry up girls! I'm 'It'! One, two, three..."

Chava tried to catch us as we ran away from her in all directions. Out of the corner of my eye, I watched Tzion, who had been left in the yard of the Rothschild building, lying on the ground and groaning. Deep down I was angry. "Is that the way to treat a friend? Why did they leave him here all by himself, with no way to protect himself?"

"Where are the boys who were here a minute ago?" asked the English soldiers as they approached us.

"What? Who?" We pretended not to know what they were talking about.

"Those boys from the Hagana who were drilling here. We heard them clearly. Where did they go?"

"We've been playing here for hours," Chava replied innocently, "and we haven't seen any boys here."

The soldiers turned away and began to search the area. "Aha, we've caught you!" they exclaimed when they chanced upon poor Tzion lying on the ground. "What are you doing here?"

"I...I...," Tzion stammered. "Uh, I fell off the fence, and, uh, my foot, I seem to have broken it!"

"Yes, yes," Rachel came to his aid, "I have been standing here the whole time. He just fell off this fence," she said, pointing to the stone fence of the Rothschild building.

At that we all began to cry and shout, "First aid! First aid! Poor Tzion! Someone get some first aid!"

Just then a whistle blew. For some unknown reason, the British commander was calling his soldiers in, and they left as suddenly as they had come. Tzion heaved a sigh of relief, and we, too, breathed deeply.

"We must begin drilling, too," announced Chana the next day, sticking both thumbs in her mouth as usual.

"Forward!" we cried enthusiastically, as Chava assumed command.

"Forward march, left, right . . . left, right . . . left, right, left . . ." We marched around the lot in single file.

"About face!" Chava ordered, and we all turned around, in a perfect imitation of the boys' maneuvers. Then Chava led us all around the stone fences between the Batei Machse houses until finally she found a fence that was high enough for all of us to jump from.

"Let's jump! Who wants to be first?" Chava moved to the edge of the high fence and turned around; she let her long legs down, holding on to the fence with her hands, and . . . hup . . . she jumped!

"Beautiful!" we cried. "Just like a soldier."

"Who is next?" Rachel came forward and repeated the exercise. After her, we all mustered courage and jumped, one after the other.

"Now run, quickly!" called our commander, and we all bolted back to the lot.

15 A Brother

In the midst of all the tension, our baby brother was born. At last, a boy! At that time, we had no idea that this little baby, who so gladdened our hearts at his birth, would have to grow up in such a difficult time. His *brit mila* was held in the Hadassah Hospital on Mount Scopus. That was the last time that we, and many of our guests, were to see the hospital for years to come. But then, as we answered "Amen" to the blessings and enjoyed the festive meal, none of us had any idea of what the future held in store. Our guests were happy; Abba and Imma were overjoyed; and we girls felt that there was nothing more we could ask for.

In honor of the baby's birth, and in keeping with our spirit of celebration, Abba bought us a wonderful gift — an icebox.

"Nowadays, cooked food can be kept from one day to the next," Abba announced proudly. The new icebox took its place in our one-room apartment, in the corner nearest the kitchen. Abba recited the blessing over joyous tidings, *hatov veha-meitiv*, and we answered "Amen."

The icebox was no more than ten cubic feet and it had two compartments: a lower door opened onto two handsome shelves for food storage, and an upper door contained half a block of ice, wrapped in a sack, which had to be lugged home daily from the iceman. During the day the ice would gradually melt, and the water would flow through a pipe from the icebox to a compartment near the floor. Our new icebox didn't save Imma much cooking, but it did keep the milk from spoiling. Until then, the milk would frequently turn sour, even though we boiled it in a big pot and stored it on the shady, northern windowsill in the kitchen.

How happy we were with our new brother and how proud we were of our new acquisition. Even the ominous clouds of war did not dim the joy inside our house.

16 The Fateful Vote

A mere four weeks after Yehuda's birth, the fateful night for which we had all been waiting arrived.

"Australia." — "Yes."

"Bolivia." — "Yes."

"Canada." — "Yes."

"Ecuador." — "Yes."
"Egypt." — "No."

These were the voices we heard on Saturday evening, the 17th of Kislev 5708 (the 29th of November 1947). Glued to the radio, we listened to the fateful United Nations Assembly vote. The proposal was to divide Eretz Yisrael into two independent countries. The committee had recently completed its investigation and presented its conclusions to the U.N. A compromise partition plan had been proposed in which the amount of land allocated to the Jewish State was much smaller than that proposed by the Jewish Agency. Jerusalem, according to the proposal, was to be an international city. Even so, this was the first time that the nations of the world had proposed to grant the Jewish people political independence!

"Great Britain." — "Abstains." — We heard the U.N. secretary on our radio.

"Iran." — "No."

The suspense grew. In our efforts to get closer to the radio, we even pushed one another aside.

"United States." — "Yes."

"U.S.S.R." called the U.N. secretary. One could have heard a pin drop in the room. "Yes."

The votes were counted. Thirty-three states had voted in favor of the proposal. A majority! We would have a state of our own — a Jewish state!

It is hard to describe the celebration which took place all that night and all the next day in the city. People filled the streets and squares, laughing and crying, singing and dancing. "At long last, an independent, Jewish state!"

The next day, the hostile faces of the Arabs on the street seemed to say "Just wait! We'll show you!" But nothing could dampen the joy which filled every Jewish heart.

Part II

Under
Siege

17 Rioting Breaks Out

For two days we were drunk with joy. On the third day we went to school as usual and finished at the normal time. As I was getting ready to go home, one of the other girls summoned me to the Teachers' Room.

"Why?" I asked.

She shrugged her shoulders. "They only told me to call you," she said and walked away quickly.

Naomi was waiting there before me. My teacher greeted me, stroked my cheek, and told me, her voice softer than usual, "Today you are not to go home to the Old City. You must go to your grandparents in town, in Beit Yisrael."

"Why?" asked Naomi, worried.

"I don't know," answered the teacher, but it was obvious that she was not telling us all she knew. "Your father just asked me to give you this message."

"All right, we'll go to our grandparents," promised Naomi, the first signs of anxiety appearing on her face.

We left school together with the other girls who were walking towards Beit Yisrael, aware of the pitying glances we were receiving.

"Is it true that Arabs beat up your father near Jaffa Gate?" Pnina, a third grader, asked us as soon as we had left the schoolyard.

"No, of course it's not true!" I replied vehemently, wondering where she had heard such a thing.

"Yes, yes, it is true! I heard your teacher telling mine all about it," insisted another girl.

"It's possible," a few of the girls concurred. "If not, why should they tell you to go to your grandparents' instead of going home? There must be something wrong."

"There must be," agreed the others. "We all heard that there were riots in the Old City today."

We kept on walking, our hearts heavy with fear. On the way we passed many people on the street, all talking about the news. Little by little, we collected bits and pieces of information and added them up. By the time we reached Beit Yisrael, we had a clear picture of what had happened. That morning, the Arabs had begun to strike and to demonstrate against the United Nations decision. The Number 2/a bus was stoned. Jewish pedestrians in the Old City were beaten.

Finally, we reached Beit Yisrael. There, at the edge of the neighborhood on Shmuel Hanavi Street, stood our beloved grandparents' house. Bobba is what we called my mother's mother to distinguish her from Savta, my father's mother in the Old City. As soon as we walked in, Bobba ran towards us and hugged us with her bony hands.

"How good that you didn't go home today! Very good!" She said, nodding her head from side to side.

"Where is Abba?" she asked at last. "Did he go to teach today?"

"Yes, he did," we answered.

"Then where is he? Did he go home?"

Bobba was worried, but we couldn't answer a single one of her many questions. Soon after, our grandfather Zeideh came home. He was very happy to see us, although he, too, was unable to hide his anxiety. Then Aunt Margalit came home from work and smothered us with kisses.

"My darlings!" she cried. Turning to Bobba but making no attempt to hide anything from us, she continued, "Don't let them go back to the Old City. It's dangerous there now that the Arabs are rioting."

For the time being we would have to stay with our grandparents until things quieted down. Two or three days passed but the riots did not stop. The Arabs set fire to the shopping center and pillaged it. The newspapers were full of other bitter news as well. All over the country riots had broken out.

18 To Meet on Happy Occasions

Days passed, and we were still at Bobba's house for it was almost impossible to get back into the Old City. Every day we joined the group of Beit Yisrael girls who walked to school together, and wherever we went, we saw people preparing for the impending war. Men and women were busy filling sacks with sand to protect their windows from shells. Protective brick walls were built in front of entrance halls and doorways. Windows were blocked up. Stores were full as people stocked up on basic food supplies. "Who knows what tomorrow will bring," they said.

We were instructed not to roam around the streets once school was over. At the sound of a warning siren we were to take cover in the nearest stairwell or shelter. While running to the shelter we were to cover our heads with a briefcase, bag, or our hands.

During that period, not a single girl from the Old City came to school. We had no idea whether Abba was teaching in his school in town or not, for we heard absolutely nothing from him. Eight days had passed, the holiday of Chanuka had arrived and we were still at our Bobba's. The dress I was wearing was all spotted and sweaty, but I had no other change of clothing. My mood was as dingy and gloomy as my dress.

"We are going to a wedding today!" Bobba announced one day during Chanuka. She thought that this news would cheer us up, but I answered angrily, "I won't go!"

"Why not? Come, it will make you happy."

"No! Never! I will not go to any wedding wearing such a filthy dress. I'd rather stay home."

"You can't, darling. You can't stay home by yourself."

"Who has a wedding at a time like this?" I grumbled. "How can anyone be happy now?"

Bobba tried to explain that in times like these it was of vital importance to start new families and to strengthen the Jewish people. But I, not understanding her words, only grew angrier. When she saw that there was no use continuing the conversation anymore, she busied herself with lunch.

After the meal, everyone dressed up in their Shabbat best and called Naomi and me — in our dirty schooldresses that we had been wearing for ten days — to come. I grumbled and complained bitterly, but to no avail. I was forced to join the party.

"Come wish the bride mazal tov," called Aunt Margalit.

"No!" I insisted stubbornly. "I don't want to."

"Here, taste this delicious cake," she said and put a piece of cake in my hand. I shrugged my shoulders, but the cake melting in my hand was too tempting. It was ages since I had even seen such a luscious piece of cake. When no one was looking I hurriedly gulped it down.

The other guests shook their heads at us, and some asked Aunt Margalit if we were her nieces. When she said yes, they sighed and called us poor little girls. I finally found refuge in a far corner where I could escape their pitying glances. Aside from my embarrassment, I was in no mood for the singing and dancing. All I could think of were my father and mother — so far away from me. What were they doing now? What was happening in the Old City? If Abba and Imma could only have come to the wedding, I would have been able to celebrate too.

"Where is she? Where did she go?" I heard voices calling my name. Coming out from my hiding place, I left my reveries behind as Aunt Margalit took my hand. "Let's go," she said.

"Let's meet again on other happy occasions!" people called to one another as they left. Now, in this time of danger, this commonplace wish took on a special significance.

19 Abba's Visit

One night we heard shooting. We were sleeping in Aunt Margalit's small bedroom when suddenly the sound of an explosion woke us all up.

"What's that? What's that?" I cried in alarm.

My grandparents were already up. Hastily, they brought us into the kitchen, which had no windows onto the street.

"What's that?" I asked again, as a second explosion was heard.

"Gunfire," answered Bobba. "They're shooting from Sheikh Jarrah." She spread a blanket for us on the kitchen floor, but we couldn't fall asleep. "Where is Sheikh Jarrah?" I asked.

"It's an Arab village on the hill facing us," answered Zeideh. "I see it's time to put sacks of sand in the living-room window overlooking Shmuel Hanavi Street. Tomorrow I'll have to get to work."

"In the kitchen too!" I demanded. "Cover up all the windows in the house!"

After a long while, the gunfire finally stopped, but we did not fall asleep until early morning. Nevertheless, we got up on time to go to school as usual.

"Abba!" Naomi cried as she walked into the living room. I looked through the doorway, and sure enough, there on the green plush sofa sat Abba! As I ran towards him, I knocked over a small vase on the table and it shattered into pieces. At first, Aunt Margalit was angry, but when she saw how excited I was to see Abba, tears welled up in her eyes, and she forgot about the vase. Abba took me on his lap and kissed me on the forehead, and I, I broke out in tears.

"Where were you all this time?" asked Naomi. "Why didn't you come to see us? Have you been going to teach?"

"No, my little one. It's hard to leave the Old City now. Today is the first time I succeeded in getting out."

"Will you be able to come again tomorrow?" I asked.

"Probably not. I have exchanged places with another teacher. He lives in town and teaches in the Old City, while I live in the Old City and teach in town. So we made arrangements to exchange jobs, and starting tomorrow I will teach in the Old City in his place."

"How will you get home now?"

"The Hagana helped arrange the exchange of teachers, and they are sending a group to the Old City in an armed convoy today. The British have issued a permit for the convoy to pass through. Until now, the children in the Old City have not been going to school, because there were so few teachers available. I will return home with the convoy of teachers. As of tomorrow, I'll be teaching in the Sephardic *talmud Torah* in the Old City."

Abba had brought us a bundle of clothing. While we were busy opening the package, the grownups had time to discuss the situation, but there were so many questions that *I* wanted to ask! What were my little sisters doing now? With every passing day I missed them more. How was our baby, little Yudale? Who was helping Imma? But Abba was engrossed in conversation

63

with the adults and I could not interrupt him.

"The Old City is under siege," he told them.

"A real siege?" asked Aunt Margalit.

"Yes, a real one."

"That means that no one can get in or out?"

"Not exactly," answered Abba. "There are convoys, but it's very hard to get a place on one. The number of passengers is limited."

"Is there shooting?" asked Zeideh, almost in a whisper. Abba purposely ignored the question.

"What about food?" asked Bobba.

"Food is brought in by convoy. There is no lack."

Nevertheless, Bobba hurried to make up a package for Imma and the children.

Abba stood up to go. "Be well," he wished my grandparents and Aunt Margalit.

"And you," he turned to us, "be good girls. You are very lucky to be here. This way you can continue your schooling in peace and quiet and not be shut up in the Old City like the other children."

"When will you come back?" asked Naomi sadly. Abba didn't answer. He kissed us over and over again, and then went on his way.

"Abba will not come back," I told my sister when he was gone. "Didn't you hear him say that he was joining the teachers sent by the Hagana? From now on, Abba will teach in the Old City."

20 Kerosene!

Jerusalem was under siege. Not only the Old City within the walls, but the New City as well. The Arabs had control of the

64

road from Tel Aviv to Jerusalem, and only large, organized convoys under armed guard could get through. Even these convoys, carrying food and supplies to the city, were regularly attacked from the Arab villages in the Judean hills. Often, they barely managed to reach their destination.

Every once in a while we would gain control of one or another of the Arab villages and clear the road, but then it would be blockaded again, until the blockade was broken. Less and less food and cooking fuel were available, and people began to worry. How would all this end?

It was afternoon; a bell rang and a voice called, "Kerosene! Kerosene!" We grabbed money and a tin can from Bobba and ran downstairs to join the long line of people anxious to refill their dwindling supply of precious kerosene. The line already stretched the whole length of the street. A horse and wagon carrying a large tank of kerosene stood in the middle of the street. The wagoner, a strong, gruff man, sold half a gallon only to each customer. All waited in line for their turns, some patiently, some impatiently. It was raining, so we turned our tin upside down, to keep the inside dry. For a long time we stood in line, yet there were still many people ahead of us. Would there be any kerosene left by the time our turn came?

Finally, only one woman was left in front of us. Soon, soon, we too would get our kerosene. When our turn came, the wagoner put his tin pitcher under the tank and opened the spigot. To our great dismay, only a few drops fell into the pitcher. There was no more kerosene left! Tears welled up in our eyes. The wagoner looked at us, and overcome with pity, he called the woman who had been in line before us and ordered, "Give back a quarter of a gallon!" At first, she refused, but when the wagoner approached her threateningly, she changed her mind. He took her tin of kerosene, returned some money to her, and sold a quarter of a gallon to us. Then he mounted his wagon, gave his horse a few lashes with his whip, and calling "dio, dio" to the horse, drove away. He left many disappointed people behind him in the street, but we ran happily upstairs to Bobba, carrying the precious tin.

"Bobba," we cried excitedly, "Bobba, look! We've brought kerosene! Now you can light the stove and start cooking!"

Bobba kissed us on the cheeks. Her eyes lit up, as she filled the tiny kerosene cooker, fixed the wicks and lit them. Then she put a pot of potato soup on to cook. A pleasant heat filled the kitchen, and we held our cold hands near the warm stove.

21 Yes or No?

"Yes or no?" Aunt Margalit asked me one day.

"Yes or no what?" I returned her question.

"Never mind. Just say yes or no. Which one?"

I thought a minute and answered, "Yes." Aunt Margalit smiled.

"Yes or no?" she asked Naomi.

"I don't know."

"Answer anyway. Which do you choose?"

"I don't know which to choose."

Naomi slipped outside and returned holding a chrysanthemum in her hand. She plucked the white petals one by one, chanting, "Yes, no, yes, no; let's see what it will be. Yes, no, yes. It's yes!"

Aunt Margalit smiled broadly and repeated, "Yes!"

"Yes what?" we both asked at once.

"Oh, nothing much," she continued, smiling as she went into the kitchen.

A few days passed and we forgot about the funny question. Then, one day, Aunt Margalit sat us down beside her on the sofa and announced importantly, "I want to talk to you, girls. You will soon have a new uncle."

"What? How?" we asked.

"I am getting married in three weeks."

"To whom?" asked Naomi.

"A young man from Hungary, a refugee from the war."

"Where can you have a wedding at a time like this?" I asked, remembering the wedding which had made me so angry during our first days in Beit Yisrael.

"In Tel Aviv."

"In Tel Aviv?" we both exclaimed in surprise.

"Yes, the situation is better there."

"But how will you get to Tel Aviv?"

"That's a good question," sighed Aunt Margalit. "I don't know. Perhaps by convoy."

The next day we found out that our grandparents would also go to Tel Aviv.

"Who will take care of us?" we asked Bobba.

"Don't worry, I talked to your Aunt Rivka, your Abba's sister. You will both stay at her house in Sanhedria for a while until we come back."

That Shabbat at lunch, we met the bridegroom. It was with mixed feelings that we greeted him, for the coming change in our daily lives worried us a little. Aunt Margalit, however, was very happy. For two weeks, delicious smells of baking filled the apartment. Bobba received extra food rations in honor of the forthcoming event. A great big tin can filled with coconut and peanut cookies stood in the cupboard, and every once in a while Aunt Margalit would treat us to a luscious cookie to cheer us up.

* * *

"I can't fall asleep," I whispered to Naomi one night, after I had been lying in bed for a long time, deep in thought. "Come into my bed, I'm afraid…"

"What are you afraid of now? There's no shooting tonight."

"Come into my bed," I pleaded, my voice choked with tears.

Naomi climbed into my bed and tried to reassure me. "It's quiet now. There is no shooting tonight. Why are you crying?"

"When the Arabs aren't shooting at us, they're shooting at someone else!" I blurted out.

"So what? What do you care if they're shooting at someone else?"

"You don't understand. They're ... they're shooting at the Old City right now!" I cried.

"How do you know?"

"I'm positive. If it's quiet here, then there ... there ... who knows what's happening there! Perhaps, perhaps at this very moment a shell is falling on our house and ..." my teeth started chattering.

"Sh ... stop crying," Naomi stroked my wet cheeks. "If all's quiet over here, it's probably quiet over there, too. I'm sure of it."

"I want to go home!"

"You can't. You must wait."

"I can't wait anymore! No more! I can hardly remember what Imma looks like. And Yehuda. I won't even recognize him."

"Puah, please, don't think about that now. Tomorrow we are going to Aunt Rivka's. It'll be so nice there. Uncle Yosef has a bookstore. He'll bring us beautiful picture books with interesting stories."

My sister talked on and on, until my eyes began to close. In the morning we woke up to find that we were both still in my bed.

Aunt Rivka came to pick us up and take us to her house in Sanhedria, a quiet neighborhood in north Jerusalem. Aunt Rivka lived in "the apartment house" — a large housing development on the outskirts of Sanhedria. From her quiet balcony one could see the bare Judean hills covered with gray-white rocks. Her house was immaculate, and there was nothing to disturb the tranquil atmosphere. Aunt Rivka took very good care of us, and our cousin Ruthie became our fast friend. We settled down for a pleasant stay as the warm, quiet household calmed me down and helped me forget my fears.

It was a cold, rainy winter. A gigantic puddle the size of a swimming pool cut off all access to Aunt Rivka's house. We all stayed indoors and had a good time reading Uncle Yosef's lovely books, until the puddle finally dried up and we had to go back to school again.

22 Chubeiza

Weeks passed. Our grandparents returned to Jerusalem, and we moved back to their house on Shmuel Hanavi Street. Every day we went to school and at night ... at night, not infrequently, we lay for hours on the kitchen floor listening to the Arabs in nearby Sheikh Jarrah shooting at Beit Yisrael.

Every afternoon the neighborhood children would all play outside in the empty lot behind our row of houses. It was winter, in the month of Adar, and after the heavy winter rains, the grass in the "field" was thick and green. We would frolic like goats, searching for chubeiza, the dark green mallow leaves — really a common weed — which grew plentifully in the lush winter grass. Along with the others, Naomi and I spent hours picking chubeiza, competing with each other as to who would pick more leaves.

Food in besieged Jerusalem was in short supply, and the wild mallow leaves became an important part of our diet. Our Bobba knew how to make tasty mallow "hamburger" patties, and we did our best to bring her as many leaves as we could.

Some of the plants also had little "buttons" which were tasty fruits to us.

"Apples, apples," I called to Naomi, eating a mouthful of chubeiza buttons. I closed my eyes and pretended that I was eating a real, juicy apple.

* * *

It was a lovely day. The sweet smell of the earth after a good rain pricked our nostrils and drew us out to the field. The rain which had fallen earlier in the week had caused fresh chubeiza to sprout up all over the plot, and we deftly picked the green leaves and small fruit. As we breathed in the pure clean air, we had no desire to go home — back to the stuffy rooms whose windows were filled with sacks of sand.

The upturned hem of my dress was already overflowing with leaves, but I kept on picking. It was twilight. Only a few children were left in the field. Slowly it got darker and darker. Not a ray of light escaped from the houses nearby, as there was a strict blackout in force.

"Let's go home already," I called to Naomi, as I suddenly realized that we were surrounded by darkness.

"One more minute... only ten more leaves."

Suddenly we heard a soft buzz over our heads, and something like lightning lit up the whole area with a bright red light, illuminating the big lot and all the houses nearby. I stood fixed in my place, gazing in wonder at the great illuminated dome of the sky, when I suddenly heard a scream which made my hair stand on end.

"It's a rocket! Run! Run!"

Naomi grabbed my hand and pulled me after her. "Fast!" she cried. "Why are you nailed to the spot? Move!"

We ran towards the entrance to our house, and just as we reached the doorway, a thunderous explosion sounded from the direction of the field. We ran into the kitchen and lay flat on the floor. My heart was beating like a hammer and my knees were shaking. The shooting continued.

"Where have you been?" scolded Bobba. It took a few minutes until my breath came back to me and I could speak again.

"What was that, Naomi?" I asked, still shaking with fright.

"A rocket."

"What? You were outside when a rocket exploded?" Bobba asked in terror. "But you weren't hurt? You're all right? What a miracle! What a miracle!" She hugged us to her as hard as she could.

"What's a rocket?" I asked.

"A rocket is a sort of light-bomb which the enemy shoots to light up a certain area. Then they can see what's there and focus their shots better."

"What a miracle!" I, too, exclaimed.

"*Baruch Hashem* we were able to get out of the rocket's light," added Naomi.

"It is absolutely forbidden to be outside at night!" warned our Bobba. For a few days after that we were not allowed to go outside to pick chubeiza at all, until gradually the memory of the incident faded from Bobba's mind.

23 A Forgotten Birthday

"Why are you so sad?" Naomi asked me one rainy morning. Instead of answering, I looked at her with a mournful gaze. Tears filled my eyes, but I would not cry.

"How can she even ask?" I thought to myself. "Doesn't she know? Doesn't she remember? Why shouldn't I be sad?"

Today was my birthday. I was seven years old, but no one knew it; no one remembered. A minute later I corrected myself.

Somebody at home did remember — Abba! He never ever forgot, and he wouldn't forget his daughter today either. I knew that.

But Abba was far away. He was in the Old City, surrounded on all sides by the enemy — besieged. Even if he wanted to, he couldn't wish me a happy birthday now. Today I would not receive a single birthday present.

Last year, when I was six, Abba gave me a beautiful black *siddur*. On the frontispiece, in gold and black lettering, was written *mipi olalim* — from the mouth of babes. That *siddur*, which I saved for Shabbat, was my pride and joy. Every Friday night I would take it with me to the Churva. Now it must be quite forlorn, sitting untouched on the bookshelf of our apartment in the Old City.

And Abba, did he still go to the Churva on Friday nights? Perhaps he could not even leave the house because of all the shooting?

Today I was seven years old, and in second grade. I wondered what present Abba would have given me. No, today I would not receive any presents. Today I would not wear my Shabbat clothes, nor eat sweets nor receive any mazal tovs. Today was a regular school day, and a damp rainy one at that. For lunch we would eat chubeiza patties, and at night we would sleep on the kitchen floor.

"Abba," my heart cried suddenly, "Abba, give me your *bracha* from afar. No, not from afar. Come and get me, come..."

The tears in my eyes wanted to seep out onto my cheeks, but I forced myself to hold them back. Today I would not cry! I was a big girl, seven years old, and I would not cry. I drifted back into my sad memories.

"Imma, Imma," I called wordlessly, "when will I see you? Do you have time to think about your seven-year-old daughter? Do you know how much I miss you?"

After lunch I received some comfort. My sister did remember the date, and she gave me a small present of her own — some of her crayons, gift-wrapped in flowered paper and accompanied by a card:

To my dear sister,
Happy seventh birthday.
I hope that we will celebrate your eighth birthday
all together in an independent Jewish state,
without the sounds of shells and shooting.

24 A Convoy Home

The month of Nissan arrived, and with it our spring vacation. Everyone was home preparing for Pesach. Everyone, that is, except for us. We were still at our Bobba's. Four months of riots were already behind us, but it was clear that the real war would begin only in another month and a half, when the British left the country.

Our Bobba was busy cleaning her house for Pesach. Since water was scarce, we cleaned the furniture and cupboards with dry rags. As we helped, we became more and more homesick. We couldn't help begging, "Please, take us home!"

Our grandparents understood how we felt and began to make plans. "We'll send you home as soon as we can," they promised.

One day, early in the morning, someone knocked on our door. It was Savta — our grandmother from the Old City. We jumped out of our beds and threw our arms around her.

"Savta, Savta," we cried with great emotion, "how did you get here? Is the siege over already? Is everyone all right?"

Savta hugged us both together. "No, girls, the siege is not over. I came in a convoy."

"Tell us about the convoy, Savta," I asked.

"No need to tell you. You'll see it all yourself today."

"We will?"

"Yes. Today. I'm taking you home."

"Home? Today? At last!"

"We're going home today! Home!" We both ran into the living room to announce the good news. Everyone sat around the big dining table as Zeideh and Bobba asked Savta about the family and the situation in the Old City.

"Are you sure it's wise to take the girls there?" asked Zeideh.

"Yes, yes! It is wise!" we interrupted.

"It is too hard for them to be separated from their parents any longer," said Bobba. "They are too homesick."

"When war breaks out, in the near future, no one knows where it will be safest or easiest. The best thing is for the girls to be together with their parents," said Savta.

"That's true," agreed Zeideh. "Besides, perhaps things will be better in the Old City. After all, the Old City is sacred to the Moslems and the Christians too. Certainly no one will dare to destroy it."

"We can never tell," replied Bobba.

"God will protect us all, wherever we are," concluded Zeideh.

Both grandmothers began to pack up our belongings. Overcome with joy, we ran to get our school bags, and greatly excited, we parted from our Bobba and Zeideh and set out on our way.

We had a long walk through the city. Savta carried our bundles of clothes, and we took our winter coats and school bags. It was a hot day, the beginning of spring. But spring and the coming holiday did not gladden the faces of the few passersby on the streets. Every sack-filled window, every protective wall, every barbed-wire fence, every set of anxious eyes announced the impending war. In place of happiness, the Pesach holiday was bringing new worries: where would everyone get wine and *matzot* for the *seder*? Where would their sons, who had joined the fledgling army, be that night? Would the British choose to make the *seder* night a night of searches and arrests? What would happen afterwards?

We walked along King George Street towards the Jewish Agency complex, where we found a large crowd of men and women already waiting. Savta made her way through the crowd, and we found ourselves at the end of a long line in front of a latticed window.

"We must get an entrance permit to the Old City from the clerk here," explained Savta.

We stood in line for a long time, trying hard to hold onto Savta amidst the great crowd. Our coats and school bags were very heavy and the sweat streamed down our faces. Just as we thought we could not hold out any longer, Savta reached the clerk at the window. After arguing, explaining, presenting her documents, filling out forms and paying the fee, Savta finally received the permits. With a long sigh of relief, we left the line.

A high meshed wire fence was drawn from one side of the street to the other, delineating a military zone. British soldiers guarded a narrow entrance on one side of the fence.

"The armored cars which will take us to the Old City will come from over there, behind that fence," said Savta. "We have to wait here." We sat down on the curb and waited.

"Are you taking those little girls into the Old City?" asked a fat woman standing beside Savta.

"Yes," she answered curtly.

"Are you crazy? To take little girls *into* the Old City — into that lion's den? What madness!" As the woman talked, she paced back and forth and gestured wildly with her hands, so that we soon became the center of attention.

"Who says the Old City is a lion's den!" Savta retorted. "When the British leave, there will be fighting everywhere."

Meanwhile, more and more people had joined the crowd.

"Are they all going to the Old City?" I wondered to myself. "Can it be such a large convoy?"

The sun beat down on our heads. We had already been sitting there for almost three hours, perhaps even longer. Finally, a few steel, armored cars drove up to the fenced-off area. Immediately, people charged the narrow gateway, everyone trying to enter at once, but the British soldiers pushed away the angry crowd.

"Only those whose names are called shall enter," announced a short man, apparently a Jewish Agency clerk. Nonetheless, most of the crowd remained at the fence.

Suddenly, we heard our names called out loud. We tried to push our way to the narrow gate, carrying all our bundles, but we could not get through. Impatiently, the clerk repeated our names. Savta fought her way through in front of us, using her elbows to break through the wall of people. At last we succeeded in reaching the military zone. A British soldier directed us to a small windowless armored "bus." Running all the way, we boarded the bus and sat down in the back. Again we sat and waited as everyone began to board.

Although it was high noon, the inside of the bus was dim. The heat was suffocating, and the windowless steel frame, baking in the sun, was like an oven. We sat there waiting for a long time, until the convoy was ready to start.

When the signal was finally given, the driver started the motor with a squeaky jerk. We began moving, leaving behind an angry crowd of those who had not been included. The convoy moved slowly and cautiously. We could see nothing outside, and the heat inside was almost unbearable. My head throbbed. Would we get there safely? Savta whispered the prayer for setting out on a journey:

"May it be Thy Will, our God and God of our fathers, that you lead us safely on our way ... and save us from every enemy and ambush..." I felt a bit better.

The armored bus made its way very slowly. Apparently we were traveling on a dirt road, for a lot of dust seeped into the bus despite the lack of windows. Then we seemed to return to a paved asphalt road, where the traveling was smoother. But the bus groaned and creaked beneath us, and then — it stopped! Had the motor burned out?

"Hit the ground at once!" the order was given. Within a second we were out of our seats and flat on the floor of the bus.

"Put your school bags over your heads!" Savta ordered. My hands trembling, I raised my school bag over my head, peeking out of the corners of my eyes at my sister. She also lay on the ground, her school bag over her head. No one made a sound. It was as though the bus were empty. In the silence I heard knocks — boom, boom, boom — like hammers in a smithy. Were those my heartbeats? No — they must have been the heartbeats — beating in terror — of all of the passengers together.

Shots. Yes, we could hear the gunfire. Would our British escorts return fire? Quiet. The shooting stopped and the bus began to move again.

"Return to your places!" called the driver, as he speeded up the bus.

Sighs of relief escaped from the passengers. I dared to peek out of the side of my school bag, and when I saw Savta already sitting on the bench in front of us, I too got up and returned to my seat, repeating the traveler's prayer to myself over and over again.

Where were we now? Was it such a long trip? It should not have taken more than fifteen minutes to cross into the Old City, yet it seemed as if we had been traveling for ages. Would we ever reach our destination? The motor hummed and the bus finally creaked to a stop.

Again? What had happened now? Were we being attacked again?

The door opened and light entered the bus.

"Everyone out!" ordered the driver. All the passengers began to push their way to the exit door.

25 Home Again

It was as hard getting off the bus as it was getting on. We had to push our way through a new crowd which was trying to board the convoy for the return trip *out* of the Old City. But we were finally back home.

Nothing had changed. The ancient wall of the city stood on our right, tall and straight, as if on guard. Beneath it lay the village of Silwan, unchanged, its little huts surrounded by cacti. Far away on the horizon rose the serene, blue hills of Moav, unaffected by the melancholy world we were living in. Before us were the steps leading down to the Kotel; and to our left was the thick, old wall of our house in Batei Machse with its latticed windows and domed roof. Our beloved house looked to me like an ancient fortress, warning the poor little huts of the Silwan, "You will not conquer us!"

We entered the open, iron gate to the familiar white stairs. Overcome with joy, we held the railing tightly as we went up the stairs to the old, familiar courtyard. Our door was open. Hearts pounding, we walked into the house. There, beside the big window, stood Imma, her back to us. Our old kerosene cooking stove was on the window sill, and Imma was frying little pancakes of stale bread.

"Imma!" My mouth formed the word, but no sound came from my throat.

"They're here!" announced a childish voice from one of the corners.

Imma turned around. Her eyes full of light, she stretched out her arms to us. We both fell into her arms and burst into tears.

"Imma, Imma, I'm so happy to be home," I whispered. "I don't know why I cried." But when I looked into Imma's lovely, dark face, I saw that she, too, had tears on her cheeks.

After that I turned to my two little sisters. Ruthie stood opposite us, giving a long speech in baby talk, accompanied by enthusiastic gestures and her charming laugh. Yehudit stood on the side, shy as ever, her thumb in her mouth, looking at us both with her great, big, black eyes. We took turns hugging and kissing them. In the end, the "Queen of the Babies" ended up around my neck, while Naomi held on to our little mischief-maker.

Together, we approached the carriage. Lo and behold — what did we see? Instead of a tiny month-old infant, lay a big baby who filled up almost the entire length of the carriage.

"Is that Yudale?" we cried in amazement. "How he has grown!"

The baby looked back at us and then slowly, a great smile spread over his face, as though he realized that we somehow belonged to him. Finally, we asked where Abba was.

"Abba went to distribute *matzot* for Pesach," answered Imma. "He is very busy now. He's almost never at home. He was appointed to the committee in charge of the Jewish Quarter residents."

"What does he do there?" we asked.

"He is the treasurer, but he does many things. There is much to do. People need work; wages must be paid; food must be distributed; and people must be assigned to guard duty."

That evening we had a delicious meal: bread and jelly and a cup of cocoa with tinned milk.

"What good food you have!" exclaimed Naomi.

"Do you know how long it's been since we've had milk and cocoa? In Beit Yisrael all we ate was chubeiza and oatmeal, and all we drank was water or weak tea," I told Imma.

"Yes, I know. The convoys have brought us the best of the food supplies sent to Jerusalem, so that people will stay in the Old City," answered Imma.

"But we saw crowds of people trying to leave on the convoy out to town today."

Imma looked at me with a penetrating gaze. I went on. "Do they think that there are no riots in town? Almost every night they shoot at us from Sheikh Jarrah."

Imma kept looking at me, but she didn't say a word. After dark I understood the meaning of her silence.

26 Attack

Nighttime.

Imma hung a blanket over the heavy wooden shutters, which had been closed even during the day, and then turned on a light. The little ones were already asleep, but we sat up waiting for Abba. Soon his familiar steps were heard, and... Abba walked into the house.

Abba! He hugged me with his big, strong hands. Once again I felt that strange something welling up in my throat and the hot tears falling on my cheeks.

"Abba, Abba," I cried between sobs. I wiped away my tears with the back of my hand. Only then did I notice how weary his face was.

"Nu, girls, it's time to go to sleep," he said finally.

"They'll sleep in the other room," he added to Imma.

"What? Which other room?" we both asked at once.

"We have enlarged our apartment lately," smiled Abba, and led us through an opening in the wall beside the bookcase to the "other room."

"Do you remember Old Rivka, who used to live here?" he asked.

"What happened to her?"

"Nothing happened. Her sons came and took her out of the Old City. She gave us permission to use her room until the war is over."

"But I'm afraid in the dark," I objected.

Abba turned on the light. Although the shutters were closed, I urged him to cover them with a blanket, just to make sure no light would seep out. Abba spread a heavy blanket on the floor for Naomi and arranged a folding bed for me, leaving its legs folded so that it was close to the floor.

That evening, a solitary shot was fired, followed by a noisy explosion. In a panic, Naomi and I lay flat on the floor. Only Abba remained sitting in his place, as though nothing had happened.

"Abba," I called, "why aren't you lying on the floor?"

"Ah, it's nothing — a few faraway shots — no more."

To me it sounded like a mighty explosion, and so close to us! Abba turned on the radio to hear the news. Naomi listened to the news and began to discuss the situation with Abba, but I interrupted them angrily:

"Abba! Turn off the radio! The Arabs will hear it and then, then they'll shoot at us."

Abba smiled. "They can't hear us."

"They can! They are close. They can hear us!" I cried.

But Abba and Naomi turned back to the radio. The shooting grew stronger and stronger. Bullets were fired from every direction, and from many kinds of weapons — all directed towards the Jewish Quarter.

"They're attacking!" I screamed in alarm.

"It only sounds that way," replied Abba. "They're not really attacking now."

My heart was frozen with fear. We had heard gunfire in Beit

Yisrael, but it was nothing like this. Especially frightening was a new type of gunfire which I had never heard before: T-t-t-t-t-t — quick bursts of fire one after the other, rat-tat-tat-tat-tat...

"What's that?" I cried, terrified.

"That's a machine gun," answered Abba.

"What? A machine that shoots bullets?"

"Yes, a machine gun."

"They press a button, and the machine shoots all those bullets? They can kill so many people so quickly? Oy!!"

"Don't be silly," Naomi laughed. "Not every bullet hits its target!"

"But many of them do, don't they? Please! Turn off the radio!" I wailed.

Imma, who had gone to sleep with the little children, called from the other room, "Turn off the radio already, Shlomo. Have pity on the child. Can't you see how frightened she is?"

"I can see, but the radio makes absolutely no difference. No one can hear it from here."

"Oh yes they can!" I insisted. "They're right here, close to us. Right down below, in Silwan, outside the wall. They'll turn that terrible machine gun of theirs on us!"

"If they can hear that well," said Naomi, "they must certainly be able to hear your screaming."

That shut me up at once.

Abba sat down on the edge of my bed. He took both my hands in the palm of his big one and held them hard, trying to reassure me.

"The war has broken out," I whispered.

"No, little girl," he said. "This is not the war yet. This must be an attack. Usually, the Arabs only shoot in the daytime, but when the British attack us, they are only too happy to join them."

"The British? Impossible!" We were shocked. "The British escorted us in the convoy home."

"Yes, but they are two-faced. They pretend to be defending us, while actually they are aiding the enemy. But soon they will leave — at long last! — and then there will be a real war. Then we will have only one enemy: the Arabs. Do you understand? Our English enemies will no longer be here!"

"But there are so many Arabs," protested Naomi.

"And they have so many weapons," I added.

"True. But Hashem will help us. He wants to redeem us. Imagine, for two thousand years we have had no country of our own, no state, no government, no army..."

"And now, do we have an army now?" we both asked.

"We have an underground army. As soon as the British leave, our army will come out into the open. We'll be able to carry weapons and to fight openly. Then it will be a completely different story."

A few shells exploded like thunder. Meanwhile the machine guns ceaselessly continued their piercing noise.

"Let me hear you say Shema now," said Abba.

We recited the Shema together. Hot tears fell from my eyes. It had been such a long time since Abba last sat beside my bed and said Shema with me. He suggested that we add a prayer tonight, *"Veliyerushalayim Ircha...* and to Jerusalem, Your city, return in compassion, and let Your presence dwell within it, as You have promised..." The ancient words calmed us. Abba recited out loud, "Pour out Thy wrath upon the nations that know Thee not... for they have devoured Jacob and laid waste his home" (Psalms 79:6-7). We fervently repeated every word after him, "Pour out Thy wrath..."

At long last, the machine gun fell silent, the shelling stopped, and only a few lone shots could be heard now and again. I fell into a deep sleep.

27 Everything Has Changed

The next morning, Imma went downstairs to bring water from the cistern. Our neighbors, whom we had not seen for such a long time, were already standing in line, water cans in their hands.

A stranger was standing there, drawing water from the cistern. He wore a heavy black coat, a round black hat, and had long *peyot.*

"What happened, Imma?" we asked her, when she returned with half a can of water. "Where is Abu Ali?"

"Abu Ali . . . Abu Ali . . . I forget . . . ah, now I remember. Once the riots started, he stopped coming. He's an Arab."

"Is Abu Ali one of our enemies, too?" asked Naomi. Imma bit her lips.

"No!" I exploded. "Abu Ali is our friend. He was always everyone's friend here. It's not possible that he could become one of our enemies."

"In wartime, every man sides with his own people," said Imma softly.

"But Abu Ali never hated us like the Arabs in the *shuk* did," I continued unbelievingly.

"And where is Baladi, the egg man?" asked Naomi.

"Yes," I repeated, "where is Baladi? Has he, too, betrayed us?"

"He doesn't come anymore either. How could he possibly come? The Jewish Quarter is sealed off. The British have put up an iron gate at the end of Jewish Quarter Road, at the entrance to the *shuk*, to keep the Jews and Arabs apart. And if any Arabs had continued to come, their own people would have considered them traitors."

"That's true," I agreed. Nevertheless, the thought that all of our Arab friends had suddenly become enemies was very painful.

For breakfast that morning we had bread and salad.

"Where did you buy these vegetables? In the Arab *shuk*?" I asked angrily.

"No," answered Imma.

"I'm glad you're keeping your promise to me," I replied in a satisfied tone of voice.

Imma smiled bitterly. "I couldn't buy in the *shuk* now even if I wanted to. Everything has changed. All the entrances to the *shuk* are blockaded. There is no longer any trade between Arabs and Jews. The only contact we have with the Arabs now is through bullets."

Naomi and I went downstairs to our lot, to a happy reunion with all our old friends, but there, too, we quickly discovered that everything had changed. The girls didn't play any of the old games anymore. They were completely occupied with military matters.

A group of Jewish underground soldiers was exercising, said Chana, but without uniforms. She proudly pointed out their post, at the edge of the lot. We couldn't see anything, and she explained that the post was under the one-story building, hidden behind sacks of sand and camouflaged with dirt. Only then did we notice the sandbags sticking out behind a dirt mound.

"And over there," added her sister Rachel, in a whisper, "over there is the British post." She pointed to the other side of the lot.

"Everyone knows that!" I cut her off abruptly. "We can see them. They have no need to hide. They rule the land."

"That's true, but you don't know about our secret plan," she added knowingly.

"What secret plan?" we asked.

"First you must promise not to tell anyone."

"We promise."

"All right. The secret plan is for our boys to take over the post as soon as the British leave."

"All the British posts!" added Yaffale.

"What's so secret about that?" we asked. "They'll just have to walk in and take over the posts when the British leave."

"No, no, you don't understand anything," Frieda told us scornfully. "You haven't been here. Of course it's a secret. The British intend to hand over the posts to the Arabs."

"Oh?" We were shocked.

"Look, look over there!" whispered Chana, very dramatically. "Look how our boys are practicing taking over the post. Watch! They are getting ready now, so that when the time is ripe, they'll know exactly what to do."

"Listen, everybody! I have something to tell you!" interrupted Batya, who had just joined the group. "Over there in that house is a cache of weapons. It's big! I saw our soldiers hiding the weapons there, yesterday. They smuggled in guns inside a sack of sugar in a convoy, right under British noses!"

On and on went the girls, showing off their military expertise, each one warning us not to divulge any of the "military secrets."

"I have twenty cartridge cases!" boasted Frieda, pulling the shiny case of a rifle bullet from her pocket.

"What do you need those cases for? They're empty. They can't kill anyone anymore," I said.

"But they prove how many bullets were fired at our yard! In Beit Yisrael I bet you never saw anything like this!"

"Yes we did too!" Naomi was insulted.

"We saw tons of bullets," I added.

"And rockets," continued Naomi.

"But there are no Arabs there," Frieda was mystified.

"Not there, but in Sheikh Jarrah there are plenty."

"Where?" a few girls asked, a circle beginning to form around us.

"In Sheikh Jarrah. The Arabs who live in the village on the

hill opposite shoot at Beit Yisrael almost every night. You were never there, so how could you know?"

"Tell us, tell us," they all begged, eager to hear our stories. So we told them of the nighttime shooting at our Bobba's house, of our diet of chubeiza and the shortage of food and fuel.

We talked and talked until sunset. Then we jumped up and warned our friends to rush home, lest a rocket fall on us all.

* * *

Friday night came, but this time we didn't go to the Churva.

"Can't we go?" we asked Abba. "We missed the Churva so much."

"We haven't gone to the Churva since the riots began," Abba answered sadly. "Any place far from Batei Machse is dangerous. We will go to *shul* in the *shtibel* in Batei Machse."

Tears welled up in our eyes. We would not be able to see our beloved *beit knesset*. Abba stroked my cheek and scolded me lightly, "On Shabbat we do not cry." But that only made me cry harder!

The next day we received another shock. We asked to go to the Kotel, but Abba and Imma explained that it was dangerous to go anywhere past the Porat Yosef Yeshiva, at the eastern border of the Jewish Quarter.

"Do you mean we can't go to the Kotel at all? But why?" asked Naomi.

"The Kotel is near Arab neighborhoods," said Imma. "Since that Sunday, the day after the U.N. vote, not a single Jew has been to the Kotel."

"Even Rabbi Orenstein, the *rav* of the Kotel, has not been to his office there," added Abba.

"That means that there are no Jews at all at the Kotel anymore?" I asked unbelievingly.

"None," was the answer.

"And now the Kotel belongs only to the British?"

"To the British?" Abba pondered the question. "Well, the British must certainly have handed the Kotel over to the Arabs by now. It must be the Arabs who are in control there."

"Arabs at the Kotel!?" Naomi exclaimed, "We'll show them! We'll show them both — the Arabs and the British together!"

Naomi paced the room, waving her fists in anger, but I burst into tears.

Arabs taking away our most holy of places — the Kotel Hamaaravi? And no more going to the Churva? And they say that it is forbidden to cry on Shabbat!

28 Deserters

Morning. I opened my eyes, rolled out of the folding bed onto the floor, and went into the other room. Abba had already returned from his morning prayers and was sitting at the table eating breakfast. Imma poured him a cup of hot coffee.

"Save the milk for the children," he said wearily, before she could pour any of the tinned milk into his cup. "Coffee without milk is enough to give me strength, as long as it is hot."

Imma sighed. "I don't believe we'll be able to boil water much longer," she said, looking hard at Abba.

"What do you mean?" he asked.

"I mean that soon we're going to run out of kerosene."

"Why?" I asked. Imma ignored my question and ordered me to get dressed. I left the room, but I could still hear their voices.

"Soon the British will leave," continued Imma sadly.

"Why is she sad about that?" I wondered, puzzled.

"Once they leave," she went on, "that will be the end of the convoys."

"What's wrong with you?" asked Abba. "Have all the dire

prophecies affected you too?"

"It's not a dire prophecy. It's simply a matter of fact. Once the British leave, the Jewish Quarter will be completely cut off ...completely."

"Why are you so pessimistic?" Abba was angry. "We will not be cut off. Our men will make sure of that. They'll continue with the convoys."

"Don't be naïve, Shlomo. You know they aren't capable of doing that. I advise you to consider what I've said before it is too late."

"Whatever can she be talking about?" I wondered sadly. "And why is Abba angry? He never used to get angry at Imma before."

Just then I remembered that today was Thursday. In Savta's house, early in the morning, the dough would already be rising. Every Thursday Savta baked *challot* for Shabbat. I hurried to finish my prayers and breakfast and ran over to her house, hoping not to miss the braiding of the *challot*. I tried never to miss a single opportunity to watch Savta. The hustle and bustle of her Shabbat preparations gave me great pleasure. Sometimes, when some of the dough was left over, she would allow me to braid two small *challot* of my own. Sometimes she would even let me spread the sesame seeds on her large, shining *challot*, after they had been brushed with egg yolk.

Savta had different types of dough for *challot*, cake, and noodles. While the *challot* were baking in the oven, filling the room with the sweet smell of Shabbat, she would roll out the leaves of the stiff noodle dough in the second bowl. She would deftly cut long, thin strands of noodles which I would carry on a white cloth out into the courtyard to dry in the sun.

That Thursday Savta had only one bowl of dough in the kitchen, and the *challot* that she braided were smaller than usual.

"Where are the sesame seeds?" I asked, ready to help

89

scatter them on the braided *challot*.

"There aren't any," she said. "No eggs either."

"What a pity," I remarked, disappointed.

"We should be happy that we still have flour and that we can heat the oven," said Savta.

"That's what Imma said. Are you also afraid that we'll run out of kerosene?"

"Not only kerosene," sighed Savta.

"Where are the noodle and the cake doughs?" I asked.

"Ah," sighed Savta, "we haven't any of those either."

Unoccupied, I left Savta's house and slowly walked down towards the lot. Naomi was already there. A group of girls was standing around a strange object.

"Shrapnel," pronounced Batya and Frieda.

"A fragment of a shell," agreed Chana.

"It's from our yard," said Batya proudly.

Just then Chava arrived and made her way to the center of the circle. She sighed dramatically and asked, "Who knows what the outcome of the argument will be?"

"What argument?" the girls asked.

"The argument between the Etzel and the Hagana."

"*The* argument between the Etzel and the Hagana?" Chana said mockingly. "As if there were only one argument between them!"

"I mean the argument about us."

"Tell us already," the girls urged.

Chava answered, "Well, it's this way. Etzel demands the evacuation of the women and children from the Old City, but the Hagana opposes it."

"Why? Why?"

"Why what?"

"Why evacuate us?" some girls asked.

"Why oppose it?" asked others.

"Well, it's this way," explained Chava. "The Etzel claim that we only get in the soldiers' way. They can't possibly fight on the backs of women and children, so they say."

"That's right," the Etzel girls hurried to agree. "Women and children hamper the soldiers."

"Why, then, does the Hagana object?" asked Naomi.

"The Hagana claims that if the women and children are evacuated, the remaining population will be too small."

"But the women and children can't defend the Quarter anyway."

"Not exactly. But the Hagana feels that the very presence of women and children — of whole families here — will hold the Quarter for us. It's the soldiers' duty to protect the residents, but it's the residents who must hold onto the Jewish Quarter."

"How silly," remarked Rachel, the Etzelnik. "How can women and children possibly help?"

"Of course women and children can help. Whoever occupies this area possesses it. It will be much harder for the Arabs to fight in a densely occupied Jewish Quarter than in an empty one, with only a handful of soldiers to defend it."

"True," agreed others. "There aren't even as many soldiers as there are buildings in the Quarter."

"Aside from that," added Chava, "the soldiers also get their food rations from the convoys sent to the Quarter. If no residents are left, no food will be sent."

"Oy," sighed Chana, "I wish they would take us out of here..."

"I wish we could leave before it's too late," her sister added.

"What? Are you so scared?" my sister scolded them. "What crybabies! 'I wish we could leave,'" she mocked Rachel's tone of voice.

"We'll hold the Quarter!" declared the Hagana girls. "We won't be evacuated! We won't!"

"You," Chava turned to the Etzelniks, "you can leave — you cowards!"

In the midst of this argument, I noticed the father of one of the Quarter's old, established families leaving his apartment in Rothschild House, carrying a large suitcase. His two older sons followed him, also carrying large bundles. They wore heavy coats and walked quickly, looking straight ahead.

"Where are you going?" I asked when Tzvikeh, the youngest son, passed me by, dressed in many layers of clothing, as though setting out on a long journey. Tzvikeh turned his head away from me and hurried to catch up with his brothers. Just then the mother and daughter came out of the house carrying bags and baskets. Turning away from our curious stares, they hurried towards the Deutsche Platz. This was too much for me.

"Shalom," I called loudly to the mother, but she continued walking towards the exit gate as though she had heard nothing.

"That's odd," commented Naomi.

"Very," agreed some of the girls.

"Perhaps they are going to a wedding in Tel Aviv," I volunteered.

"Impossible," said Chava flatly.

"A convoy has just arrived," announced Chana, pulling both thumbs out of her mouth at once.

"A convoy? So what?" asked Yaffale, uncomprehending.

"They're leaving — moving out; that's what," explained Chava in an insulted tone. "They are evacuating without even waiting for a decision on the question."

"Did you see how they were ashamed to look us in the eyes? How they left without even saying good-bye?"

"That's right . . . they're leaving . . ."

"What a disgrace," all agreed.

Just then five or six more people passed by. Another family. They, too, wore coats and carried bags and bundles. They walked by us so quickly that we didn't even have time to see who they were.

"Deserters," the whole group called after them.

"And afterwards," said Naomi, "when everything is all over, they'll come back to the homes we defended for them."

"They think they'll have it better in town," I said, "but they're mistaken, very mistaken."

"You're mistaken," disagreed two hot-headed Etzelniks. "Of course they'll have it better in town."

"Oh, no," said Naomi, "There are riots everywhere. There will be a war everywhere."

"The whole city is preparing for war," I declared.

"The whole country," Naomi added.

29 Dire Prophecies

It was nighttime. I lay in bed, tossing and turning from side to side, unable to fall asleep. All kinds of thoughts tormented me. What would happen? Would Etzel persuade the authorities to evacuate the women and children? If so, who would defend the Quarter? Where would they send us — to bombarded Beit Yisrael? To Sanhedria on the border? Where had all the families gone when they "deserted"? What if so many people left the Quarter so quickly that we found ourselves left behind and all alone?

I heard voices in the other room. First in a whisper. I listened closely, trying to figure out who could be holding a conversation at this hour of the night. I didn't have long to wait to solve the riddle, for the voices got louder and louder. It was Abba and Imma having another argument.

"There will be no happy ending here," predicted Imma.

"And I say that special efforts will be made especially here, for the Quarter is next to the Kotel and to the Temple Mount. No place is more sacred to the Jewish people. The Jewish Quarter will not be abandoned."

"I didn't say it would be abandoned, God forbid. But I think that it will be very easy for the Arabs to cut us off, and then..."

"And then what?"

"And then, how will a handful of young boys stand up against a sea of Arabs? I'm telling you, it won't take long for them to...to finish us all!"

"God forbid!" exclaimed Abba angrily.

Imma was silent. Abba sighed, "If everyone is so lacking in faith and confidence, perhaps we really will not be able to withstand them."

It was quiet. For a moment, Naomi's bed squeaked. Was the argument over? Someone was crying. Who could it be?

"It will be hell here, hell!" Imma sobbed.

It was Imma crying! What did she mean?

"Throughout the whole country it will be a war of the few against the many," said Abba. "I believe that we will win — here and everywhere else. God will help us, just as He helped the Maccabees. Have faith. Don't you realize that these are the birth pangs of the Redemption?"

Imma stopped crying.

"Today five families left, including your uncle's family," she said.

"I know."

I thought of the scene we had witnessed in the lot that afternoon, of the families laden with bundles, of the people who had stolen away like thieves. They had not even said good-bye. The girls called them deserters.

"Last week six or seven families also went," added Imma. "Only we remain...like fools."

"Where do you want to go? Where?" asked Abba, anger evident in his voice.

I tried to think. Could it be possible that my own mother wanted to leave, just like — like all those other people?

"I want to go to my parents," said Imma.

"Do you really expect your parents to remain in their home on Shmuel Hanavi Street facing Sheikh Jarrah? I'm sure they have already left. Didn't you hear the girls' stories?"

"If my parents have left their house, then we'll go to my brother Shimon in Mishkenot."

"To your brother Shimon? In his one-and-a-half room apartment, together with your parents? Don't be ridiculous. We have nowhere to go."

"Shimon will receive us with open arms."

I put my hand to my aching head. So Imma really did want to leave the Quarter! Why wasn't Abba answering her?!

After a long silence, he finally said, "I am not willing to leave! I am doing important work here and I will not leave."

"Is there a lack of manpower here? You can be replaced. You are the father of five children, three of whom are still babies. Little babies! Do you really think that I should endanger my children's lives for a cause that is lost in any case?"

Imma began to sob again. "If we stay here, we will be burned here!"

"God forbid! Enough dire prophecies! If you are not prepared to withstand difficulties, you won't survive anywhere. It will be a hard war all over the country — even in Beit Yisrael and where your brother Shimon lives."

"But, Shlomo," Imma persisted, "why can't you understand? 'Everywhere' is not here. If, God forbid, we are attacked in town, we can run away; we can go somewhere else. Here we can't leave. We are surrounded, locked in. When the Quarter is attacked, that will be the end..."

Silence. Then Imma spoke again, loudly and firmly. "I want to leave!"

"Sh...quiet! You'll wake up the girls!"

Abba and Imma began to whisper again. Naomi turned over in her bed. Had she woken up?

"What will happen if Imma convinces Abba?" I wondered.

But I immediately reassured myself. "No, Abba will never agree." Nevertheless, a few minutes later I heard him sigh, "So be it. I will go with you. There's no point in my staying here by myself."

A shadow loomed up in the bed opposite me.

"Who's there?" I asked in alarm.

Naomi got out of bed and came over to me.

"Did you hear what Abba and Imma said?" she whispered.

"I heard it all."

"Do you agree?"

"Of course not! I don't want to be a deserter."

"Then come with me," she said, and pulled me out of bed. We walked into the other room.

"You won't leave!" Naomi cried out dramatically, as we entered.

"Deserters!" I screamed with all my might.

Yehudit and Ruthie began to cry. Abba and Imma stood up. "What are you doing up in the middle of the night?" they asked, and Abba added, "I told you you'd wake up the girls."

"You won't leave," my sister repeated.

"This is not your business," Imma answered angrily.

"We are staying," Naomi pronounced decisively.

"You will stay, too," I added. "We won't let you be deserters."

"Did you hear what your daughter said?" Imma asked Abba, who was trying to quiet the smaller girls.

"Where did you ever pick up those silly names? 'Deserters' means something altogether different."

But I would not give in. "That's what the girls in the lot called the families who left today, and that's exactly what they're doing — deserting when it's their duty to defend the Quarter."

Imma laughed bitterly. "Do you really think that you and I can defend the Quarter? Maybe it's your baby brother's duty to

A courtyard in Batei Machse, the Jewish Quarter, before 1948.

Street scene in the Old City.

The Deutsche Platz (Chakura) in front of Rothschild House before (top) and after 1948.

British soldiers arrest Jew suspected of belonging to Etzel.

British "security zone"; a sea of barbed wire in the main business area of Jerusalem.

Jews detained for identification after martial law was declared in 1947.

The Jewish commercial section burned by Arab mobs after the U.N. vote.

Ben Yehuda street in downtown Jerusalem, in the aftermath of terrorist explosions, February 1948.

△ Armored convoy bringing food and supplies to Jerusalem.
▽ Jerusalemites lining up for food rations in the besieged city.

Receiving water rations.

Girls from the Jewish Quarter fill sandbags for defense works.

defend the Quarter too?"

"Yes," replied Naomi. "The people who live here will defend the Quarter by their very presence. We don't want to desert the battlefield."

Imma laughed again. "Just listen to them! Whoever put those silly notions in your heads?"

"They're not silly!" I exclaimed heatedly and promptly burst into tears. Naomi followed suit.

But Imma was firm. "We will go somewhere where we have a chance to remain alive. The defense of the Quarter is not our responsibility. We will not help anyone by staying here, and we will not harm anyone by leaving. On the contrary, I think that if we leave, the soldiers will have an easier time of it."

"Since when are you an Etzelnik?" asked Naomi.

"I'm not an Etzelnik. Plain common sense tells me to leave and to save my children's lives."

"But, Abba," I cried, holding onto his hand, "how can you agree to such a thing?"

Abba was silent for a long while. Then he spoke.

"Whatever Sarah tells you to do — listen to her voice. That is what Hashem told Abraham."

"Sarah was a prophetess," remarked Naomi.

"Yes," agreed Abba, "but Imma, every Imma, has a special sixth sense. Some people call it intuition. Imma's sixth sense tells her to take her children to a safer place. What would I do if, in the end, it turned out that Imma was right?"

It was a long night. We sat beside Abba and Imma for hours — talking, arguing, pleading, urging. But Imma and her sixth sense won out, and when dawn broke, Abba and Imma had decided that we would leave for town on the next convoy.

30 The Convoy That Never Came

After that night, Naomi and I didn't go down to the lot anymore. We stayed away from all our friends. We were ashamed — ashamed to face them and ashamed to face ourselves. We couldn't continue to play with them as if nothing had happened. How could we participate in all the discussions and plans for the future, if we weren't going to be there anymore?

Abba continued in his communal work as usual. We wondered if he had told anyone of his plans for the future. Imma did the packing, all by herself, but she didn't look at all happy.

Finally, our last day in the Quarter came. The next day the convoy would arrive. Everything at home was packed and ready. We went downstairs to the lot, hiding behind the stone fence so as not to be seen, and watched the girls doing military exercises. They were all there: Chava and Rachel, Chana, Frieda and Yaffale, Batya, Esther and Leah — every single girl — not one was missing. We saw them marching off single file towards the houses. When they had gone, we ran down to the lot. We wanted to make our farewells...I dug in the dirt and found three square stones for souvenirs. That was all I could find. Then I helped Naomi put some dirt from the lot into a newspaper cone. We took a long look at the spacious lot, at Rothschild House, at the dirt mounds and the secret post.

Just then we heard the girls marching between the houses, as Commander Chava ordered, "Left, right, left..." What would they say about us tomorrow?

The marchers were coming closer. In our hearts we bid them farewell. "Shalom," we whispered just before they returned. Then we hurriedly ran home, lest we be discovered.

We asked Imma to pack our souvenirs in one of the bundles. As she took them, we saw her wipe a tear from her cheek. Was she sorry? No, no chance of that. Imma closed the last bundle, firmly and decisively. Early the next morning the convoy would arrive. That night, on Imma's orders, we slept in our clothes.

A knock on the door woke us up the next morning. Abba opened the door a crack and looked out.

"I came to call you to an urgent meeting at headquarters." We recognized the voice of one of Abba's friends who was also very involved with the community in the Quarter.

"A meeting?" Abba asked.

The man opened the door and came into the room. He looked all about him, surveying all the bundles standing ready beside the door.

"What's happening here?" he asked, shocked.

Then he noticed that the whole family was dressed and ready to go. "What? You too?" he gasped in a broken voice.

Abba lowered his eyes. "My wife is afraid for the children," he apologized. "They're just babies..."

"There is no food in town — nothing!" he said to Imma. "I know, because I have just recently returned from there."

"There will be no food here either soon," answered Imma.

"You're mistaken. Come and I'll show you. Our storehouses are full of flour, rice, sugar, and canned goods. Half of all the food brought by the convoys to Jerusalem was allocated to the Jewish Quarter."

"We'll run out of kerosene," said Imma.

"We have a storehouse full of wood. I'm telling you that you're making a big mistake. It will be no less difficult in town and perhaps more so. Besides, what will we do without your husband? Who will take care of the people here in his place?"

He paused, and then continued, "You must not do this! If you leave, it will serve as an example for all the others to follow, and then... Well, in any case," he turned to Abba, "the meeting will begin at eight o'clock."

"But," protested Imma, "that's exactly when the convoy is due to arrive."

"No," answered Abba's friend. "We have been notified that

there will be a delay. The convoy will be late today." He sighed and quoted the proverb, "'If even the great cedars catch fire, what shall the little mosses do?' I advise you to think this through again." Then he left. Abba also put on his jacket and turned towards the door.

"Where are you going?" asked Imma.

"To the meeting."

"Have you decided to stay?"

"Have you?"

Imma lowered her eyes. "We'll see," she said.

Abba left. The convoy didn't come at eight, nor at nine. We went down to the bus stop with Imma, without our bundles, just to see what was happening. A few families were standing and waiting, their belongings piled beside them. Someone announced that the convoy would not arrive until the afternoon. Nevertheless, the people remained there, waiting. They didn't go home, for they had already decided that the Jewish Quarter was not their home anymore.

But we went home. Abba, too, returned from his meeting.

"Well, what did you decide?" he asked Imma, but she still didn't know what to answer.

"We cannot leave," Abba announced. "Neither can anyone else. The convoy is not coming today."

"And tomorrow?" asked Imma.

"At the meeting it was decided not to allow any more residents to leave the Quarter."

Imma jumped up as though bitten by a snake, "What?!"

"Blockades will be erected before the bus stop, and whenever a convoy arrives, a civil defense patrol will guard the area. No more residents will leave the Jewish Quarter."

31 The Seder

It was the *seder* night, the night we celebrate the Holiday of
Freedom. All the residents of the Quarter had received *matza*
and wine in honor of the Passover holiday. In our spacious, new
room, the table was set for the holiday dinner, and we, dressed
in our best, happily greeted Abba on his return from the
synagogue. After he had blessed us, he turned to Imma and
asked, "Shall we begin the *seder*?" He looked at Imma for a long
time, a question in his eyes: Will the Arabs let us hold our *seder*
tonight in peace and quiet?

"Everything will be all right," Imma reassured him. Since
that day when the convoy had failed to arrive, Imma's attitude
had changed completely. No longer did she foresee the worst.
On the contrary, at every opportunity, it was she who encouraged us and assured us that with God's help everything would
be all right.

Abba took his place at the head of the table, his chair
padded with pillows to recline upon, and we sat all around him.
Only mischievous little Ruthie stood up on her chair, her eyes
gleaming at the sight of the wine being poured into our glasses.
We opened our *haggadot*, and Abba recited the *kiddush*. A few
gunshots sounded far away. Yehudit, sitting next to me, jumped
up.

"It's not here," Imma reassured her. "It's far away."

We washed our hands and Abba dipped the parsley in salt
water. Then he split the middle *matza* in two and hid one piece
for the *afikomen*. We began to read from the *haggada*. The
story of our deliverance from Egypt did not seem like something far away or remote from us then. The deliverance of our
forefathers from slavery to freedom was very relevant and
meaningful to us that night. We too would soon, very soon, also
be freed. Would the British really keep their promise to leave
the country?

"We are about to experience great days," said Abba. "For the first time in two thousand years we will have a state of our own. The government will be our own, and the army and the police."

"Will the curfew be over then?" I asked, only half-believing that such a thing could really happen.

"It will be over," Savta assured me. I recalled the day that she had led us through the alleyways of the Armenian Quarter. Never would we have to undergo such a miserable experience again!

"There won't be any more searches, either," Naomi remarked happily.

"And imagine, our boys will be able to walk around in the streets and protect us if necessary, openly carrying weapons, and no one will arrest them," added Abba.

Again shots were heard, and this time they were closer. We knew very well what they meant. The Arabs, incited by their own leaders and by the British, had chosen this way to declare — morning and evening — that they would not allow the establishment of our tiny state. We began to sing a song from the *haggada*:

"*Vehi she-amda* — This wonderful promise which God has kept throughout the ages... fierce foes have fought against us in every age and land, but the Holy One of Blessed Name has saved us from their hand."

I went up to the window overlooking Silwan and sang enthusiastically, "God has saved us from their hand, and also from your hand, also from your hand!" Just then a very loud shot was heard and a bullet hit the thick wooden shutter of our window. Alarmed, I ran to take shelter in Imma's arms.

Quiet. The shots were over, but my heart was still pounding. We got up to wash our hands before the meal. Abba recited the blessing over the *matzot*. How good they tasted. After that we partook of the bitter herbs, to commemorate the suffering of our forefathers in Egypt.

"That is the way of life," commented Abba, looking meaningfully at Imma. "Freedom cannot be gained without some bitterness and suffering first."

Happy sounds were heard from inside the baby carriage. Yudale, his innocent little face plastered with pieces of softened *matza*, was celebrating the holiday in his own way, and having a wonderful time of it. He had not a worry in the world.

"How happy he is," I said. "He has no idea of what is happening all around him in the world outside."

"Nor does this little mischief-maker," laughed Naomi, as she grabbed Ruthie, who was running round and round the table. When we had gone to wash our hands, she had seized her chance and had finished off all the wine left in our glasses!

"Now she's good and drunk," said Imma, taking her in her arms. Slowly Ruthie calmed down and fell asleep. Yehudit and Yudale also went to sleep. Imma put the little ones to bed in the other room and returned for *Birkat Hamazon* and the Hallel prayers. Abba poured Elijah's cup, and Naomi opened the door.

"Pour out Thy wrath upon the nations that know Thee not," we recited aloud. Would Elijah the Prophet perhaps appear and announce the end to all our troubles?

All was quiet outside. Our candles had burned out. We reached the very last song of the *haggada*, "Only one kid, only one kid..."

Abba explained that the only kid is the Jewish nation. All through the ages, the other nations of the world have tried to devour us. But the time is nearing for our oppressors to receive their just punishment. And meanwhile, we must be patient as we suffer the pangs of redemption.

"Are you talking about war?" I asked.

"God will protect us," said Savta.

"But..."

Imma stroked my head. "Everything will be all right," she whispered softly.

32 They Really Leave

It was Shabbat, the day after Pesach. We were downstairs playing with a group of our friends. Suddenly Chana appeared with good news. "We captured Katamon! Yesterday Katamon was captured!"

We all began to shout in glee. "We did it! We captured it! We are winning the battle! God is on our side!"

We immediately formed a circle and began to dance. Only later did a few girls go to find out exactly what and where Katamon was. They quickly returned with the answer: Katamon was a wealthy Arab neighborhood in southern Jerusalem. It had been a threat to the neighboring Jewish areas, but today it was ours. The good news spread throughout the Quarter, lifting our spirits and planting hope in our hearts.

"We have a chance," people said to one another. "Let us hope."

"God has helped us so far, and He will continue to come to our aid."

We had no idea then of just how important the conquest of Katamon would be for us.

The holiday was over. Abba and Imma put the Pesach dishes away. Only two weeks were left until that fateful day — the day set for the termination of the British Mandate. A few days after the holiday, the Hagana and Etzel forces in the Old City decided to join together in a pact. Everyone was happy with this development, and we were filled with confidence, for we knew that with unity comes strength — both natural and Divine.

On Friday, a week after Pesach, the last convoy arrived.

Many people came out to greet it. Additional food staples arrived, and "our boys" even succeeded in smuggling in a few more weapons.

"That's it," one of the neighbors said to Imma. "Whatever is here now is here."

"Yes," answered Imma, "but the storehouses are full."

"The last convoy," our neighbor repeated, her eyes full of tears, "the last one."

On the following Thursday, the fourth of Iyar (May 13th, 1948), the news spread that the British were indeed getting ready to leave. All Jewish soldiers were put on alert. In the afternoon, Abba took us to the bus station to witness the historic event. The English were loading their equipment onto military vehicles. Then a row of soldiers was seen marching down Jewish Quarter Road. Indeed, a miracle was happening!

"They're leaving! They're leaving!" the children called, clapping their hands. We stood and looked after them. They marched upright with their uniforms and weapons, row upon row of soldiers. Even now, not one of them smiled or waved his hand to greet us. Cold stares, steel eyes, still hostile...

"Thank God we are rid of them," said Abba, when the last soldier had marched down Or Hachaim Street.

"Blessed art Thou...Who has kept us alive and sustained us and enabled us to reach this occasion," we recited the *Shehecheyanu* blessing enthusiastically.

Abba took our hands and pressed them hard. "We are free men now — independent! *Mashiach* cannot be very far away!"

Meanwhile our well-drilled soldiers had swiftly taken over all the British posts as they were vacated. The operation was carried out smoothly and successfully, and all the outposts in the Jewish Quarter were now in our hands.

We turned to go home, our hearts overflowing with joy. Nevertheless, our joy was mixed with deep anxiety for the future.

33 The Battle Begins

The next day, when we went down to the lot, we saw our soldiers openly carrying their weapons. Many of them even wore uniforms.

"Our soldiers have come out from underground," we called with joy.

One of the soldiers scolded us, "Go home, it's not safe for you to be running about outside. You can never tell when something will happen."

Unwillingly, we turned to go home, but some of the children stayed downstairs. There was a holiday atmosphere outside, and no one wanted to be shut up in the house.

It was Friday, and Imma was standing in our tiny kitchen, busy preparing for Shabbat. There was no way for us to hear the news, for our electricity had been cut off and the radio was dead. We knew that there were plans to proclaim the establishment of a Jewish state. Of course we were excited, and anxious to hear if indeed our independence would be declared and what name would be given to the new state, but we were cut off from the world outside. We didn't hear of the proclamation of the state on that Friday, the 5th of Iyar (May 14); we didn't know that the British Mandate was indeed over and that the English had left the country. We only heard this news much later, after we had left the Old City. Nor did we hear the bitter news of the fall of Gush Etzion until we were outside the Jewish Quarter. On that historic Friday, and during the days that followed, we knew nothing of what was going on.

On Shabbat, all was still, except for a few isolated shots here and there. In the afternoon, as we sat beside our wide window, we caught glimpses of Arabs fleeing — apparently to Jericho — by way of Silwan. This greatly encouraged us. It seemed to be a sign that they were afraid of us.

But on Sunday, the tables were turned. From early morning

on, a heavy barrage of fire was aimed at us from all sides. All our neighbors went downstairs, and we, too, took our blankets and some food and went down a flight with Savta to one of the neighbors on the second floor. With every passing minute, the fire grew stronger, a veritable concert of destruction.

We had known that the military situation in the Old City was worse than in town, but that Sunday, we truly felt that hell was at our doorstep. The enemy attacked from all sides simultaneously, using every one of the numerous weapons at his disposal, and using them all at once.

We had known all along that war would soon break out, but apparently, no one had truly estimated how fierce the battle would be, for the grownups seemed just as frightened as the children. Finally, towards noon, the gunfire began to subside.

"It's over for now," said Abba. "Let's go back home."

"Nothing is over, and it won't be over so quickly, either," Imma replied resolutely. "I'm afraid you had better be prepared to stay here for more than just one day." But more time passed, and the shooting was not renewed. Abba put on his hat.

"Where to?" we asked.

"I'm going to the office to see what has to be done. I'm sure there's a lot of work waiting for me."

"Abba, no," begged Naomi.

"I must go."

"If you at least had a steel helmet..."

"She's right," said Imma. "Perhaps they can give you a steel helmet..."

Abba laughed. "Do you think we have such a large supply of steel helmets?" He left the house and Naomi began to wail, attracting much attention from the women around us. They all tried to calm her, but to no avail. She cried unceasingly. Finally, Savta suggested that instead of crying, it would be better to pray. Her advice was immediately accepted, and we recited Tehillim fervently. Savta even gave me a small Tehillim book and showed me what to say along with the others.

Just then, a young girl, visibly upset, appeared in the doorway. It was Sara, holding a few tin cans and packages of matches.

"Empty cans! Matches!" she cried.

"What? What for?" we asked.

"Cans . . ." Sara choked on her words and great tears stained her cheeks. Her beautiful, long, black braids hung loosely about her shoulders.

"What is wrong?" one of the women asked.

"Yossi," someone answered, "Yossi, her fiance, was killed this morning at his post."

We quietly collected whatever empty tin cans and matches we had and gave them to Sara, who explained that grenades could be made from cans and that from now on we must save all empty cans. She added that, if possible, we should bring screws and nails tomorrow. Gathering up her booty, she went on to the other apartments in the block.

Yossi had been killed. Yossi, the energetic young command-er, quick as a cat. Yossi, whom we had watched so often drilling his boys in the lot downstairs. Now, on the first day of the battle, he had fallen at his post. Yet Sara was carrying on with her assignments as usual. How strong and brave she was! I, too, wanted to help my country when I grew up.

And what would they do with the cans? They would make homemade grenades. What a wonderful idea! We children energetically joined in the work. Next time Sara wouldn't have to wait for cans to be collected. We prepared a big cardboard carton and notified everyone that every empty tin can was to be deposited there.

Abba came home in the evening. He brought a mattress from our house and put it in one of the corners of the apartment we were now in. We spread a blanket out next to the mattress and settled down together for the night.

34 Abba's Will

Monday, the eighth of Iyar — a day I shall never forget.

We were all together in our neighbors' one-room apartment. Several families had moved in, each squeezing into another corner. Heavy gunfire and shells were bombarding the Quarter from all sides. Since Friday we had been completely cut off from the world, and we had no idea of what was happening outside. We were in very low spirits, fully aware of how few soldiers we had and how poorly they were armed.

All at once a hysterical throng of men, women and children rushed into the Batei Machse courtyard from the more distant streets screaming bad news: the Arabs had attacked Jewish Quarter Road! Women with babies in their arms let out blood-curdling yells. "With my own eyes I saw them with knives!" "What are you sitting here for? Run away! Run away! Soon they'll be here and they'll slaughter us all!"

In no time Batei Machse was flooded with crowds of refugees, all screaming in panic, "Gangs! Gangs of murderers! Armed rioters! Anyone who does not flee will be slaughtered!"

Panic seized us all. Grabbing whatever food and clothing was at hand, all took their children and joined the fleeing herd. Waves of people flooded the large courtyard causing mass hysteria, as the crowd surged forward in their flight from the Arab murderers.

The terror was contagious. Soon all the houses were empty. Imma grabbed my little brother and a food basket. Abba put little Ruthie on his shoulders, and we began to flee, together with everyone else. Before us, pushing and shoving, were hundreds of panic-stricken refugees — like a flock of sheep escaping from a pack of blood-thirsty wolves. The frightened mass of humanity pushed forward towards the stairs under Batei Machse at the edge of the Quarter. We all ran further and further down until we reached the last houses. Then the crowd stopped in its tracks. The humming sound of a shell could be heard over all the noise and pandemonium.

"Stop! Stop!" called a few people. "You are running straight into the firing-line of the mortars from the Mount of Olives!"

Cries of despair arose. We were trapped — surrounded! Before us — fire-spitting mortars; behind — Arab gangs; and all around — snipers. But this time, no miracle took place. The sea of enemies was not split; there was no escape. The first of the crowd began to retrace their steps, creating indescribable confusion.

"Don't go forwards or backwards! Stay here! Get inside!" The message was passed through the crowd.

Immediately, people started rushing into the nearest houses. Furnishings were thrown out and doors ripped off their hinges as people tried to make more room. The crowd burst into the apartments, and anyone who could pushed his way inside somewhere. We too crowded ourselves into a room already packed to capacity.

I don't remember if it was an apartment or a synagogue, but as soon as we entered, the men crowded to one side and the women to the other and they began to pray. I could read the fear of death in the eyes of all the adults. Seeing the men sobbing, their bodies quaking, the women weeping, and the babies and children screaming, I too burst into tears.

Imma found *siddurim* for Naomi and me. Although it was Iyar (May), the congregation was reciting the *Yamim Noraim* prayers.

"Our Father, our King, tear apart the evil decree," the men prayed aloud, the women repeating the words tearfully.

"Our Father, our King, have compassion upon us, and upon our children and infants."

"Our Father, our King, do it for the sake of those who were slain for Your Holy Name."

"Our Father, our King, avenge the blood of Your servants

which has been shed."

While I prayed, I could envision everyone slaughtered, our blood flowing like water. I looked towards the door. What were those sounds outside? Had the murderers arrived yet? My whole body began to shake.

The cries grew louder. The men prayed as if they were trying to break through the very gates of heaven. As they prayed, they beat their hearts.

"What are they saying?" I asked, paralyzed with fear.

"The confession," answered one woman, "the confession before dying."

I asked someone to find me the place in my *siddur*, but the letters danced before my eyes and I could only make out black spots.

"We have done wrong; we have been faithless; we have robbed; we have uttered blasphemy," I heard the congregation say. Together with them I cried and beat my heart:

"For the sin which we have committed before You unwittingly... and for the sin which we have committed before You by contempt for parents and teachers."

The whole congregation had finished reciting the confession. Now, full of terrible despair, we waited for the bitter end to come.

Abba gestured to Naomi and me to come to him. He took us out into one of the corners of the courtyard. I looked up at him. His face was dark and serious.

"I must talk to you," he said. "There are things that a father must command his children. You are my eldest daughters, and I must tell you what is in my heart. Soon the gangs of Arabs will arrive. This will not be the first time that Jews have been slaughtered here. Who knows what fate is in store for us. Perhaps a miracle will occur, and they will have mercy on the women and children. The men will certainly be murdered."

"Abba, Abba," we cried, unable to restrain our tears, "don't speak like that!"

Imma, who had followed us out to the courtyard and had overheard Abba's last words, scolded, "Shlomo, don't talk like that! Stop, please."

Abba paid no attention. He took my hand in one of his and Naomi's in the other. I looked straight into his blue-green eyes. They were as clear as the sea and were gazing far away — far beyond the borders of time and space.

"No one knows what will happen," my father went on. "No one knows whose life will be saved and whose will not. I want you to know, now, once and for always, that the most important thing in this life is the Torah. Nothing in the world has any real value, except for the Torah. When you grow up and are ready to get married, remember my words! If you must choose between a husband who has wealth, secular learning, honor, position and one who has Torah, what will you choose?"

"Torah, Torah," we promised, our voices quavering.

"Take care of your little sisters, and when they grow up, it is you who must pass my command on to them. Make sure that they too marry only *talmidei chachamim* — learned, God-fearing men who value the Torah above all.

"And last of all, your little brother. If it be God's will that I no longer remain with you, remember that my greatest desire was to raise him to be a *talmid chacham* — learned and wise in the way of the Torah. You must take my place."

For several long moments we stood in the courtyard and cried until we could cry no more. Abba took us back into a nearby apartment. This room too was filled to capacity with people praying loudly and tearfully. We opened our Tehillim and began to pray again.

Suddenly, a tall Jewish soldier dressed in khaki entered the room, a gun on his shoulder and a belt of cartridges around his waist. He blew a whistle and asked for quiet. All eyes turned to him. Slowly the crowd quieted down and waited to hear what he had to say.

"Our forces are beating off the attackers, and soon we will have driven them out of the Jewish Quarter," he announced. "As soon as we announce that the operation is over, we want all residents to return home."

"Home!?" cried a squat little woman in a bitter, mocking tone, as she marched up to the soldier and waved her fist at him.

"Who are you to tell us what to do?" a man in a black hat yelled.

"Don't believe him!" shouted other voices from the crowd.

"Under no condition will we go back home," screamed the short woman. "We don't want to be slaughtered!"

"Listen to me! Be quiet!" shouted the soldier. His face was red with anger, and the veins on his forehead seemed about to burst.

"Listen!" he repeated, trying to make himself heard above all the tumult. "The days have passed when you were slaughtered without a chance to defend yourselves. Now we have an army! When will you understand this?"

"An army," laughed the woman bitterly. "A handful of children and young boys. Is that what you call an army?"

"Child's play," others agreed. "Child's play."

"And arms . . . ha, ha, ha," laughed the man in the black hat. "Toys, that's all they are! Do you really believe you can ward off a sea of murderous gangs with a few boys and those toys of yours?"

Just then two young soldiers appeared. "The Arabs have been driven back. Our fighters have blocked off the entrance from the *shuk* to Jewish Quarter Road again."

A sigh of relief passed through the crowd. "Now go home! Home!" ordered the tall soldier loudly.

No one moved. The soldier lifted his rifle, aimed at the ceiling and put his finger on the trigger.

"If you don't go home, I'll start shooting," he threatened.

At that, some of the crowd began to leave the room and ascend the stairs to Batei Machse, but others remained in their places. None of the people who lived far from Batei Machse, in Chabad Street or Jewish Quarter Road, returned home. Abba and Imma picked up the little ones and their bundles, and we returned to Batei Machse. But we didn't go up to our apartment either; nor did we go to our neighbors on the second floor. For a while we walked around the courtyard aimlessly, not knowing where to go.

Then an old man and woman who lived in one of the ground-floor apartments called to us and invited us to stay in their house. Several other families were already there, sitting on blankets spread on the floor. This elderly couple had opened their doors and turned their one-room house into a shelter. We went in and were soon asleep on their floor.

35 Under Fire

The following morning none of the men went to *shul*. Prayers were held in the house. It was altogether out of the question to go outside because enormous quantities of shells and bullets were being fired on the Quarter from all sides. The lady of the house very generously opened her kitchen to us and provided everyone with hot water.

All of a sudden, Esther and Lea ran in with their little brother, all three pale and shaking. A few women forcibly pulled their mother in from the yard. She was screaming and kept trying to go back outside.

"What happened? What happened?" everyone asked.

"A shell! A shell exploded on our house. The whole wall fell in! My husband has been killed!" the mother wailed.

"No, Imma," said Esther, "he was only wounded, badly wounded. He is in the hospital. Miriam is also wounded."

The mother could not control herself. "I want to see him!" she screamed.

"It's impossible to go outside now!" her neighbors scolded, holding her tightly. One woman gave her water to drink and sat her down on a chair, but every once in a while she tried again to get up and go out. The girls sat down with us. Lea was deathly pale. She neither cried nor talked — just looked dumbly ahead. Esther muttered over and over, "I don't know how... it was a miracle... how we got here among all the shells... a miracle, a miracle..."

One woman sprinkled water on Lea's face, another brought the girls something to drink, and a third took the little boy on her lap. Slowly, they regained their composure. The children returned to their games. The old man whose house we were in, fell asleep on one of the beds.

The Eizen family was to share the last days of the war with us. Now their son Meir asked me, "Have you ever seen someone sleeping with his mouth open?" Meir pointed to the slumbering old man and laughed. I looked and saw that indeed his mouth was open and he was snoring loudly.

"No, never," I answered, "but perhaps that's how old people sleep. In any case, can't you find a better time to make fun of people?" I said angrily.

"What can we do?" Shoshana, his elder sister, said. "If we don't laugh a little we'll die of tension and anxiety."

"Nobody ever died of anxiety," I said. "You only die from shells or bullets."

"That's not so!" declared Shoshana. "You can also die from a grenade."

"Or from shrapnel," added Meir.

"No, shrapnel doesn't kill; it only wounds," said Naomi.

"My sister was wounded by shrapnel," Esther volunteered.

115

"My father was wounded by a shell," added Lea, who until now had been silent. "My father... a shell. He is badly wounded, in the hospital."

Silence. We all turned pitying glances on Lea. She lowered her eyes. Meir continued the conversation.

"You can die from a wandering bullet, too," he said.

"What's that?" I asked.

"A bullet, that, you know, wanders... a bullet that was shot by mistake."

"You don't know what you're talking about!" said Shoshana. "A wandering bullet is... well... imagine that over there, beyond the houses, sits a sniper. He sees one of our soldiers at his post and focuses his rifle on him, and then... then he shoots. The bullet flies from the gun, through the air, directly towards our soldier's head, but suddenly in the middle it changes direction, starts to wander, and then flies further and further away until it finally hits someone else and — kills him!"

"And he dies — just like that — even though no one shot at him?"

"Just like that."

"How awful," I sighed.

"The sniper himself is much more terrifying than the bullets," said Naomi.

"What, exactly, is a sniper?" asked Meir.

"A sniper is an Arab who sits far away, holding a rifle and watching us. He has the eyes of an eagle," said my sister.

"Yes, a sniper has very sharp eyes. He never misses his target," added Shoshana. "If someone like that catches sight of you, he aims directly for your head."

"You're not allowed to talk like that," scolded Naomi. "You're inviting the Devil to do his work!"

The shells which had been thundering away all this time, causing us to carry on our conversation in shouts, suddenly stopped. And then, from the silence, a voice called on a loudspeaker. "Surrender! Surrender! Do you all want to die? Surrender, now, before we slaughter you all."

This proclamation was repeated over and over again. After that, the deluge of shells was resumed, and the terrible hail of machine-gun bullets was renewed. We sat frozen on the floor — not talking or playing. Who could tell where they might be now? Had they reached our lot yet? The loudspeaker no longer broadcast its terrible message, but the words continued to echo in our ears.

"Surrender, and we won't slaughter you."

A shiver ran up my back and my hands shook. It had only been yesterday that we had all run away, only to find out later that the Arab enemy had been pushed back. Now they were threatening us again. I saw in my mind's eye the picture of the Arab vendors in the *shuk*, passing their hands across their throats the last time Imma and I had gone shopping there. I felt their burning black eyes staring at me again.

"We'll slaughter you...we'll slaughter you..."

6 Breakthrough from Mount Zion

Another lull in the bombardment. Abba went to distribute food, and Sara came to collect empty tin cans. The minute she entered the apartment she was showered with a torrent of questions. Everyone wanted to know what was going on outside, but Sara answered our questions evasively. Later, one of the civil defense guards came in and described the situation.

The hospital was full of wounded, both soldiers and civilians. There had also been losses of life. The more distant streets were abandoned yesterday, and most of the refugees were concentrated in the Sephardi synagogues and in the Shaar Hashamayim Yeshiva. Meanwhile our soldiers were bravely

117

defending what was left of the Quarter, house by house, post by post. The situation was not good.

"God will help us," sighed the guard and turned to go back to his work.

People began to speak about the Messiah. A serious conversation developed among the children as well.

"When the Jewish people go through troubles like these, it's a sign that *Mashiach* is on his way."

"Perhaps this is the war of Gog and Magog," Shoshana suggested.

"No," Naomi said, "but these are definitely the birth pangs of *Mashiach*. My father says that he will come very soon."

"Where will he come from?" asked Meir.

"Perhaps from Mount Zion," Shoshana suggested.

"It is written in the Prophets that *Mashiach* will come riding on a donkey," said Esther.

"Then how can he come from Mount Zion?" asked Meir.

"We don't know," answered Naomi. "God has promised us that He will bring *Mashiach*, and He'll know how to do it."

"I say that he'll come in an airplane," declared Meir. "I've just heard that they leveled the lot so that planes can land there."

Wednesday morning was a time of great rejoicing. During the night, reinforcements had arrived. Our forces had broken through Zion Gate, bringing in more soldiers and weapons.

As the news passed from house to house, people went outside to greet the newcomers. "We are saved!" they cried. "The road is open and the siege is over!" But snipers' bullets quickly forced them all back into their places of refuge.

Abba paced back and forth in the apartment exclaiming, "How wonderful! What daring! What bravery!" After his initial excitement had died down, he sat down beside Naomi and me. "In his commentary on the Torah, the Ibn Ezra states that the generation which left Egypt died in the desert because it was a generation of slaves who were still afraid of their masters. That generation, even had they entered Eretz Yisrael, would not have been capable of fighting the seven Canaanite nations and conquering Eretz Yisrael. Only those who were born free, in the desert, could become fearless men of war, and so it was they who were chosen by Hashem to conquer the land.

"We Jews who have experienced so many pogroms are like those Jews who left Egypt. We have been subject to foreign rule for so many years that we submit to foreign masters from pure habit. It will not be our privilege to bring the redemption. It will be this new generation who does not know fear which will be the first generation of the redemption!"

The gunfire grew stronger and shells flew; nevertheless we were all in high spirits. Only later did we find out that our elation had been premature. The redemption had not yet come. The army which broke through did indeed bring us a sizeable quantity of weapons, but the soldiers had all gone back to town, leaving behind only a small troop of middle-aged, inexperienced men. Worst of all, they were unable to maintain control of the road through Zion Gate. The Gate was blockaded once again. Once again we were surrounded on all sides and cut off from the outside world. Once again, we were under siege.

7 The Arab Legion

The following morning a panic-stricken girl ran into the apartment screaming, "The Legion is here!"

"What? What?" All were alarmed.

"The army. The whole army. The Jordanian Legion! We saw them on the Mount of Olives. Their armored cars on the mountain have heavy artillery and..."

"Why are you causing alarm?" a civil defense soldier scolded her. The girl backed up against the wall, embarrassed.

"Wh...what is artillery anyhow?" asked Meir with a child's innocence. There was no need to answer. A deafening noise, followed by a violent explosion answered his question. Everyone was terrified. The next explosion came soon after.

Suddenly, refugees from the houses next to Yeshivat Porat Yosef burst into the room.

"The Arabs are coming!" they cried. "They have captured Porat Yosef."

Hysteria ensued. Women wailed loudly; children cried. Only Savta did not panic. As was her habit, she opened her pocket-sized book of Psalms and began to pray. An hour later a messenger came in to reassure us. "Our forces are in control of the situation."

The arrival of the Arab Legion marked a turning point in the war. The shelling was endless. We realized that we were now pitted against a mighty, well-organized military force which cared not at all how much of its arsenal it "wasted" on us. These attacks were not carried out by gangs, sporadically attacking different areas. They were well-planned and carried out by a strong, serious enemy. As soon as the Legion arrived, Porat Yosef had fallen, and now the Misgav Ladach Hospital was in serious danger as well.

On Shabbat, all was quiet. In the afternoon, Rabbi Orenstein and his wife came over to visit us. At the beginning of the bombardment, they too had left their apartment at the edge of the Quarter and moved in with one of the families on the ground floor of Batei Machse.

Rabbi Orenstein was a distinguished and highly respected personality. He had been the rabbi of the Kotel and was the head of the committee in charge of the residents, of which Abba was a member.

As he sat and talked to Abba, I watched him closely. His

long, wide beard flowed over onto his chest, and his kindly face matched the pleasant tone of his speech. While he spoke to Abba, his wife talked to Imma. When her husband rose to go, she parted from Imma warmly, the two women exchanging words of encouragement.

On Sunday afternoon, one of the neighbors came in, white as plaster, and announced, "A terrible tragedy has occurred... Rabbi Orenstein and..." He was unable to finish the sentence. After he was seated, he whispered, "The rabbi and his wife were killed by a shell!"

Could it be true? It didn't seem possible. Why, just yesterday, they were sitting here, on these chairs, and talking to us...

"Blessed be the True Judge." Everyone automatically recited the blessing that is said upon hearing news of a death.

"What happened?" they asked in great sorrow.

"This morning a shell fell near the entrance to the apartment where they were living. The rabbi was washing his hands near the doorway; he was killed instantly. His wife was injured by the shrapnel which flew into the room. She passed away shortly after, in the hospital."

We were all silent. We mourned them deeply, and our spirits sank lower and lower.

So began the second week of battle. After "resting" on Shabbat, the Arabs launched a ferocious attack, bombarding the Quarter with hundreds of mortar shells and thousands of bullets. I don't know how we lived through those days, carrying on with all the normal daily activities such as eating, drinking, sleeping. To this day it is hard for me to imagine how my mother and the other women managed to take care of the babies and small children under those conditions.

I can still see Savta sitting there, reciting Tehillim. Never once did she lose her composure. She was a constant calming influence on us all. Early each morning, before the shelling began, she would run out to fetch water from the cistern. Every such venture outdoors entailed a grave risk. One woman was killed by a sniper's bullet while still holding onto her water pitcher. But we couldn't live without water. Whenever our supply was depleted, Savta would calmly go out to the cistern. The others would look fearfully over their shoulders, lest, God forbid, the shelling begin earlier than usual that day.

Abba also left the house frequently. Between one bombardment and the next, he would run out on various errands. Every time he left, Naomi would cry hysterically. The neighbors did their best to calm and comfort her. When all else failed, Imma would say to them, "Let her be. Who knows? Perhaps by virtue of the child's tears, her father will return home safely." So Naomi was allowed to cry in peace, and the rest of us cried with her.

38 The Evacuation of Misgav Ladach

We were still living with the hospitable old couple in their one-room apartment on the ground floor of Batei Machse, but it was becoming increasingly crowded as new families were constantly arriving, bearing news of another street or another house which had fallen to the Arabs.

We were being slowly strangled in an ever-tightening noose. Outside, scores of shells were exploding, as a mighty bombardment of artillery fire was under way. Stones were flying, and the air was full of dust and smoke. The lady of the house ran from one person to another, clapping her hands in distress and crying, "What will be? What will be? Try to find yourselves a place to sit."

After an hour or two the bombardment stopped, the old man fell asleep, and the loudspeaker began to call to us to surrender, over and over again. Meir was very depressed.

"How does one recite the confession before death?" he asked his sister.

"Why do you ask?"

"Because...because...so many people have already died! Who knows? Pretty soon the Arabs will conquer the whole Quarter."

"Don't say that!" Shoshana answered sharply.

"I will! I have to recite the confession."

"You know what?" said Shoshana. "Didn't you recite the confession that day we all fled?"

"Of course I did."

"Then that confession is valid now and forever and that's enough!"

"Shoshana is right," Naomi agreed, "and anyhow we're not going to die."

"Didn't you hear what they broadcast on the loudspeaker?"

"God won't allow that to happen. Everything will be all right. Perhaps reinforcements will arrive again."

Just then, in the middle of our conversation, a group of wounded boys came limping into the room.

"Wounded soldiers!" I gasped.

The old man, frightened out of his sleep, jumped to his feet, and his bed was immediately occupied by one of the wounded.

"Where are you going? The house is full already!" protested the lady of the house.

But the wounded continued to stream into the small apartment. Some had to be carried in on stretchers and were laid either on the bed or on the floor. Others, who were able to walk, found their own corners. A doctor carrying equipment and a nurse in a white coat arrived as well.

"What happened?" everyone asked at once.

"Last night, Misgav Ladach Hospital was evacuated," said the nurse. "All night long we were crowded into a single tiny apartment until we could bear it no longer and some of us left to look for another shelter."

A few of the families decided to leave immediately. Yehudit began to cry. She pulled at Imma and begged to go outside. "Blood! Blood!" she cried hysterically, trying to run out to the courtyard. Imma had to forcibly restrain her from rushing into the gunfire.

"What will happen to us now?" Imma turned to Abba. "What shall we do? Where shall we go?"

Naomi began to cry, and I followed suit. The one-room apartment had turned into a crowded hospital — no place for healthy people to remain. Abba went out to search for another shelter, and meanwhile we pressed ourselves to the wall.

One severely wounded patient cried out in pain. I turned towards him. On the bed lay Tzion, the boy whose knee had been mildly injured several months earlier while drilling in the lot. His stomach was torn and bleeding, and his pale face was distorted with pain. Crying like a baby, he called to the nurse, "Give me... please give me... oy, oy, oy."

The nurse came up to him and hid her face in the palms of her hands. "I have no more," she said and burst into tears.

"What doesn't she have?" Meir asked his sister in a whisper.

"I think she doesn't have any more morphine to stop his pain. They have run out of medicine."

The wounded were a shocking sight. Some had bandages on their heads, hands and legs. Others were not bandaged at all. Some cried out loud. One wounded boy, whose leg had been amputated, tried to cheer Tzion up, "I'm wounded too, and I'm in pain. But I'm trying to stay quiet. You try, too. It's better that way."

Abba returned to us. "I've found a place," he said. Imma picked up her bundle at once. Together with the Eizen family, we ran crouching through the courtyard and into a storeroom opposite.

39 A Musty Storeroom

Abba brought us into a long dark passageway. On one side was a tall, thick, stone wall. On the opposite side were small doorways leading to a number of small, low storerooms. Most of them were already crowded with "tenants." We and the Eizens piled into an empty compartment. The sharp odor of mold filled the windowless room. As my eyes gradually grew accustomed to the darkness, I was able to discern two wide wooden shelves hung across the opposite wall. Everything was covered with a thick coat of dust, and long cobwebs — never before disturbed by human beings — hung from the ceiling. It was obvious that no one had entered that moldy cell for years. We, however, were quite happy to have found a safe, well-protected shelter.

We sat down on the floor and listened to the shells exploding outside. Our enemy was so close that we could clearly hear each shell as it was shot from the mortar, followed by a hair-raising whistle as it flew through the air. We passed the anxious hours trying to guess where the shells would fall and explode.

"This shell will land in the lot."

"That one will fall on the house facing us."

Our guesses were made according to the duration of the whistle. Finally we would hear a deafening explosion and the thunder of walls collapsing and stones falling and scattering in all directions.

And then again: Boom!

"Another shell!" we would shout, holding our breath while it flew, whistling, through the air."

"Oy — oy," we would scream. "It will explode over our heads."

But no, thank God, it passed us and continued on its

journey, exploding on the other side of Batei Machse. Then came the swishing sound of stones falling and clattering over the lot.

We were heavily attacked from all sides. Artillery fire, mortar shells, machine guns, and bullets. A torrent of lead. Every minute another wall was hit, collapsing into a pile of stones. We could hear it all — loudly and clearly — even if we tried to stop up our aching ears.

* * *

On Wednesday, the thirty-second day of the Omer, there was a lull in the fighting, and Abba was called to help bury the dead. There are no burials within the Old City walls, but at the very beginning of the fighting, when it was clear that the siege was complete and there would be no possibility of burying the dead outside of the Old City in the near future, the rabbis gave their permission for temporary burial within the walls.

On Sunday, the first day of the war, a large common grave was dug not far from Shaar Hashamayim Yeshiva. During the last days of the Mandate, the British had not allowed us to take our dead out of the Old City for burial, and so those who passed away or were killed in those few days were also buried, together with the first victims of the war, in the common grave.

Now, the dead of the past ten days were laid to rest there too: Rabbi Orenstein and his wife; Batya's father; fighters killed at their posts; and children who had been shot by snipers while carrying messages from one post to another.

The bodies were put side by side and covered with wooden boards upon which another layer of bodies was laid to rest. Dozens of dead, most of them victims of the terrible war, were thus buried inside the Old City, until such time as, with the help of God, they could be transferred to their final resting place on the Mount of Olives.

10 The Last Bit of Bread

It was Wednesday afternoon. We children were all sitting inside the small cells of the storeroom, the adults were outside in the passageway. Despair was in their eyes. In addition to everything else, there was now no more bread. We weren't yet hungry, but a few hours later, our stomachs began to rumble. Soon we were lethargic. None of the adults said a word. Only the children demanded, "Bread! We want bread!"

Of the whole group, only two men stood up: the head of the Eizen family, his blonde beard and sidelocks white with dust, and . . . Abba, who had unceasingly and uncomplainingly carried the heavy burden of the community on his shoulders since the start of the war.

"We will go to the bakery," the two men announced.

Silence fell on the storeroom, and in the silence, the two turned to go out.

"No! No!" screamed Naomi. But Abba and Binyamin Eizen were already gone. Heart-rending screams tore the air as my sister cried out in alarm, "Abba!" Her voice carried from one end of the storeroom to the other. "Abba!"

This time no one made any attempt to quiet her. People cried silently. Would the men succeed in reaching the bakery? Would they return safely?

The shrinking Jewish Quarter was being bombarded heavily, but my sister Naomi almost overwhelmed the noise of the gunfire destroying our homes and streets. We had no idea whether the Arabs had captured the bakery yet or not. My heart felt like a shell about to explode.

"Abba, Abba, why did they let you go? Why you? There are other people here who could go! I'm not hungry, Abba! I don't want any bread. I only want you . . . you, safe and sound."

Each moment Abba was gone seemed like an eternity. The shells continued to fly. When would Abba return?

"Please, God, save him!" I cried from the bottom of my heart.

Shouts and cries of joy suddenly filled the dark passageway. They were here! They had arrived! Thank God! Just at that moment, a shell exploded in the courtyard nearby.

Everyone ran out to the passageway, jumping on the two men, each of whom carried a huge sack on his back. The fragrant smell of fresh *pitta* filled the air, causing our mouths to water. The two men were surrounded and almost trampled.

"Stand in line!" shouted Abba in an attempt to discipline the hungry crowd, but to no avail. "No one will get so much as a crumb if he doesn't stand in line," shouted Abba again, closing his hands tightly around the mouth of the sack.

Slowly, the people formed a line. Abba took out two *pittot* and handed them to the first person in line. Another two . . . and another two . . . The sack was being rapidly emptied, and there was still a long line of people, all pushing and screaming. Dozens of hands reached towards every *pitta* as it emerged from the sack. Abba shouted again, "There is enough for everyone," but the people were too panic-stricken to pay heed. Everyone knew that no one would risk his life again to go to the bakery and bake. In another hour or two, the bakery, complete with its stock of flour, would probably be in Arab hands.

Abba continued to distribute *pittot*. Each one was grabbed up the minute it emerged from the sack. No one wanted to miss out on his last piece of bread. The sacks were almost empty. Imma, who had not pushed forward until then, tried to get through to Abba.

"You haven't given me any yet!" she called in a choking voice, but she could not be heard above the din.

"Shlomo, for me! Give me, too! Your own children are hungry!" She waved her hands until Abba noticed her.

"After everyone else has received, we too will receive ours." Abba continued distributing *pittot* to the wild, unruly crowd.

Fearing starvation, they were behaving almost like animals.

Finally, the pressure lessened. Imma too received two *pittot* (no more!), and took us back to the musty cell. Each of us received a piece of *pitta*, over which we recited the blessing for bread. The little ones ate heartily, but as for me, the fresh *pitta* stuck in my throat. It was hard to swallow bread for which my father had risked his life.

1 Reinforcements

It was Thursday, Lag Ba'omer. Someone came into the store-room, bringing news . . . bad news. Of the whole Jewish Quarter, only Batei Machse, the Sephardi synagogues and Shaar Hasha-mayim Yeshiva still remained in Jewish hands. The heavy shelling continued.

"The red-headed woman who lives on the first floor was just killed in the courtyard!" someone cried. Chana and Rachel and their family came running into the storeroom from some apartment. Miraculously, they had succeeded in dodging all the shells on the way, although Chana was wounded in the knee by a piece of shrapnel. She was crying, but she soon stopped and began to supply all the children with the latest news.

Although we now held only a tiny section of the Jewish Quarter, our forces were still holding out at their posts. There were very few soldiers left, so even the wounded remained at their posts, refusing to leave. We had almost run out of ammunition, and the Arab Legion continued to advance.

The situation was very grave indeed. We, the children, looked to the adults, hoping to receive comfort and security from them, but in vain. Everyone sat or stood in silence. There was nothing to say; there were no words of comfort. All hearts were heavy. All the sunken eyes reflected terrible, deep despair. The faces were all sad and the shoulders bent. No one spoke. There was nothing to say.

Imma fed us supper: *pitta* dipped in oil with garlic. "You eat, too," I said, but she shook her head. She had no appetite. Who could eat at a time like this? Imma sat on the floor in the passageway, the baby wrapped in his blanket on her lap, her head between the palms of her hands. In a few more hours ... in just a little while ... the Jewish Quarter would fall, and then ...

Someone was standing in the doorway. All eyes turned to him.

"There is talk of surrender," he announced.

"Surrender?"

Everyone sat up and an argument immediately ensued.

"Oh, I hope, I hope we surrender already. Let's surrender and get out of here alive!"

"We can't bear any more suffering. In any case, the situation is hopeless."

"Surrender?" said others. "After such a bitter fight? After all our sacrifices? To lose everything now? To give up the Old City to the Arabs? To quit the struggle — to stop fighting? After all those long months of siege, all the bombardments, all the suffering? After all the blood that has been spilt? No! We will never surrender the Jewish Quarter! We will fight to the bitter end!"

"But why? To what purpose? Soon the Arabs will conquer the Quarter in any case. Why should we all die?"

"And if we surrender, who will guarantee that we won't die then? Do you think we can trust the Arabs?"

"I hope headquarters agrees to surrender," said Chana.

"What did you say?" her sister Rachel asked.

"I hope headquarters agrees to surrender," Chana repeated.

"Who asked headquarters? I hope the Arabs agree to let us surrender."

"Where is your courage?" asked Naomi, inflamed. "You want to surrender? I don't!"

"Do you want to die?" asked Chana.

"We can't depend on the Arabs. They'll trick us. They'll say that they accept our surrender, and then they'll stick knives in our backs anyway. That's the way they are."

A civil defense guard came in.

"Will we surrender?" everyone asked.

"No, they have promised to send us reinforcements from town."

"Reinforcements?"

"Yes, tonight reinforcements will arrive!"

The news passed from one to another, bringing new hope. We had waited so long...we had prayed...if only we could hold out until the reinforcements actually arrived...

Eagerly, we waited for dark, although inside the storeroom it was almost impossible to tell the difference between day and night.

"Is it night yet?" I asked Abba. He looked at his watch with its luminous dial.

"Yes, but they probably won't come before midnight."

"What time is it now?"

"Seven."

* * *

Our younger sisters had fallen asleep on the ground.

"You go to sleep, too," Abba told us.

"To sleep? Now? When the reinforcements are about to come any minute? Never!" I declared.

"Never!" agreed Naomi.

"Oh, yes, you will!" said Abba. "You must get some sleep and renew your strength for tomorrow."

We went back into the tiny, moldy cell. Abba brought a

candle from the passageway and stuck it in the ground near the wall. Two of the Eizen children were lying on one of the wooden shelves. Others were sleeping on the floor.

"You two lie down on a shelf, too. Here, the second shelf is empty," said Imma.

Reluctantly, Naomi climbed up onto the shelf, but I shrugged my shoulders in refusal.

"I don't want to sleep on a shelf!" I protested. "Besides, how will we know when the reinforcements arrive?"

Abba promised to wake us up — "If they come," he added to himself, lifting me up onto the shelf.

"I have never slept on a more comfortable bed," laughed Shoshana, Meir's sister.

Meir had both his legs up on the wall, to make room for his tall sister. I lay on my back, my legs also in the air, so as not to hit my sister in the stomach. My eyes were wide open, and I stared at the ceiling, watching the spiders artistically weaving a gigantic net of spider webs on the ceiling above me. The thread-like webs hung from the ceiling like light fixtures, and for some reason, they reminded me of the lamps hanging from the dome of the Churva.

"I wonder if they have been damaged," I thought to myself anxiously. "Perhaps they were all shattered to pieces by the bombardment." A big piece of dust fell from the ceiling into one of my eyes. I blinked over and over again. It was hard to fall asleep.

From the shelf opposite me I heard snoring. Were Shoshana and Meir asleep? I glanced in their direction. It was clearly Meir who was snoring, imitating an old man. His mouth was open, and he was making loud snoring noises. When this didn't get him any attention, he began to snore even louder. His snores began to sound like a donkey braying. We said nothing.

"What a strange boy," I thought to myself, " always laughing or joking, even when his heart is crying."

I closed my eyes and tried to put my confused thoughts in order. Here we were, all crowded together: fathers, mothers, children, babies, all waiting for the reinforcements. The children were sleeping. One boy was snoring. Men were pacing back and forth. Shells were flying. *Pittot.* The Arabs were coming. With knives. The Legion was here. Heavy artillery. Where were the reinforcements? How would they get in? From Zion Gate again? Would they be able to get through? Should we surrender? Yes! No! Yes! No!

Footsteps. Abba came into the cell. Joyfully, I sat up. "Have the reinforcements come?"

"No, not yet," he answered.

"What time is it?"

"Midnight. Lie down, little one. Try to fall asleep."

Again I closed my eyes. I tried to stuff up my ears, which had almost been deafened by the noise of those past few days. My whole body ached. The spider webs disappeared and a different picture took their place. I saw the sun shining again in the yard of Batei Machse. We were no longer cooped up in the dark storeroom. We were all outside. But what was wrong? Why was it so quiet? The explosions had stopped. No one was arguing anymore either.

"Have the reinforcements arrived?" I asked aloud.

No one answered.

"The reinforcements — where are they?" I repeated.

Not a sound. No answer. Everyone was asleep — sound asleep. No one heard, no one answered. Silence — the silence of a cemetery. Suddenly I heard a snore, and a voice from the ground announced, "The Quarter has fallen. Everyone is dead. I, too, am dead." The voice was Meir's.

I tried to sit up, but I was too sleepy. I forced myself to fight sleep. If only I could stay awake, not fall asleep... not die... not die like everyone else.

"*Re—in—force—ments,*" I tried to scream, but not a

sound came out of my sleeping throat. I tried to lift my arm, to move my leg, but they were paralyzed. I was chained to the ground. Suddenly I felt great pain in my back and neck. What was it? A hobnailed boot? A foot?

Someone was trampling on my neck and calling out: "Surrender at once!"

"No," I replied. "I won't surrender! I don't want to surrender!"

"Surrender or I will shoot!" repeated the voice.

"Who are you?" I asked.

"A Legionnaire," the voice answered. "We conquered the Quarter last night. If you don't surrender, you'll die, like all the rest."

"No!" I cried.

A shot. A strange liquid flowed over my body. I was lying in a sea. It must have been my blood, I thought, flowing like water. This was the end.

"God, please don't take my soul. I don't want to die... not yet. I want to grow up... to have children... to live in the State of Israel... I don't want to die! I don't want to die!" I screamed with all my might.

"Sh... *sheket*... Puah, *sheket*." Someone was caressing my face. I opened my eyes and saw Naomi leaning over me.

"Why are you crying and screaming?"

"The Legionnaire," I wailed. "The Legionnaire. He killed me."

"Silly." Naomi laughed, caressing me again. "There are no Legionnaires here. Nothing has happened to you."

"Oh, yes," I screamed in panic. "I'm covered with blood." I felt my clothes. They were wet.

"It's not blood," said Naomi. "It's just sweat. It's very hot tonight. You must have been dreaming."

"Dreaming?" It took a few moments for the thought to seep in. "Oh, it was so awful!" I checked to see that my body was still in one piece. "Where are the reinforcements?"

"There aren't any. No reinforcements. The night is over."

* * *

The reinforcements we had so hoped for had failed to arrive. Our last hope was gone. What would happen now? I went to look for Abba and found him, his eyes all red, standing in the passageway.

"Are we still waiting?" I asked.

"No, little one, it's morning already."

"But I don't want to die!" I cried. "I don't want everyone to die."

"I don't want that either, little one," he said, picking me up and kissing me on both cheeks.

"Has the Quarter fallen?" I asked.

"No, but ... "

"What will happen now?" I asked.

Abba didn't answer. He looked at me but was silent. I looked around. On every face I saw the same question, the same tired eyes, the same broken hearts.

What would happen now? The fateful question hung heavy in the air of the musty storeroom.

12 Surrender

Surrender. How much shame and degradation the word conveyed! What power it had to bow the back, to break the heart, to bend the spirit.

Surrender. Cease-fire. An end to all the bloodshed. Salvation from the valley of death. Life. Could it really be true?

Two weeks ago, if anyone had dared suggest it, I would have

stoned him. But today...today the will to live was stronger than all else.

"You must live," cried all my limbs. "Live! Don't die! Go forth from these ruins; you have dwelt long enough in The Valley of Tears."

For two weeks we had fought to keep the Jewish Quarter for the Jewish people. But during those two long weeks of fighting, the Quarter had lost its limbs, one by one. House after house, street after street, it was destroyed. For two long weeks it had defied the enemy heroically, refusing to surrender to superior strength. But now, Divine will had sealed its fate, and today we would surrender. We would be allowed to leave, to go away and begin again somewhere else — not here, in the Old City, but somewhere else in Eretz Yisrael. God had willed it.

Pieces of information began to reach us. First, a frightened girl came in, pushed through the crowd of children and adults on the floor, and announced: "The rabbis went out with a white flag, but they were shot at."

"By the Arabs?" we all asked.

"No, by the boys. Our boys. They still refuse to discuss surrender. They shot at the rabbis and forced them to retreat."

"How awful! How awful!"

Half an hour later, we received more news. "The Hagana has agreed to surrender. Rabbi Minzberg and Rabbi Chazan have gone out again carrying a white flag."

Soon it was announced that the Arabs had ceased fire. Negotiations were being held on the terms of surrender.

One by one we left the storeroom and walked out into the fresh air. We emerged slowly at first, cautiously, unbelievingly, shading our eyes from the bright daylight which almost blinded us, and rubbing our ears, those poor ears which had become so accustomed to the heavy bombardment that now they ached from the silence all around. Again and again we pinched our ears. Yes, it was really true. All was quiet. Everything was over.

There were no more explosions; there was no more shooting. Quiet. Nothing to hear and nothing to see. Genuine quiet. How heavy and oppressive the silence was.

People came out from their hiding places, from behind the sacks protecting their wrecked apartments, from the packed synagogues, from the dark storerooms. More and more were coming out into the yard. But what was wrong? The legs which had been so cramped for the past two weeks could not move freely now. Everyone walked slowly and spoke quietly. All eyes were lowered to the ground, all heads bowed in mourning. Silently we gazed at the ruins and lamented our dead.

"All residents are to be evacuated. All weapons are to be handed over to the Arabs. Soldiers will be taken prisoner." This was the decree.

All residents are to be evacuated? To where? People were wandering around the courtyard of Batei Machse, looking for the last time at its stones. Today we would be parting from this sacred, ancient place, from the Old City of Jerusalem, site of the Holy Temple. We had lost control of the Kotel Hamaaravi months ago; but now would it be lost for good? Old men and women, who had never in their lives been outside the Old City walls, would today leave for the first time. This place where they had been born, where they had grown up and studied, where they had married and raised children and grandchildren ... would they ever see it again? Today it had been decreed that they leave, and their hearts were heavy and full of sorrow.

We met Chava beside one of the water cisterns in the yard. She was silent. What was there to say? All our efforts had been fruitless, our sacrifices in vain. We were not leaving of our own free will; we had not deserted. We had tried to defend our city by remaining. We hadn't evaded our responsibilities. But now, there was no point in sacrificing any more. Chava, who had been born in the Old City, stood silently.

Chana arrived, still limping on one foot. Her sister Rachel

was with her. Frieda and Yaffale came too. The whole group gathered around the cistern.

"Do you know where we're going?" someone asked.

"To Katamon. We're going to Katamon," answered Chana, who always knew the latest news.

"To Katamon?!"

"Yes, that's where they're taking us."

"The red-haired woman was killed by a shell in this yard," Rachel told anyone who might not have heard before.

"Batya Safranovitz's father was killed helping soldiers at their post. He fought bravely and..." Frieda said.

"The wine seller died of his wounds," added Chana.

"What? Died?" I was alarmed. "When?" Lea, his daughter, was standing there, her back to the wall, extremely pale.

"What! Has your father died?" one of the girls asked.

"No, my father didn't die, but he's severely wounded... he is only severely wounded..."

But we all knew the truth. The wine seller was dead. Never again would we see that good-hearted man or buy sweets in his store. The store would remain here, in Arabs hands, if it was not already in ruins, and he, he would also remain here in Arab hands — dead. From now on Esther and Lea were orphans. There, beside Shaar Hashamayim Yeshiva, all the dead would remain: all those killed, all our sacrifices, those who were already buried in the common grave, and those who were not buried yet. They would not go with us to Katamon. They would not leave the Jewish Quarter.

Two soldiers passed us. They would not come with us either. They would be prisoners of war. The soldiers turned around and retraced their steps.

"Here is the cistern," one said to the other.

We moved aside as they approached. One of them opened the cover and looked inside. "It's all right," he said, "Throw it in!"

138

They took their guns from their shoulders and cast them into the cistern. Then they removed their ammunition belts and threw them in likewise.

"What . . . what are you doing?!" I cried, astounded. But they didn't answer.

They merely smiled bitterly.

"Your weapons! What have you done? The ammunition, the precious weapons!" I cried.

"Sh . . . sh!" Chava quieted me. "You don't understand. They're throwing away their weapons so as not to surrender them to the Arabs."

At the edge of the yard another two of our soldiers appeared. They looked around, quickly opened the third cistern and threw their weapons down. I paid no attention to Chava's explanation but ran like a madman to look for Imma or Abba. I couldn't grasp what was happening. Our soldiers were throwing their weapons away! Those precious weapons that had been so hard to obtain, that we had taken such risks to hide! Those weapons that only now could be borne openly; the precious little ammunition that was gradually running out. Who would defend us now?

I found Imma with the babies beside the storeroom.

"Imma!" I called excitedly. "The soldiers! They're throwing their weapons into the cisterns!"

"That's right," Imma answered. "They don't want them to fall into Arab hands."

"But," I protested, "we'll be left without any weapons!"

"This is what it means to surrender," Imma answered. "If they don't throw their weapons into the cistern, the Arabs will take them."

"Surrender," I repeated to myself unbelievingly. "We are surrendering."

43 Preparing to Leave

Abba came down to the courtyard. "It's time to get ready to go," he said to Naomi and me.

"Watch the children," Imma told us. "We're going up to the house to pack some things."

"Us too!" we cried. "We want to see the house again, to say good-bye."

"Not now," said Abba. "Maybe later."

Imma hugged me and asked, "What do you want to take with you from the Old City?"

"My *siddur*," I answered without a second of hesitation.

"And you, Naomi?"

"My *siddur*, too. My Shabbat *siddur*."

"I'll bring you your school bags too," said Imma. "Then you'll have all your school supplies. And clothes, so you'll have something to wear."

Abba and Imma went up, and we remained downstairs to watch the little ones. Outside, we heard something being broadcast over the loudspeakers.

"It must be an important announcement," Chana's mother told us.

We listened closely to the proclamation which was repeated over and over: "Anyone who desires to remain in the Old City may do so. Every Jew may remain in his own home, as long as he is loyal to King Abdullah."

Chana came by with the news that some people were actually happy to accept the invitation of the Arab Legion to remain in the Old City.

"Really?" Naomi was surprised. "Aren't they afraid to stay here? Aren't they afraid of the Arabs?"

"The Legionnaires have promised not to hurt anyone who stays," said Chana.

"And the people believe them?" I asked.

"There are people here who have never in their whole lives left the Old City. Old people. It is very hard for them to leave their homes," explained Chana.

Rachel came running over. "Our neighbors are staying!" she told us excitedly. "And one other family. They aren't packing at all. They have lit their kerosene stoves and are making *cholent* for Shabbat."

"Today is Friday!" the thought struck me.

"The Arabs will slaughter them as soon as we leave," everyone said.

"What stupid people! To believe false promises, to trust the enemy!"

Abba and Imma came back down, bringing two gigantic bundles with them. Abba set them down on the ground. How happy I was to see something old and familiar from the house. The bundles were wrapped in the old yellow blankets we used to play with in the house. Abba had tied them securely.

"What's inside?" I asked Imma.

"Clothes," she answered tersely.

I examined the knot, which was intended to be the handle, and tried to lift the bundle. It was very heavy.

"Who is going to carry all this?" I asked.

"Abba and I."

"What am I going to carry?" I asked.

"Here, take your school bag. I put the *siddur* you asked for inside."

My school bag! When had I last opened it? It seemed like years ago. My notebooks, my lovely blue pencil box, my reader, and my beloved little black *siddur*. I opened up the *siddur* and kissed it. Imma urged me to close it up again quickly and put the school bag on my back. It gave me a feeling of security. How good that Imma had brought it! Now I would not feel so far away from home.

Along with the bundles of clothes, Abba had brought his

briefcase which he entrusted to us to "guard above all." In it he had packed what was most precious to him: his *chumash* — the five books of the Bible — and a small Talmud Bavli. The briefcase also contained the *mezuzot* which Abba had taken off the doorposts of our apartment, and some money.

"Remember," he said to us, "only the Torah has any real value in this world." And to Imma he added, "And remember that the money in the briefcase is not ours. It was left in the committee's treasury. There is a list with the money. If, God forbid, I am parted from you, remember that this is not our money. When the time comes, the money must be distributed to its rightful owners." (And so it was, when Abba reached Katamon much later.)

"What are you afraid of?" asked Imma.

"I don't know. They announced that all men must report to the lot near Batei Machse. You can never tell what the Legionnaires might do.

As he spoke, his eyes became very sad. He looked at us all for a long time, as though trying to engrave our faces in his memory. But why?

"Whatever happens, Shlomo," said Imma, her eyes moist with tears, "trust in God. The Holy One is everywhere, even in Trans-Jordan."

Just then, one of Abba's friends who was in uniform ran up to us.

"Quick, quick!" he called to Abba. "Give me some clothes — civilian clothes!"

"Go up to my apartment. The house is open. Take whatever you want. Take the nicest suit there, you hear? It will all go to the Arabs anyway."

The man ran up the stairs, and Abba went to report at the lot.

* * *

"Why did you mention Trans-Jordan?" Naomi asked, giving Imma a piercing look.

"No reason," answered Imma. "Abba will certainly come back soon, for he wasn't one of the fighters."

"Is our house O.K.?" I asked.

Imma didn't answer. Instead she gave me a strange look.

"What does the house look like?" Naomi repeated my question.

"So, so," Imma answered evasively.

"What do you mean 'so, so'?" asked Naomi. "Did something happen?"

"We're going up to see!" decided Naomi.

"No...don't..."

"Why?"

"Because. Just don't."

"But why? Why?" I cried. "Something happened to our house, didn't it?"

"Imma," said Naomi, "a shell fell on our house."

"No."

"Artillery?" I asked. "Yes? Tell us already, Imma. Was it artillery?"

Imma nodded her head in assent.

"And what did the artillery do?" we asked.

"A great big hole in the ceiling," answered Imma.

"And our beautiful light fixture," I asked, "was it broken?"

Imma didn't answer.

"We want to go up and see!" we announced, but Imma wouldn't let us.

* * *

Little by little, old men and women began to come into the courtyard, each one with his bundle in his hand. Savta came, too, carrying a bundle. Yaffale and Frieda came with their families. Frieda was wearing her winter coat and sweating profusely.

Just then Chava appeared, running towards us from the edge of the yard. She was shouting something and clapping her hands in grief. Only when she came closer were we able to hear what she was saying.

"The Churva!" she cried. "The Churva! It was bombed out! The Churva is in ruins! Ruins . . . "

The Churva! Our synagogue! Could it be true?

"Gone. No more Churva. No dome. Nothing!" Chava wailed.

I felt dizzy. This was too great a tragedy to grasp. Why? For what purpose?

"*Baruch dayan ha'emet* — Blessed is the God of Truth!" I recited the same blessing I had heard recited upon hearing of the death of Rabbi Orenstein and his wife.

My beloved *beit knesset*, a part of myself, was gone. Our Churva was in ruins.

44 Exile

Later people would ask, How? Why? How did it happen? How did the Old City fall? Why weren't reinforcements sent? Why did the Jewish Quarter fall into Arab hands? Later, people would complain, as it were, to God, "Why did You take the Old City away from us? Why did You deprive us of the Kotel?" We thought we were so close to the Redemption, but then it was as if God had turned His back on us.

When questions like these arose, Abba would answer, "But was the Old City ever really ours? Did the Kotel ever really belong to us? Didn't the English rule us with a heavy hand? Weren't insults and degradations our daily lot at the Wall?"

Later people would consider the problem, analyze the

situation, investigate the data, try to explain, attempt to answer. At the time, however, as we stood there, loaded down with our pitiful bundles, broken in body and spirit, no one asked and no one answered. Our hearts and minds were empty.

"To the lot! To the lot!" was heard on all sides. Abba had not yet returned. How would we carry those two huge bundles? Who could even lift them? Imma opened up one of the bundles and hurriedly pulled out our winter coats, which were packed together with Abba's *tallit* and *tefillin*.

"Put on your coats!" she ordered. "Then the bundle will be lighter and you'll be able to carry it."

We shrugged our shoulders. "What, wear out winter coats today, in this heat?"

Imma asked, begged, pleaded, tried to persuade us. "All the other children are wearing coats, and even a few layers of clothing, so that next winter they'll have something to keep them warm, wherever we may be then." But we refused. Finally Imma packed everything up all over again and tied the yellow blanket together. The bundle was almost bigger than we were. Together Naomi and I managed to pick it up. Imma carried the other bundle. All this time our school bags were on our backs. Besides her own small bundle, Savta carried Yudale in her arms and Abba's briefcase in one hand. Three-year-old Yehudit and two-year-old Ruthie walked beside Imma, and so we set out for the lot.

What we saw was horrifying. Our lot had changed beyond recognition. It was covered with ruins, piles of dirt and fragments of stones. "Once I used to search the lot for little square stones to play 'five stones,' " I thought bitterly. "Now, just look at all the square stones here, huge ones from destroyed buildings, all over."

Of all the houses around the lot, only sections of walls and parts of fences were still standing. Even the façade of the beautiful, massive Rothschild building was gaping with bullet holes. Whole wings had been torn from both sides of the building, and its stone fence was in ruins. Opposite us, we could see the bare skeleton of the once-magnificent Tiferet Yisrael synagogue, looking like a wounded animal. Destroyed.

Something strange was spread out on the ground at the edge of the lot; it looked like a giant, colored tablecloth. Naomi gasped.

"What is it?" I asked.

"The flag! It's their flag — Abdullah's flag! They have conquered us, and we..."

"We...we have surrendered," I finished the sentence.

A huge crowd of women, children, the elderly and the wounded were assembled together in the lot. Never will I forget that depressing picture: those fallen faces, those dragging limbs, those eyes full of unfathomable suffering and sadness. A crowd of mourners. Not one or two individuals, not one family, but a whole community of bereaved.

And all those bundles. Bundles wrapped in rags, tied with old faded blankets. No suitcases, no duffel bags. Just piles and piles of bundles on the ground — bundles that could be carried on someone's shoulder or lifted by a weak arm or put in the hands of small children. All kinds of things wrapped in torn sheets; all one's belongings held together by faded blankets.

Refugees. War refugees. Survivors. Refugees fleeing from their homes, leaving their birthplace. People whose homes had been destroyed, whose loved ones were gone. Alone and bereaved, barely escaping with their lives...and their bundles.

Every time I pass this place, I see that terrible sight again. What a depressing picture it was. And we were part of it.

* * *

"Are we going into exile?" I asked Imma as we joined the community of refugees.

"To which exile?"

"To the exile of Babylonia?"

A bitter smile spread across Imma's face.

"We're going to the exile of Katamon."

"Is Katamon as far away as Babylonia?" I asked.

"Not quite," she replied.

"But it's just the same as the exile to Babylonia," I insisted. "This is just how the Jews looked after the destruction of the First Beit Hamikdash, before they set out on their journey. I saw it once, in a picture."

"And just like they looked after the destruction of the Second Temple, during the war with the Romans," added Chana, whose family was standing next to ours.

"I feel like the Jews who were expelled from Spain," said Naomi. "We are being expelled from the Jewish Quarter."

So we stood amidst the stricken crowd, waiting for our orders. We did not cry, not one of us. We were beyond tears, beyond despair. The dust choked our throats, unrelieved by tears. The sky was overcast from the heat. We sweated profusely, and our tongues stuck to the side of our mouths.

I looked all about me, searching for the men. Hadn't they too been told to report to the lot? Finally the order to start moving was given, bundles were loaded onto shoulders, legs began to march. The crowd was moving, but where was Abba? Wasn't he coming with us? Of course he would come. He wasn't a soldier, only part of the civil defense. He took care of the residents. Hadn't they finished classifying the men yet?

Everyone was walking. We had to move too. Together, Naomi and I lifted the heavy bundle. With my free hand I held onto three-year-old Yehudit and followed Imma and Ruthie. Savta walked behind us, carrying Yudale. There was a huge mass of refugees in front of us and almost as many behind. What a wretched parade. A caravan of exiles.

147

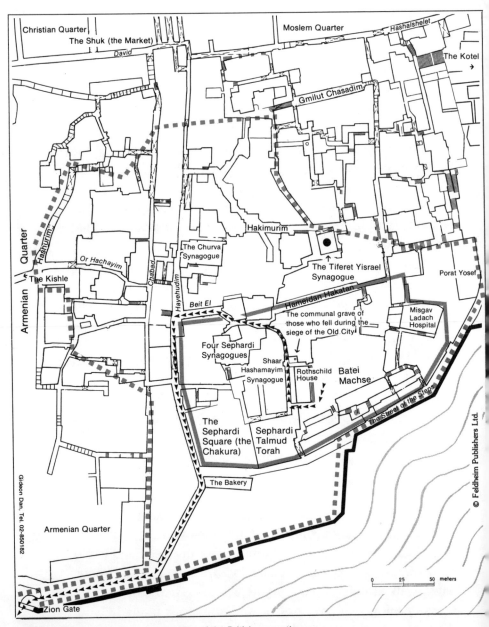

Christian Quarter

The Shuk (the Market)

David

Moslem Quarter

Hashalshelet

The Kotel →

Gmilut Chasadim

Hashurim

Quarter

Armenian

Or Hachayim

The Kishle

Chabad

Hayehudim

Hakimurim

The Churva
Synagogue

Beit El

The Tiferet Yisrael
Synagogue

Porat Yosef

Hameidan Hakatan

The communal grave of
those who fell during the
siege of the Old City

Misgav
Ladach
Hospital

Four Sephardi
Synagogues

Shaar
Hashamayim
Synagogue

Rothschild
House

Batei
Machse

The Street of the Steps

The
Sephardi
Square (the
Chakura)

Sephardi
Talmud
Torah

The Bakery

Armenian Quarter

0   25   50 meters

Zion Gate

Gideon Dan, Tel. 02-850182

© Feldheim Publishers Ltd.

■ ■ ■ ■ ■ The Jewish Quarter at the time of the British evacuation.

━━━━━ The area still held by Jewish forces on May 28th, the day of the surrender.

▶▶▶▶▶▶ The route by which the Old City inhabitants were evacuated on the day of the surrender.

45 A Road Full of Obstacles

It was now Friday afternoon. As we set out on our way, I sent a last glance towards the lot where I had spent such wonderful childhood days. My entire world was being left behind. My legs wouldn't follow my command; they stopped and stumbled every minute, refusing to move. I looked at the large courtyard with the water cisterns, our weapons deep inside them. One last farewell glance at the third floor, and then I forced myself not to look any more, lest I fall behind the moving mass.

Batei Machse disappeared from sight. The house with the wide window disappeared too. Soon the Arabs would come and take everything we had: our new icebox, the bookcase with the handsome clock above it, the big table, the folding bed — everything except what we were carrying in our bundles.

Naomi and I stopped. For a moment we rested the big bundle on the ground. We switched hands. Imma looked behind her.

"Hurry up, girls! Faster!" she called.

"Abba . . . ," I said.

"Abba will come later. Don't worry."

We left the lot and started walking down a narrow street. To my dismay we now met the enemy face to face, on both sides of the street. Legionnaires stood dressed in khaki uniforms and special caps. Full of glee in their victory, they stood and watched the mournful parade pass by. They were armed well, guns on every shoulder, full ammunition belts, long chains of bullets across their chests.

"These, then, are the soldiers who fired their cannons at us," I thought to myself. "These are the men who manned those terrible machine guns, who stood behind the mortars. It must have been one of them who shot the shell which killed Rabbi Orenstein and his wife." One of them had killed Batya's father, and another the wine seller. These were the soldiers who had

149

shed our blood, who had destroyed and laid to ruin the Jewish Quarter, who were exiling us from our city, like the Babylonians ... like the Romans. These are the enemy, so close now, only one step away.

"How much ammunition they have! How many bullets each soldier has!" I wanted to exclaim out loud, but fear kept me silent. What would happen if one of them suddenly began to shoot?

"Puah, come. Come on. They won't hurt us," said Imma, noticing my anxiety. "That's what they promised when we agreed to surrender."

Shaking like a leaf, I followed Imma and Ruthie. We walked over pieces of broken glass and stone. We passed stores half ruined, walls pierced by bullets. Here the wine seller's store ... Esther and Lea's father. I peeked inside. Perhaps ... perhaps I would see him in there, leaning against a pillow, ready for business? He'd look at me with his great big eyes and hand me a piece of licorice. But no, the store was empty, and broken bottles littered the floor.

Our bundle was heavy, and our hearts were heavier. Again we stopped. Again Imma urged us to go on. With great effort we picked up the bundle — just like big girls! We must help Imma. Abba had been delayed, and she was depending on us to help her. With a few more steps we would reach Jewish Quarter Road, and from there we were not far from the Sephardi Square.

From afar I noticed Yosef's candy store — "our store." I was happy to see that it was almost undamaged. But, wait, what was this? Why was the door wide open? Was Yosef crazy? Wasn't he coming with us? I stopped for a minute to see what had happened to him. Shocked, I saw that Yosef was not in his store at all. Instead, it was full of armed Arabs, red-checked kafiot on their heads.

"Iraqi soldiers!" Savta gasped behind me. The Iraqis were looting the store wildly — spilling all the candy from the sacks, emptying all the shelves, gorging themselves.

As we neared Jewish Quarter Road, a terrible tumult reached our ears. Turning the corner, we caught sight of an Arab mob coming towards us from the *shuk*. The Legionnaires stood between us, their hands linked to one another to form a human chain, barring the rabble from attacking us.

"Attack them!" chanted the inflamed mob.

Yehudit began to scream, and I, seeing the blood in their fiery eyes, froze in my steps, unable to move. My teeth chattered and my whole body quaked. Imma and Savta exchanged glances.

"If only we get out of here safe and sound," I could hear Savta mutter.

Imma walked faster, almost ran, with little Ruthie and her bundle.

"Get moving!" Savta scolded us.

I tried to lift the bundle together with Naomi, but my trembling hands wouldn't obey me. Imma looked over her shoulder, and, seeing that we were not moving, cried, "Enough, enough. Leave the bundle right there. Leave it and start walking."

"Leave the bundle? Here?" asked Naomi.

Imma ran back towards us. "It doesn't matter," she said.

We left our family's clothes beside a fence on the side of the street. "Pretty soon Abba will come," I thought to myself. "He'll recognize our bundle. He'll recognize the yellow blanket and pick it up."

Instead of the heavy bundle, Savta gave Naomi Abba's briefcase, and I was given Imma's bag. "Take good care of it," she said. "It has the things we need the most: a few diapers for the baby and my silver candlesticks. When we get to Katamon, I'll light Shabbat candles."

"Yes, today is *erev Shabbat*," I recalled.

Our burden lightened, we walked faster, past the little

151

coffeehouse, along the street, past our stores. Everywhere, uniformed Legionnaires and Iraqis in red kafiot were gorging themselves, plundering, pillaging, shattering everything.

"Everything is being taken!" Cries of despair were heard from the refugees. "Our houses ... our stores ..."

Some Arab soldiers were seen dragging a sewing machine and other valuables from the houses. Stunned, we passed them with their booty. How eagerly they swooped down on their prey! How fervently they attacked, ravaged and laid waste.

"Oy, vay! Is this what they intended to do to us?" cried one woman as she ran past us, tearing her hair.

Suddenly I smelled smoke. Sparks flew in the air. What could that be? "Who could be lighting a bonfire now?" I asked myself. "Lag Ba'omer was yesterday, not today." Because of all the people in front of me, I couldn't see what was going on, until, suddenly, everything became clear. A scream of terror flew from my throat, "Fire! Fire!"

"Fire! fire!" screamed the crowd.

"Fire! The Arabs are setting fire to the stores!"

On both sides of the street, flames filled the stores, and tongues of fire licked the narrow street where we were walking. One flame blocked my path, and I stopped in my tracks. My .mother was far ahead and Savta and Naomi were nowhere in sight.

"Imma!" I screamed, terror-stricken.

Yehudit grabbed hold of my dress and danced all around me, screaming hysterically. The people behind us simply passed us by, skipping over the fire as they proceeded on their way. As the fire grew bigger and bigger, we stood there in despair, screaming with all our might, "Imma! Imma!"

Finally, Imma heard us and came running back. She was all loaded down — a big bundle in one arm, and little Ruthie in the other.

"Jump! Jump!" she shouted to us.

"No, No!" I screamed. Yehudit also refused to budge. Finally, someone held out a hand to me. I jumped over the fire, pulling Yehudit after me. Then once again, Imma was far ahead of us, and I, seven years old and scared out of my wits, was trying with all my might to take care of my three-year-old sister and to catch up with my mother. With a heavy school bag on my back and a big bag in my hand, I pulled my hysterical little sister as hard as I could, each time she refused anew to keep on walking between the tongues of fire.

"Just don't let go of her hand," I repeated over and over to myself. "Just let us get out of here safely."

So we walked the whole way, jumping and skipping over the tongues of fire, holding on tightly to each other, both of us screaming intermittently at the top of our lungs.

Suddenly I felt a bang on the head. I looked up and was terrified to see rows of bullets touching my head. A Legionnaire! He was so close to me that I almost fainted. He reached out and took Imma's bag from my hands. A sharp pain split my arm. I didn't even get a chance to see his face before he was gone, wearing his Legionnaire's cap, and carrying Imma's bag. Imma's bag... the bag with the silver candlesticks.

To this day I remember exactly how that bag looked. It was light beige with green stripes all around. Imma had entrusted it to me, but now... he had taken it away. I hadn't taken care of it; I hadn't held on tightly enough. I began to wail loudly. Hearing my cries, Imma turned back to me.

"What's happened?" she asked in alarm.

I pointed to the Legionnaire — far away by now — but could not utter a sound.

"What's happened? What's happened?" she repeated.

I finally succeeded in uttering the words, "Your bag... your bag..."

"Never mind, never mind," Imma comforted me, "it's not important. Just keep walking, keep walking!"

Again Imma moved forward, and we followed her as though pursued by a demon. We left the burning Jewish Quarter behind and caught up with her as we reached the Sephardi Square. There, finally, we were able to stop and rest. At first, Savta, Yudale and Naomi were nowhere to be seen. Then they came running up, puffing and panting. Savta and Naomi were both excited and alarmed. Naomi was crying. They had been walking together, Savta carrying Yudale and Naomi carrying Abba's briefcase. A Legionnaire approached Naomi.

"You poor little girl. Let me help you," he offered. The briefcase was very heavy, and Naomi happily handed it to him. But the minute he took it, he began to run. Savta, who had seen what had happened, quickly handed Yudale to Naomi and began to pursue the Legionnaire.

"Give me that briefcase!" she yelled at him. "*I'll* carry it."

Savta was furious, and the Legionnaire, taken aback at this unprecedented show of aggressiveness, apologized. "I just wanted to help her. I wasn't going to take it." He returned the briefcase.

"Did you ever see such *chutzpa*?" exclaimed Savta angrily. "To steal from a child! But I wouldn't let him. From now on I won't let this briefcase out of my hand."

Having finally reached the Sephardi Square, we were able to put our bundles down and stand freely or sit on the large stones scattered everywhere, while we waited.

I had no more bundles to carry, only the school bag on my back. We all sat down on stones, but I was afraid of remaining out in the open. Out of habit, I began to look around for some shelter, but Imma reassured me, saying that here there was no need to go indoors. The Legionnaires had promised to guard us, as part of the surrender agreement. I looked around. The sky was red, and the smell of fire and smoke filled the air. Pale and stricken, Imma sat on a large stone, two-year-old Ruthie in her arms and the one big, remaining bundle on the ground.

"Have the Arabs finished capturing the Old City?" I asked her.

"Yes," she replied.

"Tell me then, why are they still destroying it? Why are they burning down the stores, if everything belongs to them now?"

Imma didn't answer. There was no answer. I cried bitterly, "Why are they setting fires? Why are they burning everything? Why?"

46 The Gate to Freedom

It was almost twilight, and we were still waiting in the Sephardi Square. People paced back and forth impatiently.

"Why are we still waiting here?" some protested angrily. Various conjectures were formed.

"Perhaps the gate is closed," proposed one rawboned woman, whose skinny braids peeked out from the kerchief on her head.

"There may be stones blocking the way which have to be cleared away," suggested another woman who was carrying a sleeping baby, while a little boy held on to her dress.

"It must be because of a roadblock!" guessed an old man, waving a cane in his hand.

Everyone was anxious. Who could tell how long the Legionnaires would succeed in restraining the Arab rabble? Who could tell how long they themselves would keep from shooting? And worst of all — perhaps, perhaps the Arabs would change their minds, God forbid, and not let us leave.

I shared the general apprehension. Nevertheless, I was glad for the delay. Now Abba would certainly have time to catch up with us, I thought. Soon he would arrive, and we would all leave the Old City together.

A little later we found out the cause of the delay. Two men had been sent to make contact with the city. They were to make sure that the road was open and safe, and then they would bring trucks to transport us to Katamon and supply the manpower to guard us.

People began to move again. I looked anxiously towards Jewish Quarter Road. Wouldn't Abba come from there? Why was he so late? Imma got up from the stone where she had been sitting.

"Let's go," she said, picking up Ruthie.

"And Abba?" I asked.

"He'll come with the other men," she answered.

"When?"

Imma shrugged her shoulders. "We can't wait here. We must go with everyone else." As she spoke, she picked up the heavy bundle. Naomi, all worn out, helped her carry it. Ruthie's little head lay on Imma's shoulder; she was sound asleep. Savta walked slowly, holding the baby and the briefcase she had saved.

"My Savta is a heroine," I thought. "How she chased that Legionnaire! And I . . . I allowed Imma's bag to be stolen!"

I walked beside Savta, my school bag still on my back. I wanted to carry Abba's briefcase. I wanted to help too, but it was so heavy.

"Never mind," said Savta. "You take care of your little sister. She's *your* 'bundle.'"

Yehudit walked beside me, sobbing as she went, and I wept with her. Imma walked; Imma ran; she went constantly forward. She paid no attention to our crying, made no effort to quiet us, just pushed us to keep going on. She almost ran towards the gate, wanting only to get out, before it was too late.

"You can't depend on the Legionnaires," she said.

But Abba, when would he come? Would he come too late,

God forbid? I was plagued with anxiety until a comforting thought suddenly struck me. Why, he would come from another direction! He must be taking a different route! Yes, that must be the answer. The men had left by way of another gate, just as the Israelites, crossing the Red Sea, had taken twelve different paths. Each tribe had taken a different route and stepped onto the shore at a different spot. That is what had happened to Abba. He must now be leaving via a different gate. That was it. We would meet him in Katamon. Perhaps he was even there already. Could it be that he had got there before us? This new idea invigorated me, and with renewed strength, I marched after Imma.

Someone announced, "The blockades have been removed, but large stones are strewn all over. Walk carefully!"

We walked slower. Yehudit tripped over a stone, and cried harder. Laboriously, we made our way towards Zion Gate.

There it was . . . the gate to freedom! Soon, soon we would be free. We would pass through the gate and finally be outside the walls that had closed us in for so long. No more siege; no more blockade. No longer would we be surrounded by enemies. Could it be true?

Again I thought of the Babylonian exiles. Which way had they walked? I thought of Tzidkiyahu, the vanquished king of Judah. He, too, had run away with his family. He had fled through an underground tunnel dug by his servants, but just as he reached the end and was about to emerge, he found his enemies waiting for him at the mouth of the tunnel.

What if we were not safe either? Terrible thoughts filled my mind. Who knew who might be waiting for us outside the gate? "They reached the gates of death" (Psalms 107:18). So had one old man in the square recited. What did he mean? Could this be the gate to death? Was death lying in wait for us outside? Perhaps the rabble, whom we had seen on the way, was waiting for us there? Perhaps, God forbid, we would be attacked

157

by some other Arab army with whom we had not signed a treaty?

A lone shot was heard. What was that? A wandering bullet, or were they shooting at the refugees? Cries of alarm. People began to run, to stumble over the stones and to push each other. Amidst the tumult we heard that a little girl had been wounded in the leg. Hysterically, everyone hurried towards the gate, running, pushing, paying no attention to anyone else.

"Forward! Hurry! Faster!" Imma urged us on, as she herself ran, carrying both the baby and the bundle with that supernatural strength which people possess only in times of danger. We hurried after her, but for some reason, the people just in front of us were walking very, very slowly, while the panicky mass behind us continued to press forward, pushing us as it moved. One desire filled all hearts — to move forward — to reach the gate and get out of here — out!

So we were pushed forward, amidst the raging crowd. The pressure was intense, the heat and lack of air unbearable. I fought with all my might not to be trampled by the mob, but my younger sister was almost crushed. With my last ounce of strength I screamed, "Help! The child! The little girl!" Alarmed, Imma threw down the bundle she was carrying, grabbed Yehudit and lifted her up.

"The bundle! The bundle!" Naomi, who had helped Imma carry it all this way, cried out. "I can't... by myself... "

"Leave it there and come on!"

"In the middle of the road?"

"Never mind, never mind... the main thing is to get out safely."

Our last bundle was abandoned in the middle of the road.

I looked up and caught sight of the gate which was our goal. But a wall of people forced us to stop moving. A barbed wire blockade was stretched the whole width of the gate! There was only one narrow opening through which two people could barely pass at once. I looked behind me and saw the human mass continuing to press forward.

A few giant images stood out in this moving mass: women carrying mattresses on their heads. Anxiously, I watched them coming closer. Soon I would be trampled! I closed my eyes. "This is the end," I thought, "the gate of death."

We had survived everything — the terrible war, the Arab mobs, the Legionnaires, the tongues of fire. We were almost out of danger, but now, this was the end. The Angel of Death was standing at the gate, waiting for us. And Jews! It had to be done by Jews! They were out of their minds. Pretty soon they would crush us . . .

"*No mattresses!*" I suddenly heard a loud voice yell. I opened my eyes and saw a tall soldier standing in the passageway facing us.

"No mattresses!" he yelled again, outshouting the noise of the crowd. I looked behind me. The women were not obeying his order. Their muscular arms held the mattresses up high, pushing away everyone who stood in their path.

"You won't be allowed through the gate with mattresses," the man warned again with great authority.

"We will, too, get through," replied the angry women as they continued to march forward, their mattresses on their heads.

"No!" called the man, and, waving his fist at them, he closed the narrow passageway. For a moment, all movement stopped. Then the angry crowd stormed the gate.

"I will open it again only when the mattresses are discarded," yelled the soldier.

The crowd turned its rage on the women with the mattresses. A mattress was seized and thrown away above the people's heads. At that, they gave in. The mattresses were left on the side of the road.

We were close to the gate, but caught between the pushing mob, we were unable to move either forward or backward.

Imma was holding the two little girls in her arms, and Naomi and I were on the ground, fighting to free ourselves and not be crushed. Behind us, people continued to push harder and harder.

"Push! Push hard! Use your elbows!" Imma shouted at us.

We tried — we wrestled, we kicked — but unsuccessfully. We were hampered by the school bags on our backs, as those behind us grabbed onto them, attempting to pull themselves forward.

"My school bag!" I cried.

"My school bag!" Naomi cried.

"Take them off!" shouted Imma. "Leave them here!"

"Leave them here?"

"Yes, yes. Fast! Hurry! You have no choice," ordered Imma.

"Leave my school bag?" Naomi repeated her question, unable to comprehend.

"It's not important; you'll get another one; take it off!" Imma cried.

I tried to free myself of the school bag, but could not. Naomi helped me and I helped her. Finally, our school bags with all their contents were left behind, wedged between the people inside the gate. They must have fallen to the ground and been trampled by the crowd. My school bag, my blue pencil case, my beloved *siddur*!

Once free of our bags, we were able to edge ourselves forward towards the passageway. My head was spinning; my breathing was heavy; my temples throbbed. I don't remember how I walked, but I'm sure it wasn't my legs that carried me. I must have been pushed through the gate by all the people. As I came out, I remember a blast of air on my face and then I fainted. Someone held a canteen to my mouth, and I felt the water touch my lips. As I sipped the cold water, I regained full consciousness.

"We're out! We're out!" I heard Naomi's voice at my side.

160

She gave me her hand and helped me stand up. I leaned against the high stone wall next to the gate. This was the Old City wall, and we were outside!

"We're out! We're out!" I cried in joy. "At last!"

I looked around in wonder, not believing what I saw. All around us stood young men and women, angels of mercy, holding out helping hands, carrying babies and children, giving water to the people streaming through the gate — to freedom.

17 Night on the Mountain

Above the wall, a pale white moon began to rise in the gradually darkening sky. I breathed in as deeply as I could. Back there, at the gate, we had almost suffocated. Imma put the two little ones on the ground, stretched her bones and gave a sigh of relief. "Thank God, thank God," she repeated for the tenth time.

"Where is Savta?" Naomi asked.

Only then did we realize that we had lost Savta and the baby in the tumult at Zion Gate.

"Savta will get here soon," said Imma, filling her lungs with air just as I was doing.

"Do you think it's possible she left before us?" asked Naomi. Worry stole into my heart. How could we find out if Savta had managed to get through the gate safely? And what about our baby? What if, God forbid, something had happened to them?

Unable to wait any longer beside the gate, we had no choice but to depend on a miracle. I have only vague memories of being led down some path to a large courtyard. We walked up wide, white marble stairs into a large, imposing building — a church that had been captured from the Arabs on Mount Zion. Once inside, we walked up many stairs and passed through large halls.

"Whose baby is this?" we suddenly heard a voice ask.

A girl, a WIZO volunteer, was walking back and forth across the hall with a baby in her arms, searching loudly for its mother. Imma ran over, looked at the baby, and cried, "He's mine! He's mine!" She took the baby from the girl's arms and pressed him tightly to her heart. We all smothered him with kisses.

"Yudale! Our little Yudale! Where were you?" we asked.

"Who gave him to you?" Imma asked the girl.

"I don't remember . . . I don't remember . . . such a tumult!"

As we were busy searching for Savta among the refugees filling the halls, we were suddenly ordered downstairs to leave the building. At the entrance, we joined a group waiting for further instructions. A guide asked for silence.

"You were lucky to leave the Old City safely," he said. "Under the terms of surrender, the Arab Legion promised to escort you out of the city wall, but no further. Now that you are outside, no one can guarantee your safety. Each one of you is responsible for himself. There is no assurance that they won't start firing at us. Therefore, listen carefully.

"When we leave here, we'll be out in the open. Tonight there is a full moon. You must stay as close to the wall and walk as quietly as possible, so that you are neither seen nor heard. Do you understand?"

Everyone murmured in assent.

"Follow the instructions and trust in God's mercy. Now, let's go!"

We left the safety of the building. Bright moonlight flooded a wide street paved with small square stones and flanked by two high walls on either side.

"Stay close to the wall," the order was given. Just then I stumbled over a stone and fell down.

"Sh, sh," everyone hissed.

"Where is the wall?" I asked myself.

Naomi helped me get up. "Walk quietly!" she whispered.

"Don't make any noise." We clung to the outer wall of the building we had just left. Part of the street was in the shadow of the wall, and we walked, silently, in that shadow. Again, death was nearby.

Suddenly, a loud voice broke the silence. "Matilda!"

"Sh, sh," the angry crowd hissed again.

"Ma — til — da," the voice called. There on the bright side of the street, loomed Savta's generous figure! Our Savta! Apparently she had been searching for us inside the church all this time and had not heard any of the guide's orders.

"Matilda! Children! Where are you?" she called, not noticing that only she was breaking the silence.

"Here," Imma answered weakly.

The people at the edge of the line grabbed hold of Savta and brought her into the shadow of the wall. "Stick to the wall!" they whispered angrily. But Savta had heard Imma's voice and hurried past them to join us.

Silently we marched along the street until the people up front reached the end of the protecting wall.

"Can everyone hear me?" asked our guide quietly.

"Yes."

"We are at the end of the wall. Crouch down and cross the street as quickly as possible. Keep in order!"

We bent over and crossed single file, continuing along a narrow alleyway to a large building. We were brought inside to several large rooms where we prepared to spend the night. Blankets, brought especially for us, were spread on the floor. WIZO volunteers walked around distributing drinks and candles. Many women covered their heads with a kerchief and lit the candles.

"What are they doing?" I asked Imma.

"Lighting candles for Shabbat."

"Why don't you light too?"

"Because ... because it is already dark outside. Shabbat

began when the sun set, and now that it is already dark, it is forbidden to light the candles."

"That's right," said Naomi. "Now it's forbidden to light any fire at all."

"It's forbidden!" I shouted.

"Sh, sh," said Imma. "You are right, but those women don't know that. Let them be."

The light of the candles flickered on the bare table. No cloth had been spread.

"The candles don't help anyhow," I said crossly. "It doesn't feel like Shabbat tonight."

"What a Shabbat! What a Shabbat!" agreed a little girl sitting on one of the blankets in the corner.

"What a Shabbat," I took up where she had left off. "No table or tablecloth, no *kiddush* or *challot*, and no... no Abba!" I covered my eyes with my hands like Imma used to do at home when she would light Shabbat candles. I tried to picture Abba sitting at the head of the table, reciting *kiddush* over the wine, the table covered with a white cloth.

"Abba," I whispered, choking with tears, "Abba, where are you?"

"Maybe Abba is in Katamon already," I reminded myself and remarked to Naomi. "Perhaps Abba is waiting for us to make *kiddush*." Naomi looked at me doubtfully and made no reply.

We lay down on one of the blankets that were spread on the ground. Our small, exhausted bodies sorely needed a rest. Lea, one of our neighbors, was lying next to me. My little sisters fell asleep immediately, but Naomi and I turned from side to side. Accidentally, I kicked Lea.

"Be quiet! Lie still!" she scolded angrily.

I burst into tears. "Why don't you sleep with your own children?" I retorted.

Lea looked at me strangely. "My children? My children are prisoners of war," she answered, turning her head away.

"Bad girl!" Imma scolded me. "Lie quietly and stop disturbing everyone."

"You should be ashamed of yourself," Naomi joined in, whispering into my ear. "Don't you know that one of her sons was killed and the other wounded?"

"No... I didn't know."

I lay quietly and must have dozed off, until I awoke to a tumult. In the dim candlelight I saw everyone scurrying about the room. Imma was standing up and calling, "Get up! Quick! Get up! We're going."

I rubbed my eyes, but Imma wouldn't let me tarry. Everyone was up and hurrying towards the door and the volunteers were folding up blankets.

"What's happening? Are we running away again?"

"What's going on?"

Yudale was already in Savta's arms. Imma pushed us towards the door, hurriedly picking up the two little girls. "Hurry, hurry! Don't be the last in line."

"Are we running away?" I asked again. "Why?"

We went out into a long hallway, following the stream of people before us. Imma pushed forward, urging us to walk faster and faster. "We mustn't be at the end," she said.

"But what happened?" Naomi asked.

"They announced that it is too dangerous to remain on Mount Zion overnight. We must go down and cross over into the New City."

This news aroused our fears once again. Panicky, we made our way through the crowd, above all not wanting to be among the last ones out. Everyone was pushing towards the exit which was guarded by two men. My heart was pounding. What if we didn't manage to get out in time?

Imma pushed forward, the two little girls in her arms, Naomi following her and pulling me. I held onto Savta and pulled her after me, so that we wouldn't lose her again. A man was shining a flashlight on the two big stairs outside the door, warning us to walk carefully. Imma went through while Naomi and I were at the top stair. Suddenly the guard hit my hand and detached it from Savta's.

"That's all," he said, closing the door behind me. Savta remained inside! I screamed and Naomi burst into tears. Imma beat the door with her fists and shouted, "We're together! We're together!" Finally the door opened and after a heated discussion, Savta and Yudale were allowed to come with us. The next day we found out that all the people who remained behind had to spend the night on Mount Zion, despite the danger, for there were not enough vehicles to transport all the refugees to Katamon that night.

The door closed behind us and we found ourselves outside, still at the top of Mount Zion, surrounded by the threatening night. Once our eyes had grown accustomed to the dark, we saw that everyone was descending the steep incline on the mountain, half walking, half running.

There was no road, and once you began the descent, there was no stopping until you reached the bottom.

"Take the baby," Savta said, as she looked at the difficult descent and resigned herself to her fate. "I'll stay here."

"Oh, no!" said Imma. "It's not so bad! You're coming with us. You'll go down just like everyone else."

"No, children," Savta shook her head firmly. "No, that is too much for me. There is no way I can get down that mountainside. I...I will certainly fall."

"That's true. How will we get down?" Naomi asked, her hand trembling in mine. I felt my knees go weak. I wanted to say something to Savta, but my lips were chattering. Just then, several Gerrer *chassidim* approached us. One of them took the baby from Savta. Two strong figures took Savta by the arms, and masculine voices urged her to begin the descent. Someone came over to help Imma with the little girls.

166

"You two are already big," they told us. "Run! Run down the hill until you get to the bottom."

"Run!" Imma called to us, as she began to slide down the incline, holding onto frightened little Yehudit. As they went down, dirt and stones began to slide and roll, making an awful noise.

"Immale, the mountain is moving!" I screamed, terrified, watching Imma slide further and further away.

"You're already grown-up," the men said. "Run!" But at that moment, I felt so little, so helpless, so lost...Behind us we heard Savta's discouraged voice as she refused to move, the young *chassidim* encouraging her and urging her on.

"We have no choice," said Naomi, no less scared than I. "Let's run."

"Yes, we're the big ones now. There's no one left to help us."

Someone gave us a light push from behind. We tried to hold on as the ground slipped away from under our feet, but it was too late to stop. We ran and ran, holding hands and taking half of the mountain with us, our feet stumbling over the sliding stones. Finally, we came to a stop and fell straight into Imma's outstretched arms. I burst into tears.

18 The Road to Katamon

"Matilda! Matilda!" Our ears picked up the sound of someone calling amidst all the tumult.

"Who is calling me?" asked Imma, her eyes searching through the crowds.

"Matilda, Matilda," the excited voice called again. "It's your brother, Shimon."

Amidst the crowds of people, I managed to pick out my

Uncle Shimon. He was wearing a Hagana uniform with a beret on his head. It was he, none other! Words cannot describe our joy and excitement upon seeing him. No longer were we isolated. We had succeeded in remaining alive and in renewing contact with the city and with someone from the family.

"What are you doing here?" Imma asked at last.

"We came to help," he answered, giving orders right and left. "Where is Shlomo?"

Imma shrugged her shoulders.

* * *

After that, everything happened quickly. Canvas-covered army jeeps were parked at the foot of the mountain, most of them already full. Soldiers from the Hagana urged us to get on quickly. Imma took Yehudit and Ruthie and got onto a jeep, and Yudale was put on her lap. Savta, panting and sighing with relief, had also arrived safely by then and was helped into a jeep.

"Get on already!" Imma called out to us. But we remained outside, glued to one spot.

"Shabbat," Naomi cried. "It's Shabbat!"

"Shabbat! Shabbat!" I repeated, my whole body quivering. "It's Shabbat! Are you all crazy?!!"

"It's all right! Today it's permitted," Savta screamed back at us.

"Get on!" Imma called.

"But we can't ride on Shabbat."

"The duty of saving a life overrides the laws of Shabbat," someone called out to us from inside the jeep. A girl's head peeked out. "Saving a life overrides the laws of Shabbat," she repeated in an authoritative tone of voice. It was Chana, our wise little friend.

Nonetheless, it was hard for me to follow this order. How

awful — to travel on Shabbat!

"Today it's a *mitzva* to travel, in order to save lives," Chana repeated persuasively.

Our feet refused to do that which they had never before done. Every cell in our bodies rebelled. To touch the jeep? To get on and ride?

"Whose lives have to be saved?" we asked hesitatingly.

The motor started and let out a long harsh sound.

"We are all traveling today," the passengers inside said.

"If we don't leave quickly, we're all liable to be killed," said Chana's mother. "We must save our own lives."

"The same Torah which forbids us to travel on Shabbat commands us to travel if our lives are in danger," added Savta.

Naomi began to climb inside. Someone grabbed me by the waist and pulled me forcefully in. Just as my feet left the ground, the jeep began to move. I fell in, right on top of another girl lying on the floor.

"Ouch!" she screamed.

"Oy, my foot, my foot!" screamed Chana. "They closed the door on my foot!"

Poor Chana had to travel like that all the way to our destination. Luckily, the foot that was caught in the door was not her injured one.

"Why are we traveling on Shabbat? Why are we in danger?" I persisted in asking. "Aren't we safe yet?"

"Over there ... the Angel of Death is waiting!"

"No, no," I disagreed. "The Angel of Death stayed at Zion Gate. I saw him standing there when we passed him on our way out."

"And I saw him on top of the mountain!" maintained Rachel.

"And I saw him on the mountains all around us," said Chana. "He stands there keeping watch and he spits fire."

"Stop it," scolded Savta. "What kind of talk is that?"

"We're on our way out now," Imma tried to reassure us and

to chase away the memories of that horrible experience. "Soon we'll be in Katamon."

Katamon...the magic word. It quickly put a stop to our morbid conversation. Each of us attempted to describe the place she imagined.

"In Katamon there are skyscrapers," Rachel finally volunteered enthusiastically.

"Nonsense," Imma scolded. "Only in America are there skyscrapers."

* * *

We drove on, squashed together inside the little jeep, bumping along in the dark with the lights out so as not to be seen by the enemy. Our hearts surged, torn between hope and anxiety — great hopes for a new life, a life of peace. Yet we were full of apprehension about the unknown future.

Katamon. The jeep shuddered, expelled one more suffocating cloud of benzine, and hurled us forward once more. Then the motor stopped with a squeak. The back door opened, and Chana's foot was freed. Our exhausting journey had come to a happy end.

We were led into a large building where blankets had been spread out for us in one of the halls. Exhausted from our ordeal, we dropped down in one of the corners and immediately fell asleep. Our greatest desire was to give our aching limbs a rest during the short hours that were still left of that longest, most terrible of nights.

photo on next page:
Savta (holding Yudale), Naomi and Yehudit paused for one last look
before the evacuation to Katamon

Part III

Refugees

49 A New Morning

A new day dawned. Bright sunlight danced on the window panes of the latticed windows, its rays kissing the faces of the sleeping children as if attempting to console us for our dark yesterday. A tumult of awakening filled the hall.

We roused ourselves from the short night's sleep and went outside to investigate our new surroundings. The sun shone brightly on the white stairs and the wide entrance and on the small sign — in English and Arabic — on the handsome façade of the building: Hotel. Pure, clean air filled God's world, clean air untainted by fire or smoke. A peaceful world with no shells exploding, no bullets whistling by. A world with no destruction or ruins, and no war. Could it be true?

We ran to call Imma. Our younger sisters had woken up and were looking about in apprehension. Yudale had just opened his eyes. Imma picked him up from the blanket he had been sleeping on, only to reveal a huge wet spot where he had been lying, reminding her that she had no change of clothes for him. Imma took off his wet clothing and wrapped him in a small blanket which Savta had somehow or other held on to. We all went out into the yard, and Imma spread Yudale's wet clothing out to dry on one of the fences.

"Where are his diapers?" asked Savta.

"Together with all our clothes," Imma answered.

Tears welled up in my eyes. Yudale's diapers were not together with all our other clothes, I realized angrily. Yudale's diapers had been in Imma's beige bag. What could the Legionnaire be doing with my poor little brother's diapers? Perhaps at this very moment he was throwing them into the street. Oh, how we needed those diapers now!

Imma looked at me compassionately, and silently stroked my head. Mischievous little Yudale jumped out of her arms, pulled off his blanket, and began to crawl all around the patio. One of our neighbors lent Imma a pair of pants for him, but these quickly suffered the same wet fate as his other clothes.

"Lunchtime," a few women announced, as they walked in carrying food.

"Food, food!" cried the little ones. "We're hungry!"

"We're hungry!" we, "the big sisters," repeated. Imma and Naomi hurried across the street. There, in one of the houses, a communal kitchen had been set up. Volunteers had cooked soup and prepared tea for the "refugees from the Old City" as we were called from that day on. Imma and Naomi soon came back with slices of bread, jelly and wedges of yellow cheese. It had been a long time since we had eaten anything, and we partook of the cold food with gusto, happy to satisfy our hunger.

Sitting there on the stairs at the entrance to the hotel, eating together with the other families of refugees, we first heard the bitter news: The men had all been taken prisoners of war!

50 The Bitter News

Prisoners of war!

To this day I have no idea who brought us that news.

173

Perhaps it was the refugees who were forced to spend the night on Mount Zion and only began to arrive in Katamon on Shabbat morning. In any case, the news spread like wildfire — a devastating blow to us all, before we even had time to begin to recuperate from our bitter experiences.

All the men had been taken prisoners of war! We were left alone, a community of women, children and aged people — homeless, uprooted, bereft of all our possessions, broken in both body and spirit. Women, both old and young, began to weep and wail, crying for their loved ones and tearing their hair. Others wept silently. The children were panic-stricken and began to scream at the top of their lungs, running to and fro under everyone's feet.

"They cheated us!" protested a few women. "They promised that only the soldiers would be taken captive, but now they have taken them all! What liars! What liars!"

"Who knows what they'll do to them over there," others cried anxiously. Feelings of helplessness, anger and despair engulfed us all.

Prisoners of war. At that time I didn't grasp the full import of those words. I only gathered, from the reaction of those around me, that something terrible had happened — something so terrifying that even the adults were left helpless and in tears; something that made everyone cry. And so I, too, cried.

After an hour or two the wailing subsided. People began to get up and investigate their new surroundings, tend to their children, and walk around the building. Only one little girl persisted in her heart-breaking sobs — my nine-year-old sister Naomi. Fearful for Abba's fate from the very beginning, she would burst into hysterical crying every time he left the house, continuing until he returned safely. Now, after hearing the bitter news of his imprisonment, she refused to be comforted. Naomi sat at the head of the stairs, her bitter sobs echoing throughout the building. Friends and neighbors gathered around my sister, attempting to comfort her and stop her crying, but all in vain.

"Don't cry, Naomi," Chava said. "Look at us. We've all stopped crying."

"My father has also been taken captive," volunteered Yaffale.

"My father, too... my father, too," others joined in.

"And my two brothers," said a dark-haired girl whose name I didn't know.

"A-bba!" Naomi continued to sob relentlessly.

"Why are you crying so much? You must stop," Savta said. "You can't go on crying forever."

"All of the men are prisoners of war, not only your father," Chana added.

"Yes," her sister Rachel agreed. "And sorrow shared is sorrow halved."

"How can the fact that we all share a sorrow comfort us?" I asked. "On the contrary, it's much more sorrowful that there are so many captives."

"That is a saying of our Sages, and if they said it, it must be true," Chana's mother joined the conversation. "The prisoners will be able to help one another."

"To help?" Naomi burst out. "How? In the hands of the Arabs? They are prisoners! Do you realize what that means?"

"They are better off than we are," said Chana sagely.

"Why? Why?" we all asked.

"Because they will be fed two eggs a day, but we, here in besieged Jerusalem, may yet die of starvation."

"Two eggs a day?" we all exclaimed. "Who told you that?"

"I know it. Every prisoner receives two eggs a day," Chana answered, her eyes twinkling.

Eggs! We had not seen eggs for such a long time we had almost forgotten what they looked like. But even this failed to impress Naomi.

"What does food matter?" she exclaimed. "The prisoners

are in chains! Their hands are tied and they can't move."

"Of course food is very important," Chana persisted. "Without food, no one can stay alive. Aside from that, do you think that we're going to enjoy peace and quiet here now? Of course not! We're still in the middle of the war here, but for them . . . for them it's all over."

"That's right," Rachel agreed. "Who can promise us that the Arabs won't try to recapture Katamon? But the men will remain there, in captivity, until the war is over."

"Until the war is over," my sister murmured, hot tears rolling down her cheeks. "Until the war is over, if they're lucky."

"The war," a few women clapped their hands in distress.

"Yes, the war is not yet over," said others.

But Naomi was stubborn. "Abba, A-bba!" she wept, dissolving once more in tears. "My father is being held captive by the Arabs — in enemy hands, with no weapons! Abba!"

"Your father has no need for weapons," said all the mothers and grandmothers around her. "Your father and all the other fathers are far away from the war now. They're in Trans-Jordan."

"But he is in Arab hands!" she screamed, in a voice so loud it must have reverberated from one end of Katamon to the other. "The Arabs! They are liable to . . ."

Imma hugged Naomi. "Stop it already," she said. "The Arabs can't do anything to him."

"But he has no weapons," my sister protested. "The Arabs are liable to . . . I once read that during the World War they lined prisoners up along a wall and . . ." Naomi began crying all over again.

"Quiet. Sh . . . sh," Imma said. "During the World War it was different. Today there are rules of war. There is the Geneva Convention."

"What is the Geneva Convention?" several children asked.

"The Geneva Convention is an agreement that was accepted

The Churva Synagogue before 1948 and afterwards.

Arab snipers in the Old City. Below, ducking sniper fire in the streets of Jerusalem.

Rechov Hamadregot (the Stepped Street) inside the wall, leading up to Batei Machse.

The outside of Shaar Tzion (Zion Gate), pockmarked by heavy shelling.

Old City refugees leaving through the Zion Gate.

(above) Postcard from Trans-Jordan captivity
(below) Postcard from the Min Hahar family to Trans-Jordan.

Jewish prisoners held captive in Trans-Jordan.
Harav Min Hahar standing at right.

The first group of Jewish prisoners returning home.

Ceremony in Batei Machse Square celebrating 13 years of the reunification of Jerusalem. Harav Min Hahar is speaking.

The Kotel as it appeared before 1948 and as it appears today.

by most nations to protect all prisoners of war."

"How does it protect them?"

"It states that no prisoners may be harmed, that food and all their other daily needs be provided, and that the wounded and the sick receive the necessary medical treatment."

"We also have Arab prisoners of war," Chana exclaimed suddenly.

"That's right! We have also taken Arab captives," others repeated.

"So what?" Naomi retorted angrily.

"That's very important," Chana explained. "The Arabs must want us to take good care of our captives, and therefore, they won't harm the prisoners they have taken."

"Besides," added Chana's mother, "after the war, we'll be able to exchange prisoners."

"Exchange prisoners? What does that mean?" the children asked.

"After the war," Chana's mother explained, "each side will want to receive its prisoners back, and then...then the prisoners of war will be exchanged. We will return the Arabs we have taken captive, and, in return, the Arabs will return all of our men from Trans-Jordan, and then..."

"Then all our fathers will come home!" one of the children exclaimed.

"But what will happen until the war is over?" someone asked.

"Yes, who will guarantee that the Arabs honor the Geneva Convention and don't harm the prisoners?" asked Naomi, the stream of tears continuing to flow from her red eyes.

"The British will make sure that the Arabs honor it."

"The British?!"

"Yes, the British are an enlightened nation..."

"The British — enlightened? Have you forgotten so quickly?"

"Well, they follow the rules of war, and they will force the

Arabs to honor the agreement. The Arabs need British aid to fight us," added Chana's mother.

Her words reassured us all, all except my weeping sister. She continued to cry for a long time after that, until, still crying, she finally fell asleep...

51 A Luxury Neighborhood

On Shabbat afternoon, just after Naomi had awoken from her restless sleep, Chana, Rachel, and a few other girls passed by.

"We're going for a walk," called Rachel. "Come with us."

"For a walk? Where to?" I asked.

"Come with us. Come and you'll see for yourselves how beautiful it is," the girls all called out together. Naomi, still in a bad mood, shrugged her shoulders.

"Come on. It will do you good," Chana urged her again.

"But how can I go for a walk while my father is imprisoned?" Naomi protested. Imma and Savta also encouraged her to go out, at the same time warning us all not to wander too far away.

We left the building and began to walk down a newly paved asphalt road, flanked on both sides by imposing stone houses and beautiful gardens. Never in our entire lives had we seen such beautiful grounds. Bougainvillaea with purple flowers poured over the fences and climbed up jasmine bushes, whose delicate white flowers filled the air with an intoxicating fragrance. Huge lilies, in every color imaginable, bloomed in the gardens, staring haughtily at us "refugees" who had come to admire their beauty. Roses covered the balconies in front of the houses, their pinkish petals falling over the white stairs.

"Let's go in," suggested Chana, stopping before a lovely two-story home of pinkish stone.

"Let's go!" we all agreed.

Chana pressed the handle of the small gate in the fence, but when it didn't open, she nimbly climbed over it and jumped into the yard. A cry of admiration burst from her mouth, emboldening us to follow her example. Once inside, we found ourselves in the midst of a magnificent garden. Following the white gravel path, we came to an enchanting patio on one side of the house. Above our heads, laced on a trellis, hung large green clusters of grapes, peeking at us from behind luxuriant, broad grape leaves. Beside us, on the concrete floor, stood a round, stone table.

"Almonds! Plums!" we heard some of our friends call from the back of the house.

We hurried after them. Trees heavy with fruit grew in round, sunken pits enclosed by low stone hedges.

"We'll come back tomorrow and pick fruit!" Chana cried enthusiastically.

"Pick?!" I was astounded. "Why, this garden doesn't belong to us!"

"You're right. It's not ours. Not ours," several girls agreed.

"Not ours?!" exclaimed Chana. "Of course it's ours. Whose else then?"

"Really, whose is it?" we asked each other.

"It belongs to the Arabs who lived here," I suggested.

"And I say that everything here belongs to us," Chana repeated vehemently. "Everything here is ours, do you hear? We have conquered Katamon, and the whole neighborhood and everything in it belongs to us."

"Yes, you're right," the girls agreed. "It's all ours."

"So then, today we won't pick anything, because it's Shabbat, but tomorrow we will all come back to pick fruit. Now let's have a look around inside the house."

We entered an imposing hallway and went straight up to the apartment on the second floor. The door had been forced open, evidence that someone else had already "visited" the site. We walked in, but immediately stopped in our tracks, stunned by the overwhelming luxury we saw. Never in our lives had we seen such a splendid home! It was several moments before we could gather up the courage to step on the Persian carpets covering the smooth floor tiles in the ballroom-sized hallway.

"How lovely," we exclaimed.

"Look at this floor!" exclaimed Yaffale, as she bent over and rolled up the expensive Persian carpet, the better to examine the tiles. We all followed her example, getting down on all fours to run our hands over the floor which was as shiny as a mirror. We had to see for ourselves if a floor could really be so smooth.

Then we turned to examine the heavy ornate furniture standing in the room. Beneath a latticed window stood a fancy green velvet sofa.

"What plush upholstery!" Frieda exclaimed.

"It's velvet," I said, remembering my grandmother's house in Beit Yisrael.

"And what's this?" asked Yaffale, sinking into a soft velvet armchair.

"That's just a regular upholstered chair," said Frieda.

"No, it's a child-sized sofa."

"It's called a *fauteuil* in French," stated know-it-all Chana. "There's another one — over there! They are both *fauteuils*."

"Armchairs," I disagreed. "These are called armchairs."

"Liar!" a few girls charged. "Only in America do they have armchairs."

"Well, I say these are armchairs. My uncle in Rehavia has armchairs."

"In Rehavia? Perhaps Rehavia is just like America. But these chairs here are *fauteuils*," the girls all agreed, as usual accepting Chana's word.

One after another, we tried sitting in the plush armchairs, unlike anything we had experienced before, quarreling over them and thoroughly enjoying ourselves. Then we walked all around the apartment, examining everything, running our hands over every piece of furniture to make sure it was real and not just a figment of our imagination.

"Come here! Fast!" Rachel called from a room at the far end of the apartment. "There is something fantastic here!" We hurried over to her, trying to guess what. She opened the door slowly and dramatically, letting us into a small room whose walls were covered from top to bottom with shiny, turquoise tiles. Set in the floor was a gigantic blue basin, similar to a pool.

"What is this?" we asked, surprised.

"I think it's a bathtub," Rachel answered.

"I once saw something like it, somewhere."

"Yes, my uncle in Haifa has something like it. It's called a bathtub, and this is the bathroom. It's a room where you wash up."

It gave us great pleasure to run our hands over the shiny walls which Chana told us were "tiled." We tried turning on the faucets but quickly closed them, as the air pressure in the waterless pipes made an awful noise.

We looked at ourselves in the mirror, which was fixed in the wall above the blue sink. We admired the beautiful outdoor scene painted on six ceramic tiles on the wall above the bathtub.

What luxury! A bathtub! We had barely imagined that such a thing existed. In the village up north where we had once lived, we had had a shower, but in the Old City, we made do with standing in a washtub and pouring water over ourselves from a big pail which had been heated on the kerosene heater. When had we last washed ourselves? We tried to remember but could not. Was it possible that we had not washed-up since the war began?

We spread out again throughout the apartment, opening and closing doors and windows, closets and drawers. Everything was so interesting — so amazing — as if we were on another planet. We heard an unusual sound. Gathering from all corners of the apartment, we followed it to one corner of the hall where Yaffale was standing beside a dark piece of furniture we had not yet examined. She was quite frightened.

"What is this?" she cried. "All I did was touch it and it..."

"Don't be afraid," said Chava. "It's a piano."

"A piano!" we all exclaimed in unison. "So big?"

"Yes, this is a piano," Chana confirmed after a close examination.

"No, it's not," Batya disagreed. "Only the 'Voice of Jerusalem' radio station has a piano, not private homes."

"Well," Chana concluded, "wealthy Arabs must also have pianos in their homes, as you can see with your own eyes. We'll come back tomorrow and take turns playing it."

"Yes," Rachel added. "On Shabbat it is forbidden to play the piano, but we'll come back tomorrow! I am first in line to play."

"And I'm second," called Yaffale.

"No, girls," Chava corrected. "Just as it is forbidden to play on Shabbat, so it is forbidden to talk about playing it tomorrow. On Shabbat it is forbidden even to discuss our plans for the weekday."

"Then we are not allowed to plan to pick plums tomorrow either," said one of the girls. "Then what should we say?"

"Oh...just that it's nice to have plums and to play with the piano when it's not Shabbat."

"Fine," agreed Rachel and Yaffale. "When it's not Shabbat, like tomorrow, it should be lovely to play with the piano."

"Are you crazy?!" someone exclaimed. "It's not our piano. We have no permission to touch it!"

"That's right. It's not ours," I chimed in. All the time we were in the apartment I had a strange feeling, and every once in a while I would glance uneasily at the door, half expecting the Arab owner to walk in and catch us red-handed.

"Let's leave here already," I suggested. A few girls agreed with me immediately.

"Why should we go?" asked Chana.

"Because...because this house doesn't belong to us," we said, shrugging our shoulders.

"Haven't I already told you that all of Katamon is ours?" Chana repeated impatiently. "That means this house and all the other houses. We have conquered them. Have you forgotten?"

"Yes, but what shall we do if the owner suddenly appears?" I asked.

"Ha, ha, ha," Chana laughed heartily. "Have you ever seen such scaredy-cats? Should the owner appear...ha, ha, ha,... straight from Cairo..."

"Who told you that he's in Cairo?" we all asked.

"Haven't you heard? When our soldiers conquered Katamon, all those rich sheikhs ran for their lives. They deserted their homes and ran far away to Cairo. They fled and will never return!"

"Did Katamon surrender without a fight?" I asked.

"On this street there was no fighting, but there was a very bloody battle over the Church of Saint Simon."

"Really? It's true that all these houses are in perfect shape," commented Yaffale. "Apparently there was no need to fire so much as a single shell here."

Her comment reminded me of the sight of the ruins of the Old City and of the Arabs who hadn't stopped destroying, ravaging, gutting and laying waste everywhere, even after we had surrendered; of the rabble so eager to plunder, unable to wait for us to leave before ravaging our homes. I recalled in anguish what Chava had told us about the Churva. Once again I saw the tongues of fire licking at the stores on Jewish Quarter Road. Tears choked my throat.

"*We* won't break a thing! *We* won't ruin the houses!" my friends declared, as if they had read my thoughts.

"These houses are not ours, no matter what," I insisted.

"Whose are they, then, if not ours?" Chana asked angrily. "*They* are in *our* houses in the Old City!"

"I don't know whose they are."

"Well, I do know!" retorted Chana. "These houses have no owners now, and anyone who wants to can come in."

"Let's go back home anyway. Our parents will be worried about us," suggested Frieda.

"Home? And just where is home?" asked Rachel, smiling bitterly. "Besides, have you forgotten that all our fathers are prisoners?"

Her questions brought us sharply out of our fairyland and back to bitter reality. We walked down the stairs and out of the building, promising each other that we'd return for another visit to this amazing house. What a sharp contrast it was to our miserable situation!

52 Penniless

On Sunday morning, relatives from all over Jerusalem came to visit us "refugees." Someone told Imma that Rivka Cohen was looking for her. Hoping that Bobba and Zeideh had come also, we went outside and were swept along with the crowd up the street.

"They're pushing me!" I screamed in terror, grabbing onto Imma's dress. After that terrible ordeal at Zion Gate, even the sight of a small crowd was enough to scare me out of my wits.

"Here they are! Here they are!" I suddenly heard voices nearby cry. Before I could even manage to see who it was that had come, we were all locked in each other's arms, in a frenzy of hugging and kissing. Finally, completely out of breath, I succeeded in disengaging myself from all the arms holding me.

There was Aunt Margalit! And my beloved Bobba and Zeideh, and Aunt Rivka, the only one who behaved calmly.

"Oh my, how Matilda looks!" Aunt Margalit said to Aunt Rivka, clapping her hands in dismay.

Hearing that, I turned to look at Imma. Only then did I notice the black circles around her big dark eyes, even more noticeable because of the contrast to her pale, drawn cheeks. And that look in her eyes — so strange and so sad — like one risen from the dead.

Everyone was dismayed to hear that Abba had been taken prisoner.

"Didn't you hear before?" asked Savta.

"We heard, but we didn't want to believe it. We hoped that perhaps somehow Shlomo had remained with you," Bobba and Zeideh answered.

"Then," Aunt Rivka repeated in distress, "Shlomo has really been taken captive."

Imma nodded in affirmation.

"What do you need?" Aunt Rivka asked, the first to do anything practical.

"What doesn't she need?" Savta answered her with a question.

"The baby," Imma said, pointing to the wet rags that he was wrapped in. Aunt Rivka understood immediately. While Zeideh, Bobba and Margalit continued to shower Imma with questions, Aunt Rivka walked away from us and disappeared into one of the houses.

"Why didn't you take any clothes for the children?" Margalit scolded Imma.

"Didn't the Arabs allow you to?" asked Bobba.

"The Arabs allowed us," Savta answered, "but it was impossible."

"We couldn't..." Imma said.

"Still, you must have taken something," Margalit repeated,

unable to comprehend what had happened.

Imma grabbed the collar of her dress. "This is all I took," she said.

"If so, then they don't even have any clothing," Zeideh told Bobba. "They have nothing."

"Denuded of all your possessions!" exclaimed Margalit, who was in the habit of sprinkling her conversation with literary expressions. "Didn't you bring *anything* with you?" Margalit continued her cross-examination, refusing to believe that her sister had really lost everything.

"The children," Imma answered sadly, "but don't ask how!"

"Yes," I thought to myself, "let them not ask us how." Imma was right. How could we possibly explain to them? How could we tell them of the terrible exodus we had undergone? How had my sister described it? "The expulsion from Spain." How could we even talk about it now, when we were so weak and tired? They wouldn't understand anyhow. How could they possibly understand why we had left our clothes and all our belongings at the side of the road, one bundle after another? And how could they understand how Death had pursued us to Zion Gate and beyond?

"Where is your jewelry, Matilda?" Aunt Margalit returned to her cross-examination. She took Imma's hand in her own, turned it over, and exclaimed in despair. "Why, you aren't even wearing your ring, your precious diamond ring! Why? Don't try to tell me that *that* was too heavy!" She stared at Imma in reproof, then finally burst out, broken-heartedly, "Why, you are absolutely penniless!"

I thought back to that awful day of our surrender. Who could have thought about jewelry then? My dear parents had invested all their physical and spiritual energy in providing us with the things we needed most: clothes, diapers, school bags, candles and candlesticks for Shabbat, *siddurim* ... and ... in Abba's briefcase, Torah and Talmud. "Who needed jewelry?" I asked myself. "What value could a diamond ring have had then?"

"Margalit, my dear," Imma finally spoke, "you have absolutely no idea what hell we went through. We ... we have risen from our graves!"

"From your graves!" Zeideh repeated.

"God help us!" exclaimed Bobba, shaken through and through.

"Blessed is the Holy One Who has kept you from death!" exclaimed Zeideh.

"Thank God, you are all well and unharmed," Margalit quickly agreed. She hugged Imma, whose eyes were filled with tears. "Don't worry, don't worry, you can get new clothes. The main thing is that you are still alive. As for the ring ... Well, let that be a *kappara* — an offering for our sins," she added, kissing Imma on both of her tear-drenched cheeks.

Just then Aunt Rivka came back, a bundle under her arm. "Here, I've brought some clothing for the baby," she said to Imma.

Imma's face lit up. "Clothing? How wonderful! Where from?"

"I looked in one of the Arab houses," Aunt Rivka answered.

We opened the bundle and were thrilled to find tiny undershirts and pants, a pair of pajamas, shirts for the baby, underwear for us, a towel, and ... diapers.

53 Prisoners of War

My father was a prisoner of war. It took several days for me to realize fully what that meant. Gradually I gathered the full import of the fact that my father was in a prisoner-of-war camp in Trans-Jordan, and we would not be reunited with him in the near future.

Abba had not followed in our footsteps. He did not see our big bundle, wrapped in the yellow blanket at the side of the road. Nor had he reached Katamon via an alternate route as I had imagined while waiting in vain for his arrival. Unfortunately, Abba had been taken in the opposite direction — to Trans-Jordan, the land of King Abdullah. The journey we had taken to safety had taken us even farther away from him. My father was now a prisoner of war in an Arab country. He and the other men had bought us our freedom at a very dear price.

From bits and pieces of conversation, questions and answers, and the expressions on the adults' faces, I put together a horrifying picture: my father and the others were in a P.O.W. camp in the middle of the desert, far away from us, surrounded by a barbed-wire fence and guarded by armed Arab soldiers. They were helpless, weaponless, in Arab hands! Not only my father but all the prisoners of war, even our soldiers, had no weapons and were completely at the mercy of the Arabs.

I asked Imma, Savta, and anyone else I could find, innumerable questions. What did the P.O.W.'s eat? Did they have enough water to quench their thirst? Did they sleep on the ground? Was it always hot in Trans-Jordan or was it cold at night? And most important, were the Jordanians honoring the Geneva Convention, or — God forbid — were they beating our men ... or worse?

One question in particular bothered me: did we know the exact location of the P.O.W. camp? If not, then, God forbid, we might shoot in their direction and wound our own prisoners.

I was tormented by nightmares. Sometimes I dreamt that Abba was very thirsty. I would picture him lying in the dunes, pleading for a sip of water, just about to faint of thirst, God forbid. I would search frantically for water, but in vain. There was none.

In another dream, which repeatedly returned to torment

me, I would picture Abba standing close beside me. I would try to grab onto his arm when suddenly a barbed-wire fence would spring up to separate us. Abba was inside the fence; I was outside. Abba and the fence would move further and further away from me. I would pursue him with all my strength, but, to my dismay, every step would increase the distance between us. Finally, Abba would disappear from sight.

Not infrequently, I would have the most frightening dream of all. I saw a very high wall, with a long row of men — their faces to the wall and their hands tied behind their backs — lined up against it.

"The prisoners!" I would scream and look from one to the other, searching for my father. Finally, I would catch sight of him, his back to me. "Abba!" I would cry, but he would neither hear me nor answer. I would look at his cuffed, weaponless hands — no rifle, no pistol, no hand grenade. Silence . . . silence interrupted only by the sound of the Arab guards pacing back and forth in their hob-nailed shoes with their bayonetted rifles, scornfully surveying the silent, wretched line of captives. Suddenly one of the Arabs would stop, lower his rifle, and take aim, and I would awake with a scream.

Sometimes I succeeded in closing my eyes again, and now only half asleep, I consciously "dreamt" a better ending to the nightmare: The Arab would be aiming his rifle, almost ready to shoot, when a voice proclaimed, "The Geneva Convention." The Arab would lower his rifle, while all the other Arabs looked about them, searching for the source of the warning. Only I would recognize the voice, so familiar to me. It was, of course, Imma's.

54 The House at the Top of the Hill

For about a week we all lived together in the "hotel" and ate our meals together in the communal kitchen. The days passed as if in a dream. In small groups, we girls would go from one garden to the next, picking unripe fruit — plums which set our teeth on edge, almonds whose shells were still green, and green grapes. We took turns playing the piano, and we visited all the Arab houses, never tiring of the wonderful sights. Exhausted from our wartime experiences, we tried to suppress our anxiety about the unknown future.

My little brother was quite content, crawling energetically around the balcony, holding onto the railing and trying to pull himself up on his tiny feet. I loved to hold him in my arms and look at his placid, innocent face.

"How happy this little one is," I would remark to Imma. "He doesn't know anything. He doesn't know that his father is a prisoner, nor that he is homeless. Even his lack of clothing doesn't bother him."

Imma had found a small enamel washbasin and some soap in one of the houses, and so was able to wash Yehuda's clothes and hang them on the fence to dry. Naomi and I were still wearing the same polka-dotted dresses we had worn when we left the Old City. Their pink color had turned gray from all the dust we had accumulated in our wanderings, but we had nothing else.

One morning Imma was told that the hotel was being dismantled and that each family should occupy one of the nearby apartments. Savta volunteered to watch the children and urged Imma to go quickly and find us suitable living quarters. About two hours later, Imma returned from her search to take us to our new home. We walked two or three blocks and then climbed to the top of a hill.

"Why so far away?" Savta asked.

"Because all the houses nearby have either been occupied already, or else they have been emptied completely of all their furniture. This is the closest thing I could find. Besides, it has two very important features: a shelter, a real shelter, in the basement, and a water pump in the yard."

"Don't depend on the pump. It's probably not working now," Savta said deprecatingly.

"The pump works," Imma assured her. "The people in the first aid station on the top floor told me so. They even promised to give me the key."

"Now that sounds very good!" said Savta, quickening her step. "We'll have water and good neighbors too!"

Puffing and panting, we finally reached a small, stone house, half of it one story high and the other half two stories. There were two spacious apartments on the first floor. The Zeltzers, Chava's family, were already living in one, and we took the other. Imma proudly showed us the lovely apartment she had chosen: two handsome rooms plus a spacious kitchen and a real bathroom with an indoor toilet. Best of all, the apartment had a large porch, the whole length of it enclosed in glass window panes, one of which could be opened.

"A porch to play on!" we exclaimed in delight.

The kitchen and one bedroom were empty of furniture, but in the other bedroom were two beds with mattresses. And best of all, there was a tiny crib no more than three feet long.

"A crib for Yudale!" we cried in joy.

We laid him down in his new crib, but the little mischief-maker immediately grabbed hold of the top bar and stood up on his feet.

"Well, I see that we'll have to put him to sleep in the crib only at night," Imma noted.

Savta and Imma left us to watch over the little ones while they went to hunt for more furniture. They went down the hill and came back an hour later, carrying mattresses on their backs. Throwing them down on the floor of the empty bedroom, they hurried out again to get other things that we needed before nightfall. The sun had already begun to set when Imma and Savta came back carrying the last things that they had succeeded in finding that day, an empty pail and a jerry can.

By nightfall we had amassed a considerable amount of property. We had two beds with mattresses, a crib, two more mattresses, blankets, a folding bed, a heavy wooden chair which, if necessary, could also serve as a small table, a large mat, a hammer and a few nails, some plates and spoons and two brand new, unused cups which we brought to a *mikveh* as soon as we could.

The last rays of the sun lingered over the house on the top of the hill. Savta hurried to the communal kitchen, now a long way from our new home, for our supper. Imma, with our help, put the two mattresses and the folding cot in the empty room and began to make the beds.

Savta brought our supper and set it down on our lone chair. We sat ourselves around the chair on the mat on the kitchen floor and began our meal. Just then there was a knock on the door. A middle-aged woman and a boy stood in the doorway.

"We are from the station upstairs," they told Savta, who had opened the door. "Do you need anything?"

"You're from the first aid station?" asked Savta. "No, thank you, we're all quite healthy. Thank God, we don't need anything."

"Thank you very much anyway," added Imma.

The woman glanced around at our empty kitchen. "Why, you don't have *anything*!" she exclaimed, her eyes full of pity.

"Besides little children..." added the boy.

"Why are you sitting in the dark?" the woman asked. "Don't you have candles?"

"No."

"Come with me, girls," she said, turning to us, "I'll give you candles and matches." We followed her upstairs to the top floor.

"Poor people!" I heard her whisper to the boy as we entered the station. "What an empty house."

The boy gave us two candles and a pack of matches.

"Just what we needed," Savta said when we returned.

Soon the door opened again, and the woman and boy came back into the kitchen carrying a square black table between them.

"We can easily get along without this table in the station," they said, as they set it down in the middle of the kitchen.

"Thank you! Thank you! It's really very good of you," Savta and Imma thanked our good neighbors. A few minutes later they returned with two rectangular wooden chairs.

"Come with me, little girl, and I'll give you one more thing," the woman said, watching Savta break a cucumber in half with her hands. I went back up with her, and she gave me a small knife and two glasses. I tried to avoid her tender, compassionate look as I walked toward the door. Earlier in the day I had not thought of our family as poor, penniless refugees. But this good-hearted woman with her pitying gaze had reminded me of what I was trying to forget. My eyes filled with tears.

I walked back into the kitchen carrying the small knife and the two glasses. Everyone was already seated around the table. Savta and Imma each sat on one of the chairs, holding one of the little girls on their laps. Naomi quietly offered me "half" of her chair. Yudale crawled around on the floor, carrying a chunk of bread. Sitting at the table donated by the people from the first aid station, we chewed on dark bread and jelly, yellow cheese, and sardines.

"Our first meal in our new home!" declared Naomi.

None of us answered her. We continued to chew on our bread in oppressive silence.

"Where is Abba?" Yehudit suddenly asked, just as Savta

began to pour cocoa from a bowl into the two glasses I had brought.

"Abba will come another time," Imma answered. From her voice I could tell that she, too, was swallowing her tears.

After we said the Grace after Meals, Imma put the baby in the crib. Yehudit and Ruthie went to sleep on one of the mattresses.

"I'm afraid they'll fall out of the bed in the middle of the night," Imma said.

Naomi and I were left to decide who would sleep on the folding cot and who would get the second mattress.

Imma and Savta retired to the other bedroom for the night. Naomi and I decided to change places every night, and she lay down on the mattress, giving me first chance on the cot. Having no pajamas, I lay down in my clothes and closed my eyes.

Back home in the Old City, there was an empty, forsaken folding cot, I thought to myself. Perhaps someone else was already sleeping in it. Back home, at this hour, my father used to come in and sit beside me, take my hand in his great big one, and recite the Shema with me. Who would say the nightly prayers with me now? Not that I couldn't do it alone, but...

"I — m — ma!" I called.

No answer from the other room. The even breathing of the two exhausted women told me that they were already fast asleep. Naomi tossed and turned in her "bed" on the mattress.

"Have you said Shema yet?" she asked.

"No."

Naomi got up and sat beside me. Her small hand reached for mine, and together we recited the Shema. Then, loudly, we added the prayers which Abba had said with us during the fighting:

"Pour out Thy wrath upon the nations that know Thee not... And to Jerusalem, Your city, return in compassion, and let Your Presence dwell within it, as You have promised..."

194

At the end, Naomi added, "And return our father to us, in Your compassion..."

And I answered, "Amen!"

5 Beginning All Over Again

One who has always lived a normal life, in a normal house, may very well attach great importance to its furnishings, realizing that no house can be a home without a table, chairs, beds, and a closet. Today, one would certainly have to add an electric refrigerator, a gas stove, a washing machine — things which did not even exist in pre-war Jerusalem — to the list.

But then, when we were busy setting up house all over again, beginning with nothing, we quickly came to appreciate the immense importance of seemingly trivial objects, such as a comb, a mirror, scissors, a needle and thread, a pencil and paper, a rubber band or a piece of string, without which life became very difficult indeed. It is almost impossible to imagine how difficult.

"The house is empty," the lady from the station had remarked to the boy last night, and they had gone and fetched us a table and two chairs. But we, who had already begun to eat on the mat, did not miss the furniture as much as we later missed all these "trivial" little items.

Aunt Margalit had called us "penniless and poverty stricken," and she was right. Our house was completely empty, and we urgently needed to furnish it. There were as yet no stores, nor did we have any money, so the next morning we went with Imma to the deserted Arab houses at the bottom of the hill to see what we could find. Savta stayed home to watch the little ones.

"A mirror!" cried Naomi from one of the rooms of a

195

luxurious Arab house. Following her voice, we came into a room containing a large mirror attached to a lovely, pale, wood dresser.

"How handsome!" we exclaimed in admiration. "But how can we take it with us?"

Imma bent over and examined the drawers, "We really need these, too," she decided, "to store the clothing Aunt Rivka brought us."

Imma spilled the contents of the drawers onto the big double bed in the bedroom — picture albums, cosmetics, and other miscellaneous items we had no use for. But there was one great find among the cosmetics — a comb! Imma looked around and found a screwdriver to remove the mirror from the dresser. She placed it carefully on top of the bed. It was no small feat to transfer the new piece of furniture to our apartment, but when we had put it together again in the empty bedroom, with the mirror in place, our joy was unbounded.

One of the most splendid features of our lovely new apartment was the tiled white bathroom. Built into the bath-room floor was a handsome white bathtub with shiny faucets and even a shower. We had a bathtub with faucets, but . . . we had no running water.

Water was a precious, scarce commodity in those long days during the war. Neither we nor any of our neighbors had running water in our houses. Here and there were yards with water cisterns. People would gather around them, pail in hands, waiting their turn to draw water. Sometimes water had to be brought from far away.

Our yard, however, was blessed with a pump. This was one of the main reasons Imma had chosen the house, so far out and at the top of the hill. The first aid station was also probably located there because of the pump. Imma had been entrusted with the key to the pump — an iron handle. Once the handle was attached to the pump, two or three pushes sufficed to fill a pail of water. The people at the station warned her to use the water sparingly, but word of the "magic" pump spread quickly, and soon the whole neighborhood began to come to our yard, making it necessary to keep the pump locked, and to fix hours for drawing water.

Once we possessed a comb, we and the Zeltzer family chose one warm morning as bath day. We could not even remember when we had last enjoyed such a treat. We all gathered wood for the fire, heating the water in a large, old, somewhat rusty tin which we had found. We set the tin on a stone base over the fire. When the water had boiled, it was poured into a pail and from there into the shiny white bathtub. The first to enjoy the luxury was Yudale, after him Ruthie and Yehudit, and finally Naomi and I. Imma and Savta washed our hair a few times with laundry soap from the communal kitchen. The joy we felt, sitting in the hot water in the white bathtub, scrubbing the dirt off our skins, cannot be described. Afterwards, it took us a full hour to comb our hair.

Later, as we stood before the large mirror admiring our clean faces and neat hairdos, which we had finally managed to complete, we were unable to decide what gave us the most pleasure — the chest of drawers, the mirror, the bathtub, or that little thing called a comb!

6 The Attack on the Hill

So involved were we in solving the difficult problems of daily living, that we almost forgot about the war. One day, we received a reminder. It was a miracle that it did not cost us our lives.

It was a quiet afternoon. The Zeltzers had gone to visit their married daughter in the Shaarei Chesed section of the city, equipped with a shopping list of things we needed. Before leaving, they told us not to worry if they didn't return until the next day. The day before, Savta had gone to visit Aunt Rivka. At that time, Aunt Rivka and her family were living with their aunt in Machane Yehuda, near Jaffa Road, as they had been forced to leave their home in Sanhedria on the border because of the shelling. For some reason, the staff of the first aid station wasn't there either.

We girls were peacefully playing downstairs near the house. Meanwhile, a group of children gathered in the yard to draw water. As the sun began to set, Imma came down to close the pump.

"But I didn't get water yet," complained a little boy.

"Neither did I!"

"Nor I!" the children protested angrily.

"It's late now," said Imma. "Go home and come back tomorrow."

"But it took us so long to get here. Let us fill up a few pails before we go," the children begged.

Imma could not say no. She began to pump the water herself to fill their pails, trying to finish as fast as possible. Suddenly there was an explosion.

"A shell!" someone cried.

Terrified, we abandoned our games and ran for the stairway. Just then, a second shell landed nearby with a tremendous roar.

"Immale!" the children screamed in terror. Panic-stricken, they began to run in all directions.

"To the shelter!" Imma shouted.

A few children obeyed her order and hurried after us to the stairway, leaving their pails, full or empty, in the yard. But others tried to run home. Imma grabbed them.

"No one goes home!" she ordered. "Everyone into the shelter!"

Two children tried to escape. "We'll run as fast as we can. Before you know it, we'll be home," they argued.

"No!" Imma was adamant. "Not now. The whole area is exposed. You can't go home until all is quiet again."

Naomi and I stood in the doorway, screaming in terror, "Imma — IMMA!" calling her to come to the shelter.

"You two go downstairs right now!" she shouted, seeing us still in the doorway, and we obeyed. Then a third shell exploded not far from the house. The next shell was even closer, convincing even the most stubborn of the children to go down to the shelter. Imma came down last of all and locked the door behind her.

"Where is the baby?" she asked when her eyes had grown accustomed to the dark. My heart stopped beating. In all the tumult none of us had remembered that the baby was upstairs sleeping in the crib — alone in the house! Without a second's hesitation, Imma flew up the stairs to our apartment. Still another shell landed nearby. We began to scream hysterically. Another fateful minute or two passed, and then Imma came down to the shelter, carrying the baby.

No sooner had she closed the door behind her when a terrific blast was heard. The walls shook. It seemed as if the whole house was being lifted up, as in an earthquake, and was about to fall on top of us. Terrified, we shrieked and screamed together with all the other children in the bomb shelter, until we felt that the house had ceased to move. All was quiet — the quiet after the storm.

"They must have hit their target and decided to end the attack," Imma said at last.

For a long time, all the children stayed down in the shelter with us, paralyzed by fear. Only after it was clear beyond doubt that the attack was over did they dare venture out to go home. Imma opened the door of the shelter. "It's already dark out. How will you go home?" she asked.

Three children left first, waiting a while outside until their eyes had become accustomed to the darkness.

"I can see the way," one of them announced.

"Are you sure?" Imma asked.

"We're sure!"

"Leave your water pails here. Tomorrow you can come back to get them," she told them.

The three broke out in a run for home.

"Moshiko! Moshiko! Sarika!" we heard a voice calling in the darkness. "Where are you?"

"Here we are, Imma, Savta," the children answered. "We're here."

They went towards the voice, and, to our delight, we heard them meeting their mother or grandmother. The other children also mustered up courage and left. Imma wanted to go back up to the house, too, but we insisted on remaining in the shelter until morning, and it's a good thing we did.

At dawn we went upstairs and were overwhelmed by the destruction. Fragments of brick, plaster and glass were scattered all over the floor and the beds. Our precious mirror was smashed to bits, and all the windows were shattered. There were big holes in all the walls, testimony to the huge shell which had passed from the eastern end of the building right through the walls of both apartments and into the western wall. Scattered among the wreckage on the floor and the beds were small bullets, the size of marbles. Yudale's crib was full of them. Overcome with emotion, we picked up a few.

"What are these?" we asked Imma, who was wandering from room to room, exclaiming over and over again, "What a miracle! What a miracle!"

"Don't touch them!" she hollered at us. "Some of them might still be live. They're liable to explode!"

A short while later three uniformed men arrived in a small car.

"The British!" I cried in alarm.

"Stupid!" my sister scolded, almost ready to slap my face. "Those are policemen — Israeli policemen. Don't you see that they're not wearing British uniforms?"

"Israeli police? How wonderful!"

The policemen approached Imma and asked for details of the attack. They wrote it all down and measured all the walls and all the holes. Then they collected all the shell fragments and all the bullets, unable to hide their emotion. They showed their collection to Imma. "One hundred!" one said. "There are one hundred of these in a missile. One hundred lead bullets!"

"An anti-tank missile!" the other exclaimed. "Do you know what that means? An anti-tank missile! It's a miracle that the house is still standing."

While they continued to take measurements, the Zeltzer family arrived. They were quite upset to find their apartment in ruins. Everyone said the same thing. "What a miracle! What a miracle!" From all over the neighborhood, people came by to see what had happened.

The children who had been in the shelter with us the previous night came to get their pails of water. Their mothers and grandmothers also came, not failing to thank Imma for saving their children and to bless her and wish her a long and happy life.

Moshiko and Sarika's grandmother was the most grateful of all. She kissed Imma and showered her with a thousand blessings in Ladino, calling her *Buena Vizina* — a good neighbor.

The policemen finished their investigation and called to Imma and the neighbors.

"You must leave the house," they said. "Go find yourselves another apartment somewhere down the hill. The line of children coming for water must have drawn the attention of the Arabs. They are not that far away, and they can see the hilltop easily through their field glasses."

As they spoke, they closed the pump, removed the handle, and took it with them.

"No more water!" they announced to all. "From now on, there's no more water here. Is that clear?"

Later, when the staff of the first aid station arrived, they were also told to leave the house at once. Imma tried to request a postponement.

"How can I move to a new apartment in one day?" she pleaded. "How can I move everything so quickly?"

"Miracles don't happen every day," the policemen told her. "You may not remain even one more night on an exposed hill like this one!"

Having no choice, Imma ran to look for another apartment. There were no vacant apartments in our vicinity, so we were forced to move to the other end of the neighborhood. Imma found a lovely second-floor apartment on a small street (later called Rechov Mechalkei Hamayim), but it was completely bare of furnishings. During the few hours left before dark, we — Imma, Naomi and I — moved the most essential items to our new apartment. The rest we abandoned, leaving them in the destroyed house at the top of the hill.

57 Black Chairs

Our house on Mechalkei Hamayim Street was a duplex. Each apartment had a separate entrance and was surrounded by a garden with a grape arbor, fruit trees and plants. A hexagonal pool with a fountain in the center was built into the garden. Originally, it must have been full of clear water, but by the time we moved in, it had dried up and was filled with old leaves, dirt, and moss. A few stairs and a concrete path led to the stairway at the side of the house and up to our apartment on the second floor.

Entering the apartment, we found that one family had already moved in, but the thought never entered their minds — just as it didn't occur to anyone else in those days — to occupy more than two rooms. The whole floor had originally been built as one apartment, for there was only one kitchen, one bathroom, and one balcony on each floor. We, who were used to living in crowded conditions, could not grasp the astonishing fact that this huge area was intended to house no more than one family!

We split the huge apartment with our neighbors — two rooms to each family. We took the kitchen and balcony, and our neighbors had the indoor bathroom. We were a bit disappointed not to have a bathroom but thrilled, on the other hand, with the lovely white-tiled kitchen. The floors of the two spacious bedrooms were also covered with handsome, brightly colored floor tiles.

Sunshine flooded into the rooms through wide windows and fancy doors with flowered glass panes and lacquered woodwork. Everywhere it was evident that this was a luxury apartment and that the previous tenants had been quite wealthy.

"Every change is for the better," Imma commented as we moved in. Of the many possessions we had acquired in the house at the top of the hill, we were only able to bring a few, and so, the day after we moved in, we had to begin all over again "acquiring" furnishings from nearby houses. The area was already heavily populated by Old City refugees, and the few apartments left had all been partially or completely emptied.

Nevertheless, we found a few things in the building opposite us — a huge, turquoise, double bed; strange, over-sized chairs; and other heavy, impractical furniture. Since it was impossible for us to carry our other beds such a distance (except for the folding cot), Imma decided to take the turquoise bed. It had to be taken apart to get it downstairs and into our house. I don't know how she did it, but Imma managed all that heavy work very well. The huge bed was set up in our apartment. It provided more than enough room for all four of us girls to sleep.

Two enormous black chairs were the subject of many angry discussions between me and Imma. Too embarrassed to admit how frightened I was by their size and threatening black color, I tried to think of all kinds of reasons not to take them, none of which sufficed to convince Imma.

"These are the only chairs there are, and so we're taking them," she stated flatly. Against my will, I was forced to help her carry them home, and that night I had nightmares.

Several days later, Savta came home and heard of our "adventure" in the house on the top of the hill. She promised never to leave us alone again. She examined all our new acquisitions, and, catching sight of the over-sized black chairs, she turned up her nose.

"They have graven images on them," I said, seeing that she, too, did not like them. "Graven images!"

"What are you talking about?" asked Imma.

"Here, look," I said, pointing at two figures carved on the armrest.

"She is right," Savta agreed. "You know, these black chairs remind me of a church. Where did you get them?"

"From the house across the street."

"It couldn't be a church, could it?"

"I don't think so," Imma answered apologetically.

"All right. We can solve this problem," Savta told me. "Bring me the hammer." I hurried to do as she said, and when I had brought it, Savta broke each of the images on the armrests with one blow.

"Now are you happy?" she asked.

I shook my head. "Their black color..." I complained.

"When we get some paint, we'll paint them a different color," Imma promised me. But the black chairs were destined for another fate.

Our communal kitchen had been dismantled, and now food rations were being distributed in the office of the Park Lane Hotel, one of the houses refugees had stayed at during our first days in Katamon. Some of the rations were donated by U.N.W.R.A., the United Nations Works and Relief Agency, and they were distributed to each family according to its size. Naomi and I spent hours in line, waiting for our kilogram of brown sugar, oatmeal, rice, or cornflour for the baby.

There was never enough water for everyone, and this was a constant cause of dissension. Not infrequently, fistfights would break out over the distribution of water. Some of the cisterns in the neighborhood were completely empty by now, and the remainder could not supply us with sufficient water. Every so often a truck carrying a small water tank would drive up to the corner of our street, and meager portions of water would be rationed out. Besides the tiring chore of waiting in line for food rations, Naomi and I were also charged with "catching" the water truck in time to be among the first in line, thus ensuring ourselves one of the precious tins of water.

We found kitchen utensils in the deserted Arab houses, and Savta and one of the neighbors *kashered* them in a large tin of boiling water heated on a bonfire downstairs. The utensils were then immersed in a nearby cistern and were thus permissible for use according to Jewish law.

There was no kerosene to be had, so the children gathered wood and thorns from the empty lots, and our mothers cooked our meager rations from the Park Lane Hotel over bonfires outside.

As time passed, we exhausted our supply of wood. After one person accidentally stepped on a mine and was killed, we were no longer allowed to wander around empty lots. We were left with no choice but to burn wooden objects, some quite valuable. Doors, window frames and shutters from the deserted houses served as excellent fuel for our fires. Tree branches, and sometimes whole trees, were cut down in the gardens. Next in line were the less valuable pieces of furniture. Drawers, small tables, and even curtains were thrown into the fire.

One morning, when we could find nothing else with which to light our fire, Savta decreed, "The black chairs!"

I rushed to help her take the big chairs downstairs. As the hammer rose and fell, the heavy black chairs came apart. Pieces of black firewood were stacked in a corner of the stairwell, and when the hard work was over, the bonfire was lit. Silently, Imma put the coffeepot on for tea and cooked some cornstarch cereal for my little brother. Savta and our neighbor put two pots on the fire, and soon the steaming fragrance of the two soups, lentil and bean, spread throughout the yard. Happily, I stood there, watching the gay fire crackling over those hated chairs. Now I was finally rid of them! But Imma walked sadly upstairs.

"Where will I find other chairs?" she asked.

58 A Pair of Scissors

Word of our rich neighborhood — deserted by its Arab tenants and only partially repopulated by the refugees from the Old City — spread quickly throughout Jerusalem. Other refugees from dangerous areas such as Sanhedria and Beit Yisrael, who had left their homes on the border and had moved in with relatives in the center of town, now moved into the empty houses in Katamon.

But many more people came for an entirely different purpose. During all hours of the day, the houses and streets teemed with people from all over town looking for booty — first in Katamon, and later also in Baka and the German Colony. Despite the danger in the streets, crowds of people came searching for valuables of all shapes and sizes — from jewelry and silverware to pianos and Persian carpets.

We refugees had not yet recovered from our initial shock. Still broken in body and spirit, we watched the people swarming through the streets of Katamon, dragging pianos and heavy furniture home with them. It didn't make sense to us — to worry about such futile objects during such troubled times. Bereft of all our belongings, we were preoccupied with our search for the bare essentials. Thus, at the same time that we were busy collecting simple household articles like underwear, kitchenware and blankets, the houses were gradually being emptied of their valuables.

The new Israeli government tried to put an end to the looting by forbidding the removal of property from the houses, but they did so before we were able to re-equip ourselves with the bare essentials we so desperately needed. Police were put on guard on every street, waiting in ambush to catch the looters.

The question of whether we should search the houses or not was of prime importance to us. Even the children would discuss the problem seriously with their friends, and not infrequently, the adults would join in with their opinions.

"If our government prohibits it, then there's nothing more to say!" declared Naomi.

"Don't be naive!" Rachel scolded her. "Everyone else is doing it, and so shall we!"

"Even if everyone else is doing it, that doesn't make it right," said Frieda.

"*We* are allowed to search the houses," decided Chana, taking her thumbs out of her mouth in order to settle the argument.

"What do you mean — we?" we all asked at once.

"'We' means 'us' — the refugees from the Old City. The government wasn't referring to us when it made the decree."

At this point, some of the mothers who were sitting on a fence nearby and feeding their babies joined in the discussion.

"Of course the government wasn't referring to us. Everyone knows that we left the Old City with only the shirts on our backs. Besides, the Arabs took all that we had, and this is one way of collecting at least partial reparations."

"That's right," several of the girls agreed, "and besides, the government awarded Katamon to us."

"Yes," others agreed. "When we first came, all the houses were open to us, but now they have been closed, all because of those hooligans!"

Imma praised Chana, agreeing with her and commenting on her intelligence. It was clear that the government's prohibition did not apply to us. In any case, we had nowhere else to turn to for the bare essentials that we lacked. Savta agreed wholeheartedly, adding that we only took things from the Arab houses that we desperately needed, and this could easily be proved. We were not "crazy" — dragging away pianos and silver and other useless articles. Wagging her finger in warning, she added, "Those fools will walk over a mine one day with their pianos!"

One morning I went with Imma to look for household items. We were inside a beautiful house which had already been emptied of most of its contents. Bright sunshine streamed through the windows onto the floor, and roses peeked through the open window. Two young men were busy taking apart some piece of fancy furniture, apparently a buffet.

"What in the world do they need the buffet for?" I thought. Imma looked at them in disdain and walked into another room. I searched for "finds" in the kitchen.

"Come here!" I suddenly heard Imma call, joyfully. "Come and see what I've found!"

I ran to her. In her hand was a pair of scissors! Large sewing scissors. Her eyes glowed with joy.

"Just imagine," she said, stroking the sharp scissors with her fingers, "now I'll be able to do anything. I'll be able to cut up all those Arab dresses and sew skirts and other clothes for you." Imma already had needles and thread. How she needed these scissors; how she had missed having a pair. Although our mother knew how to sew, we had been wearing the same old dresses for weeks, the same dresses we wore when we left the Old City.

"How wonderful! I will get to work today!"

Not wanting to leave the apartment empty-handed, I picked up a lovely little stool that I had found in the kitchen. Happily we left the building.

Just then a policeman turned the corner and came towards us. To my surprise, Imma quickly slipped the scissors into the pocket of her dress. Was she afraid of being caught red-handed? Weren't we allowed to be here? Anxiously, I looked in the direction of the policeman. He was coming towards us. Why had he chosen to pick on us?! Panicky, I tossed the stool behind a rosebush. The policeman stopped in his tracks a few steps away from us.

"What are you trying to hide there?" he asked Imma in a threatening tone of voice.

Her cheeks reddened. "What am I trying to hide? What am I trying to hide?...Diamonds!" she said, slowly drawing the scissors from her pocket as she spoke. Opening her hand, she raised it slowly up to the policeman's eyes, the scissors lying in the palm of her hand. Her eyes glittered in helpless anger.

"Here, take it! Take my diamonds! Please, help yourself!"

Taken aback by her behavior, the policeman stammered, "Wh...what...I only asked..."

But Imma was still angry. All the rage, the frustration, the pain, difficulties, worries, and anxiety that had accumulated in her heart in the last weeks burst out all at once.

"I am from the Old City, if you really want to know. Can't you find anyone else to arrest?"

Unchecked, the words flew from her lips. "All that rabble, carrying away all those treasures under your very noses! You don't arrest any of *them*. But my precious scissors you're ready to confiscate. Do you have any idea whatsoever how desperately I need them?"

The policeman stood beside us, his hands behind his back, smiling apologetically.

"Please, lady, I had no intention...I didn't know...Take the scissors! Take anything, anything you want! You may help yourself to anything in any of the houses."

But Imma was too upset and too embarrassed. She apologized for her outburst and thanked him for his generosity, her eyes lowered to the ground. She did not go back to look for anything else in the house, but I, I retraced my steps and retrieved the little stool from behind the rosebush.

59 A Shelter in the Hallway

The house where we now lived was spacious and well built. It lacked only one thing — a shelter.

"One can never tell what tomorrow may bring," Savta cautioned us. "We must be prepared for the worst."

Imma and our neighbors agreed. First they scouted around for empty sacks. Then we were put to work filling them with dirt from our garden and from the empty lot next door. The first sacks were hoisted upstairs to the second floor and lined up in the long narrow passageway leading to the staircase. Next, all the windows in the staircase were stuffed, and the big double door in the entrance was blocked with sacks, leaving only a narrow opening.

"Well, that's that," Savta said, satisfied that the job was finally completed. "This will be our shelter."

The first bombardment found us well prepared. Our shelter was more or less ready, and we were maintaining a blackout at night anyway, because of the shortage of fuel. Tired from running about our new neighborhood all day long, we were all fast asleep. Imma, exhausted from the demands of her dual roles as father and mother, slept the soundest of all.

I woke up to the sound of Savta's urgent warning, "Matilda, they're firing! Matilda, they're firing!"

I rubbed my ears but heard nothing. As I turned over in bed, I suddenly caught the sounds of gunfire, and I jumped to my feet. My whole body was quaking with cold and fear as I stuck my feet into my shoes.

"Faster, faster!" Savta urged us. "Take your blankets and run to the stairway."

The younger children woke up in alarm and immediately burst out crying. I grabbed my blanket and put it over my shoulders. In the darkness I saw Naomi doing the same.

"The children!" Imma screamed.

The gunfire grew fiercer. Naomi grabbed Ruthie from Imma's arms. "Help me, help me!" she cried to me, but I was too muddled to be of any help. I picked up as many blankets as I could carry, and together, we ran out to the stairway. We went down one flight and crowded together with our neighbors at the bottom of our shelter.

Speechless and shaking in the dark, we sat opposite the window stuffed with sacks and listened to what was going on outside.

"That same awful, miserable machine!" I cried to myself, after identifying the prolonged blast of the cursed artillery, emitting non-stop bursts of fire in the midst of the bombardment.

My teeth were chattering and my body was shaking. I

pushed myself closer to Imma. "What will be? What will be?"

Savta began to recite Tehillim out loud, and we repeated each passage after her. This helped to raise our spirits somewhat.

"The war is still going on," said sixteen-year-old Tova. "Do you hear, Akiva? They are shooting at us again!" she addressed her brother, who was being held prisoner in Trans-Jordan.

"Yes," Savta answered her, "the prisoners of war are safer than we are right now."

"See, Naomi," I pinched my sister's arm hard, "Abba has it good now. No war is being fought where he is now."

"I hope so," she sighed with all her heart.

The shooting did not stop until almost dawn. The women tiredly began their workday, and we went down to the empty lot next door. Perhaps we would find something that could be used to fuel the bonfire.

60 To Break or Not to Break

Habit is a powerful thing. One can become accustomed to anything, even to bombardments. We were treated to the same "entertainment" almost every night. Savta, our human alarm system, would hurry us down to the stairwell, and there we would sit for hours, wrapped up in our blankets, listening to the explosions. Nevertheless, as time passed, we slowly began to come back to ourselves, like people recovering from a mortal disease. The wounded also became reconciled to their fate and began to appear in public. Young boys began to walk down the streets limping on crutches, or with scarred faces, or with shirts hanging limply about their shoulders, covering the stumps of their missing arms. Even Tzion, who was mortally ill the day we surrendered, was seen walking on his crutches, debating with friends, and even laughing.

"What is better?" Rachel shot this question at us one day as we were jumping rope. "A father with only one leg in Katamon, or a father with two legs in Trans-Jordan?"

"You silly girl," her sister scolded, "don't ask questions like that!"

"How wicked of you!" Yaffale also rebuked her. "At least you could have asked 'Which is worse?'"

Only then did I understand that she was talking about Nechemia, our neighbor on the first floor who was hobbling about on his one foot along the concrete path in our garden. There was a large scar on one of his cheeks, and his mouth had been twisted by the fragments of a shell that had wounded him before the surrender. Nearby, his young children were playing.

"I will *too* ask questions like that!" Rachel insisted. "I will *too* ask! And if you don't answer me, I'll take away the rope."

Rachel held on tightly to the jump rope, staring at Nechemia's children, undisguised envy in her eyes.

"'Quiet, girls," said Chava, who was especially good at quenching fires like these. "I haven't told you about the statue yet."

"Statue? What statue?"

"Come and I'll show you."

We hurried after her down the street. On the corner, we suddenly caught sight of a statue on a pedestal inside a garden.

"An idol!" Rachel exclaimed in disgust. "Let's break it!"

We had all picked up stones and were just about to smash the statue when a policeman appeared on the scene.

"You mustn't do that!" he chided us.

"Why not?" we protested.

"Because," he answered, "we are not Arabs. We don't destroy."

"That's right," rejoined Rachel. "We are not Arabs, and that's exactly why we want to smash this statue. We don't pray to graven images."

The policeman shrugged his shoulders. "Don't pray, but don't break either," he concluded.

We wanted to continue the debate, but Chava warned us not to talk back to a Jewish policeman. "At long last we have Jewish policemen, and we must obey their orders. Had he been British, it would have been another matter."

Chava was right. A Jewish policeman was something else altogether. He didn't have that mean look in his eyes, as did the policemen we had formerly known. Even his rebuke warmed our hearts. And how handsome he looked in his blue uniform with the shiny badge!

Proudly, we watched the policeman disappear in the distance, and, one by one, we dropped the stones we had been holding.

The following day, we found the building, which was a church, and the garden and statue all enclosed by a tall, barbed-wire fence.

61 The List of Prisoners

An Arab house furnished with the bare essentials, a bonfire downstairs for cooking, a water truck, food rations from the Park Lane Hotel, and even a shelter. It seemed as if all our basic needs were provided for. There was nothing else we needed — except for Abba, the most important of all.

Where was he now? What was he doing? Were the Arabs hurting him? Did he need anything?

Anxiety for our fathers hung like a heavy cloud over every household. Not only at home but everywhere we went — standing in line for water or for food rations, in the abandoned Arab houses where we continued to search for "finds," while visiting neighbors and friends — we all shared the same burdensome worry.

"What if the P.O.W.'s never even reached Trans-Jordan?" Frieda wondered out loud one day right in the middle of a game of tag.

I, too, had been having a hard time with my secret fear for Abba's well-being. Hearing Frieda, I also spoke up.

"Yes! Or perhaps they were taken to Egypt or even Syria, or perhaps to some country even farther away."

"Perhaps..." stammered Yaffale, "perhaps they didn't take them anywhere."

"What do you mean?" asked Chana.

"I mean that... perhaps... perhaps something happened to them on the way."

"Stop it! That's enough!" Rachel chided us, and she stuck her fingers in her ears.

My temples throbbed. What if something had happened to them on the way? Yes, my sister must have been right. The Arabs must have lined them all up against a wall and...

I glanced at Naomi. Now she would probably be seized with a hysterical fit of crying. But no. Instead she came up to me and took my chin in her hand in a motherly fashion.

"Stop it," she pleaded. "What kind of a black mood are you girls in?"

"But who knows? Why haven't we received any news of the prisoners?" a few voices asked.

Just then, Tova, one of the older girls, burst into our group in a storm of excitement. Completely out of breath she waved her hands excitedly and cried, "A list! A list!" It was impossible to get her to explain what she was talking about, so we followed her as she ran down the street and up the stairs. She ran first to her mother and then to mine, announcing, "A list! A list! A list of the prisoners!"

"What? Who?" we asked, confused.

"There is a list... the list of prisoners has arrived," she said,

215

puffing and panting and wiping the beads of sweat from her forehead.

"Where?"

"There, in the office."

Imma threw her apron onto the table and ran downstairs with our neighbor. "Watch the little ones," she called back to us. All our friends ran home to deliver the good news. The list of prisoners had arrived.

"What kind of a list is it?" I asked Savta, when they had gone. "Why is everyone so happy?"

"It's a list compiled by the Red Cross and..."

"Here, let me explain it to you," Tova interrupted Savta. "A Red Cross representative has visited our prisoners in Trans-Jordan. The Red Cross representative visits every country which holds captives and checks to make sure that it is abiding by the Geneva Convention."

"Ah, the Geneva Convention," I nodded my head to show I understood.

"And so," continued Tova, "the Red Cross representative visited our prisoners in Trans-Jordan."

"So, now, the Arabs will not be able to do them any harm; is that right?"

"Right."

"You see," I turned to my sister, "now there's nothing to worry about."

"I hope not," she said, half to herself.

"Then what is that important list that everyone was talking about?" I asked.

"The representatives of the Red Cross visited the prisoners and wrote down all their names. That is, the name of every man they met."

"Then their list proves that they really are in Trans-Jordan," said Naomi.

"Yes, it is a live greeting!"

* * *

Eagerly, we waited for Imma to return from the office with a "live greeting" from Abba. Two hours passed and she was not yet back.

"What's taking her so long?" we asked over and over again, as we went from one window to the next and on to the balcony.

"The office must be overrun with people, and the lines must be very long," Savta tried to reassure us.

Finally we caught sight of Imma walking up the street. With heavy steps she walked up the stairs and in through the open door. Completely exhausted, she threw herself down on the turquoise bed. We ran to fetch her a glass of water.

"Is it all because of the long line?" I asked, looking straight into her tired eyes, and at the cup which trembled in her hand.

"Oh ho, what a line!" she sighed, and caressed my face.

Then, she exchanged a few words in Yiddish with Savta. From the look on their faces, it was obvious that something was wrong.

"Abba!" Naomi cried. "Where is Abba?"

"Abba is there," Ruthie answered, pointing at the door with her small hand.

"Abba went away...Abba will come back next week," Yehudit added.

They both climbed onto the bed and sat down beside Imma.

"Abba is in Trans-Jordan," said Savta. "Where else?"

Imma took hold of Naomi and tried to reassure her. "Abba is with all the other prisoners," she said finally.

"Then what's wrong? You must tell us what's wrong," Naomi demanded emphatically.

"Nothing."

"Did you find his name on the list?" my sister asked.

"I read hundreds of names and..."

"And what?"

"Many of the names are illegible. There are many typing errors. The Red Cross representative is not Jewish, and he had a hard time copying down the Hebrew names."

"Tell me, what about Abba?"

"They must have made a mistake in spelling his name. After all, it is so long and complicated..."

Silence.

"What did they say in the office?" Savta finally asked.

"They also said that his name must have been spelled incorrectly. They suggested that I come back tomorrow. There was such a crowd today that no one had time to help me check it out carefully."

The next day we went with Imma to the office. The clerk was very sympathetic and tried to help us. By then he had a much shorter list of names that had not as yet been identified. After much deciphering, we decided that perhaps the name "Solomon Miner" was referring to Abba — Shlomo Min-Hahar. The clerk promised to verify it through the Red Cross and advised Imma to check back with him in a few days.

One week later, we finally received the verification we had so hoped for. Abba was indeed in Trans-Jordan.

62 A Baby Is Born

It was a pitch-black night. Katamon was under a complete blackout. People went to sleep early so as not to waste precious candles or kerosene. Although kerosene was now being distributed from time to time, it was measured by the drop. Imma was saving the small amount she had for an emergency, and meanwhile, we went to sleep early every night.

That night, however, we didn't even have time to close our eyes before a blinding light split the darkness, illuminating our house for a minute before we were plunged back into darkness.

"What's that?" Yehudit asked innocently.

"A rocket!" I screamed in terror and leapt out of my bed, my blanket over my head to protect me. I grabbed my little sister, covered her with the blanket, and ran to the stairway. Used to these nighttime exercises, we arrived before even one shot had been fired.

"What happened this time?" Imma asked, as the bombardment began. "They've begun early tonight."

"Yes," our neighbor answered as she joined us, her slippers in her right hand and her blanket over her left shoulder. "I didn't even have time to fall asleep."

Her daughter Tova was already sitting on a stair, wrapped up in her blanket, her teeth chattering. Shells were exploding one after the other, and the windowpanes shook loudly.

"They say that the priest of Saint Simon church signals to them." Tova displayed her proficiency in gathering the latest news.

"Who says?" Imma asked, an undertone of fear creeping into her voice.

"That's what I heard."

A deafening explosion put an end to the conversation, and we all moved a few steps further down. The next explosions brought us all the way down to the bottom of the stairway, but then a shell, which exploded close to the house and nearly lifted the front door off its hinges, made us go back up to the top of the stairs.

"It's safer up here," Savta said.

"It's awful here!" said Tova, who had remained, along with her family, down below at the bottom of the stairs. "It's too bad we didn't go to our neighbors on the first floor."

All was quiet. Was the attack over, or was this merely a lull in the fighting?

"I'm going to run for it," Tova announced. The door opened

with a squeak, and we heard the sound of feet racing down the concrete path around the house. Silence. Our neighbors had left us.

"Let's run too," begged Naomi.

"But... if we don't make it...," Savta began. A shell exploding nearby put an end to the discussion.

"The front door is open!" I screamed in terror and ducked under Imma's arms. Another series of shells and gunshots, and then all was quiet again.

"Now!" said Imma. "Let's run fast!"

Imma was so determined that there was no way Savta could oppose her. I don't know how, but we all ran, together with the little ones and with all our blankets, down the stairs into the garden, along the long concrete path, and then up the broad white stairs in front of the house to the first-floor apartment.

Imma pounded on the thick, latticed, wooden door with all her might until someone opened it. Several other families who lived nearby were already sitting in the hallway shelter on the first floor. Blankets had been spread out on the ground for everyone.

We squeezed in among the others on the floor and tried to fall asleep. But there was no sleep for us that night. The shelling was particularly heavy and frightening. It was clear that the Arabs were launching a massive attack in an attempt to recapture Katamon. We began to recite Tehillim out loud.

All of a sudden, the door to Nechemia's apartment opened, and his wife, Tzippora, who was in her ninth month of pregnancy, ran screaming into the hallway. We could not get her to tell us what was wrong. She ran back and forth, beating on the front door with her fists and trying to open it, but her husband and eldest son pulled her back into the apartment. Again she ran out and attempted to leave the building, and again they kept her back.

"What shall I do?" she cried in despair, after they had set her down on a chair and sponged her face with cold water.

Only then did we realize what was happening. Tzippora was in labor — on this terrible night! The poor woman rose from her chair again, but two women blocked the doorway.

"It's impossible to get to a hospital tonight," they said. "You'll have to give birth here."

Her contractions got stronger, and Tzippora ran back and forth, screaming in terror.

"She's hysterical," the neighbors whispered, nodding their heads to each other. One after the other offered her own advice on how to deal with the situation.

Suddenly, Tzippora stood still and demanded that someone go to call Dr. Holdah, the doctor who had come with us from the Old City to Katamon. Her oldest son went to call the woman doctor. An hour passed, but neither the boy nor Dr. Holdah arrived. Tzippora continued her dreadful screaming. All efforts to calm her down were fruitless. Finally, Savta took matters in her own hands.

"I will deliver your baby!" she said firmly.

"No, you are no midwife!"

"My sister is a midwife, and I have helped her several times. I know what to do," Savta insisted.

The confident tone of Savta's voice and the lack of any other alternative finally convinced Tzippora to go back into her own apartment with Savta. The rest of the family joined us out in the hallway, and the door closed behind them.

Inside the house, we heard a kettle of water being put up to boil on the kerosene stove to sterilize the necessary utensils. Tzippora must have calmed down, for we no longer heard hysterical screaming, only sighs of pain. Outside in the hallway, we too calmed down, for we knew Tzippora was in good hands. With God's help all would end well.

By that time we were indifferent to the sound of the shells exploding outside. I tried to catch a snooze, but just then a soft cry was heard from inside the apartment...the cry of a newborn baby. Was he protesting against being brought into a world of war and destruction?

"Mazal tov! Mazal tov!" The women kissed each other while we children began to dance on our blankets.

In our excitement we didn't even hear the door open. Dr. Holdah and the boy stood in the doorway, greeted by shouts of joy. The doctor was led into the apartment, and at dawn, when the firing had subsided, mother and child were transferred to a hospital.

63 The Letter

A letter had arrived! Hard as it was to believe, we had received a letter from Abba. Imma had to assure us over and over again that it was really so, for the letter was in English, and we were not familiar with Abba's handwriting in that language.

"Are you sure that Abba really wrote the letter?" I asked Imma for the thousandth time, as we were on our way home from the office.

"Yes, it really is Abba's handwriting," Imma assured us over and over again. Her eyes shone with joy as she held the precious piece of paper on which a few English words had been written.

We had received word of the letters only that morning. Like lightning, the message had spread throughout the neighborhood — there were letters for us in the office! Along with everyone else, we raced down to the office, where we found a large, excited crowd already beleaguering the clerk. We had to wait in line, if it could be called that, for several hours, but finally the letter we had so longed for was in our hands.

A letter from Abba! A letter from Trans-Jordan!

When we were some distance away from the noisy crowd, we sat down on one of the stone hedges, and Imma read us the letter in English, translating it word for word. The letter was short, only five lines, and written with a pencil. Abba wrote that he was feeling fine and asked us to try to answer his letter. On the last line he sent regards to Savta and signed his name. The return address was: P.O.W. Camp, Arab Legion, c/o the Red Cross.

We each held the small piece of paper in our hands and kissed the precious letters. On the way home, we asked Imma why the letter was so short. Hadn't Abba any time to write to us?

"It must be because of the censorship," Imma reasoned.

"What is censorship?"

"Censorship is inspection. The Arabs and perhaps also the Red Cross inspect all the letters. They read every letter before mailing it to us, to make sure that no military information is sent out."

Back home, Savta's eyes filled with tears at the sight of a letter from her captive son. At noon, Tova, who had been waiting in the office all morning, came into our apartment carrying a letter.

"It's from my brother," she said. "Can you translate it for me? I don't know any English." Tova hurried to call her parents, and Imma read the letter to them and translated it.

"It's too bad that the letter is in English," Tova said. "We will have to answer it in English too."

"How do you know?" Naomi asked.

"That's what they told me in the office. I was one of the last in line, and they told us that we could answer the letters, but they must be written in English on a single sheet of paper. We must bring them to the office, and they will send them on to the Red Cross. Can you help us write a letter to my brother?"

Imma nodded her head in assent.

"And, oh, I forgot the main thing," Tova called out as she walked out the door. "The letter may be no more than twenty words long... and it can't say a word about war or politics."

In the afternoon, many other women brought their letters to us, all with the same request. Many of them had learned to converse passably in English during the Mandate, but few could read or write English. Imma had her hands full translating all their letters. Until nightfall she was busy reading letters, and so the letter to Abba had to be postponed until the next day. In the morning Tova brought over a packet of writing paper and two pencils that she had found in one of the houses. Imma sat herself down beside our only table in the white-tiled kitchen, and we all stood around her.

A twenty-word letter! We had wanted so very much to write Abba about all our terrible ordeals on the way to Katamon, about the house at the top of the hill, about our life in our new neighborhood. We wanted him to know how anxious and worried we were about him. How could we squeeze all that into twenty words? Who was responsible for this decree?

"We have no choice," said Imma. "We can only send our regards. Perhaps it is all for the best. It's best for Abba not to hear of all our troubles right now. We don't want him to worry too much."

"Then what shall we write?"

"Write 'Dear father, How are you?'" I suggested.

"No," said Imma, "that's a waste of words. Abba already wrote us that he is fine."

"Then write 'We received your letter,'" Naomi proposed.

Four English words appeared on the paper.

"But I only said three words in Hebrew!" Naomi protested.

"Yes, but unfortunately it takes four words in English to say the same thing."

"Now write 'We hope to see you,'" I wanted a sentence of mine to be included too. But the English translation was five words long, instead of the three in Hebrew.

"What kind of a language is this?" we grumbled.

"Just what we could expect from the English," Savta said. "We finally got rid of them, so now it's their language giving us trouble."

For a long time we labored over the letter, writing sentences and erasing them, exchanging one word for another, until Imma finally had a twenty-word letter. After she had copied it over, Naomi and I took the letter to the office, leaving Imma at home to help the neighbors who came knocking at our door all day long.

54 Our Apartment Grows Smaller

The Department for Abandoned Property was the government office in charge of the property that had been abandoned by the fleeing Arabs. Since it was already illegal to take spoils and policemen had been stationed to enforce the law, the department heads had to find something else to do. They held conferences, brought up proposals, discussed them, and before long, reached an important decision.

Since the residents of the Old City were used to living in crowded conditions, it was argued, they had no right to spread themselves out all over the neighborhood at government expense. Our lovely, spacious apartment in Katamon would be reapportioned according to the number of members of each family.

What would be done with the vacant apartments? Some well-placed people said that the department intended to rent them out to fill the government's empty coffers. Others did not think that the government would try to get rich through business deals at a time like this but that the apartments were needed to house refugees from other areas.

One way or the other, the Department for Abandoned Property got to work, and rumors spread that officials were going from one house to the next, crowding families together.

Imma and Savta considered the matter seriously. Imma had a feeling that the officials would say that our family wasn't large enough to deserve two rooms and would force us all to live in one.

"That would be unfair," said Savta. "I have the right to live in an apartment of my own. In the Old City I had my own apartment."

Imma was reassured. "That's a good claim," she said.

That particular day neither Savta nor Imma was at home. Savta had gone to Aunt Rivka for a day or two, and Imma had gone to town to buy a few necessities. Before she left, she gave us a list of instructions of what to do and how to take care of the little ones.

"If by any chance the officials come when I'm not here," she said at the end, "don't forget that Savta is a family of her own."

"Of course, of course," we both answered together.

Imma went out and we began to carry out her instructions. We fed the little ones, straightened up the house, changed the baby, and then sat down to play.

Someone knocked on the door, and before we could get up to open it, a strange man and woman walked in. The woman carried a folder, and the man held a sheaf of papers in his hand.

"Where is your mother?" the man asked.

"Imma went to town," we answered.

The man turned to go, but the woman held him back.

"It makes no difference," she said. "The girls can answer our questions."

She walked into the room and looked about her. The handsome broad door between the two rooms was wide open. The woman looked meaningfully at the second room, which

226

had its own entrance from the common hallway, and ordered, "Take out the list!"

The man spread out the sheaf of papers in his hand.

"We are from the Department for Abandoned Property," he said. "We have come to investigate."

My heart began to beat faster. So they had come at last, just when Imma wasn't home. What had they come to investigate? We had no time to wonder.

"What is your family name?" the man asked.

Naomi told him and he searched for it on his list. I studied the two of them. The man was simply dressed in a pair of khaki pants. The woman wore slacks and a green silk blouse. She had short blond hair and wore lipstick.

"Here, I've found it," said the man. "How many people are you?"

"Just...just a minute," I said. "We're five children and..."

"How many?" the woman asked impatiently.

"Let her think," said the man. "Five children and your mother makes six, right?"

"Also my father," I said.

"Your father must be in Trans-Jordan," the woman scolded me.

"Yes, but he will come back, with God's help," said Naomi.

"Of course," agreed the man. "But right now he doesn't live here."

"True," we agreed. "But when he comes home, he'll live here."

The woman was angry. A deep wrinkle appeared on her forehead. "Better not talk too much to someone like that," I thought to myself, meeting her severe gaze.

"Then there are six of them," she said. "What is written on your list?"

The man skimmed the lines. "Six," he answered finally.

"Just...just a minute," I protested. "Also Savta."

227

"Savta! Did you ever?" the angry woman exclaimed.

"No," said Naomi. "Savta is a family of her own."

"Forget about Savta," said the man. "You are a family of six. Now show me the apartment."

"This is our apartment," said Naomi. "One room and the kitchen." As she spoke, she gestured to the room where we stood and the kitchen adjoining it.

"And where is the toilet?"

"Outside."

"Fine," the man nodded in assent.

"And what is that?" they asked, pointing to the other room.

"That is Savta's apartment," we answered.

"Apartment? I only see a room, a second room."

"No," said Naomi. "That is Savta's apartment."

"Savta. Where is Savta?" the man asked.

"Savta went to visit Aunt Rivka. She'll be back tomorrow."

"So, Savta went visiting...Did you hear that?" the woman repeated. She turned back to us and shook her finger threateningly. "No one lies to me, little girl!"

The man tried to say something, but the woman interrupted him, the wrinkle on her forehead deepening.

"Just look! See how they teach little children to lie. Their grandmother must live with the aunt. Ah, what an upbringing!" As she spoke, she walked determinedly towards the second room.

"I am not lying," I wanted to tell her. "I never lie. The Torah commands us to keep far away from falsehood, and Abba...my Abba knows how to bring us up. Almost every day he used to remind us that God's Name is Truth, and that one should always tell the truth." I wanted to tell her all that, but her cheeks burned with anger, and there were sparks in her eyes as she took the folding cot in her hands and began to push it along the smooth floor into the room where we were standing.

The little ones burst into tears and clung to us. Naomi tried to protest.

"That is too Savta's apartment. She'll come back tomorrow and..."

"Keep quiet!" the woman yelled. "And you come here." The man hesitated.

"Why, this is our job," she chided him, raising her head importantly. "A family of only six cannot be permitted to occupy two rooms!"

"We know all too well how you lived in the Old City," she turned to us. "There you had nothing, but here you have taken everything."

"In the Old City we had a lot of things," I said. "A bookshelf and clothes closet, a clock and a new icebox."

"Yes, but there you lived in one room."

"We did not. We lived in two rooms," said Naomi.

"At the end..." I added.

"You are lying again!"

"N...no," answered Naomi.

"Keep quiet, I told you!" Then, turning to the man, "Let's go!"

They walked into Savta's room and pushed the chest of drawers into our room. Then, with no prior warning and all in a fury, the woman began to throw the blankets, clothes and other things that were in the other room onto the chest and the blue bed, urging the man to help her as she worked.

"Quickly! Quickly!" she urged him. "Time is short and we have a lot of work!"

The little ones began to wail loudly. We stood, shocked beyond words, and watched what was going on. Hearing the crying, our neighbor and her daughter Tova came in. Before they could grasp what was happening and begin to protest, the other room had been completely emptied, and all its contents strewn about our apartment.

The couple closed the wide door tightly, and the man

removed the handle so that the second room was completely closed to us. Our neighbor yelled and protested, but the angry woman would hear none of it.

"Don't stick your nose into other people's business!" she scolded. "Go back to your own apartment. We're coming to check up on you next."

Meanwhile, the man had gathered up his lists. The two of them left, taking the door handle with them and leaving behind crying children and an overturned apartment.

We were completely at a loss until Imma finally came home. By the time she came upstairs, she had already heard what had happened from our neighbors. They advised her to go to the office and explain that Savta lived in her own room next to us. However the office was closed in the afternoon so Imma calmed her hysterical children and then began to straighten up.

The next morning, even before Savta returned home, new tenants moved into the second room: a lone woman, a little girl and a suitcase. The department representative who brought them told them they could use our washroom. When Imma tried to protest, she was told to complain to the department. Imma did lodge a complaint, but it took a week for the matter to be settled. Meanwhile, we were crowded together in one room, which was much smaller than our one-room apartment in the Old City.

A week later, the man appeared again, the door handle in his hand. He reopened the door between our two rooms, but at the same time he closed off all the doors leading out to the spacious hallway, which, until then, had been used jointly by everyone. The new tenants were moved into the hall. Then we found out that the new woman was not at all homeless. She had an apartment in Me'ah She'arim, she told Imma, but she wanted to try out this new neighborhood. If she liked it, she would stay.

To our great relief, she didn't like it. After a short time, she went back where she came from, together with the girl and the suitcase. But the Department for Abandoned Property would not give up, and a short time later an old couple were housed in the "third apartment" on our floor.

65 School for Two

Her name was Sophie. One morning she appeared in our doorway, her blonde hair carefully combed and curled around her head, her bright eyes looking at Imma. She was ill at ease. It was just after Savta had complained that we were growing up wild, not learning anything.

Sophie had been a student of Abba's, so she said, and when the Old City was cut off, she was left owing Abba a lira and a quarter for the private lessons he had been giving her. Now she had walked from town out to Katamon to pay her debt. She took a few coins from her purse, handed them to Imma, and went her way. A few minutes later she came back.

"Excuse me," she said. "I am so mixed up. Now that your husband is a captive, it must be very hard for you to take care of everything all by yourself with all these little children. How can I help you?"

"Thank you very much," replied Imma, "but it's not necessary."

"Please let me help you," the girl pleaded. "I am a new immigrant, and I had a hard time learning Hebrew until your husband helped me. Thanks to him I am now capable of being a teacher. I would like to repay him for what he did for me."

Her straightforwardness and persistence convinced Imma, who relented and asked Sophie to buy a few things for her in town. "That will be a great help to me," she said.

"I'll be happy to do it," said Sophie, "but that wasn't what I meant. Perhaps . . . perhaps . . . has a school been opened here yet?"

"No," we answered.

"Fine," she said. "Then I will teach the girls. What do you think of that idea?"

Imma was very enthusiastic. On the spot they agreed that Sophie would come two or three times a week to teach Naomi and me.

Two days later Sophie came back with supplies — *siddurim*, books, notebooks, and two pencils.

"What kind of a school is this?" I complained. "Two students and one teacher!"

"Every school begins small," answered our teacher.

Naomi held her head up proudly and refused to sit beside me, even during prayers, as she was in a higher grade.

Nevertheless, we did pray together. It was the first time in so long that we were able to pray from a *siddur*. The classes began. While "third grade" was being taught, "second grade" had recess.

When "school" was finally over, I ran downstairs and hid in a corner of the garden. I was running away from Imma, Sophie, Naomi, and everyone else. When I had asked Imma if I could go to school, I didn't mean a school like that. I missed school — *real* school — the kind you have to rush off to in the morning, to walk a long way down crowded streets to reach, your school bag on your back, and then ride home from it on a bus! I wanted a school with chairs and desks, with chalk and a big blackboard on the wall and a teacher hidden by a forest of waving hands. A school with a yard teeming with children, balls flying overhead, and jump ropes. A school that you came home from tired, after having bought some Turmos for a mil or hot peanuts from a tall Negro wearing a broad-rimmed straw hat.

Nevertheless, it was with great interest that I sat and listened to Sophie when she came back two days later. I hadn't learned anything for such a long time that everything interested me. Sophie gave me a *chumash Bereishit* and a notebook. In her school we learned Torah and arithmetic, Hebrew, and even gym. At recess I played by myself. Sometimes we even had a lunch break, and then Sophie would chat with Imma, and Naomi would graciously sit beside me while I ate.

Sophie's lessons were interesting, but Imma told us to be careful not to make her angry. Nor were we allowed to try to make her laugh, although Imma didn't warn us against it. There was something about the simple, almost severe, manner in which she dressed which left no room for laughter. It had none of the gaiety of young girls. Perhaps, too, it was her shoulders, which seemed to be carrying the weight of the world. And above all, it was the sad look in her eyes, so serious, so adult . . . When eyes like those looked at you, the slightest smile would die on your lips. Where Sophie came from I didn't know, nor did I dare ask. I only knew she was a new immigrant.

Our teacher's visits were a great help to Imma. There were as yet no buses to Katamon, and Sophie would buy Imma things she needed in town and bring them to her. Once it was thread, another time wool and knitting needles. Little by little, I became accustomed to my school and my teacher. On those days when Sophie didn't come, I missed her greatly. Once, three days passed with no sign of Sophie. Since we had no telephones, we had no idea what had happened to her.

"How many lessons did Abba give Sophie?" I asked Imma.

"I don't know. Maybe ten, maybe twenty. I have no idea. Why do you ask?"

"I was thinking. Perhaps she is finished paying Abba back for what he did for her, and she won't come to us anymore."

Imma laughed. "Sophie must just not be feeling well. She promised to keep on coming until a school is opened here."

And, indeed, a few days later, Sophie did come back — to my great delight. This time she didn't come alone; she brought a little girl with blonde braids, a new student for our school. Her name was Shula, and her family were refugees from Neve

Yaakov, an agricultural settlement north of Jerusalem which was captured by the Arabs. Shula was also in the second grade. I was happy to have another pupil in my class and someone to play with at recess.

Everything was fine until our big fight. One day Imma came back from an abandoned Arab house with a present for me — two big thick crayons, the kind used in kindergarten.

"How wonderful!" I cried happily, taking the two crayons from her hand. One was black and the other green. Imma brought me paper, too, although one side was covered with Arabic. But the second side was blank. Since I had not drawn a picture in months, my heart was filled with joy at the sight of these objects. Happily, I sat down on the floor.

What could I do in two colors? My imagination, fired by the sight of the crayons, helped me solve this problem easily. At the bottom of the page I drew a black line — the ground. Above it I drew green grass, black tree trunks with green branches and leaves, a green house with a black roof and a black fence. Above them I drew a green line for the sky and a few black birds in the air.

My joy was so great that the next day I showed my picture to Sophie the minute she walked in the door. Seeing my excitement, Sophie stroked my beaming face and complimented me on the picture. Torn with jealousy, Shula looked at my precious picture.

"What kind of a picture is that!" she declared scornfully. "Whoever saw black ground and a green sky?" Mockingly, she laughed. "Look, look! A black roof instead of a red one! Is that what you call a beautiful picture?" she asked Sophie.

I turned white with anger. Sophie answered for me.

"Aren't you ashamed of yourself?" my good-hearted teacher scolded. "She finally has two crayons and you laugh at her! You should have given her a few of your own crayons a long time ago!"

Then she put her hand under my chin and said, "Never mind. Sooner or later, Abba will come home, and then you'll have everything, even crayons. Everyone will come home. The war here in Eretz Yisrael is different. There, those who were taken away never ever came back."

"Where is 'there'?" Shula asked curiously.

Sophie didn't answer. She was looking at us, but it was clear that she didn't see us. It was as if she were in another world, as if she were "there."

When Sophie and Shula had gone, Naomi confided that she was jealous of me. "I don't even have anyone to fight with," she said.

"As if you don't fight enough with me!" I replied.

"You don't understand," she said angrily. "I fight with you like a sister, but not like one of my friends..."

* * *

It was a very hot day, a *chamsin*, and we were finding it hard to sit and concentrate. As Sophie was reading us a story, drops of sweat gathered on her face, and she wiped them away with a freshly ironed handkerchief that she took from her shirt pocket each time.

"Why don't you roll up your sleeves?" Shula suggested, and Sophie took her advice.

"What is that scribbled on your arm?" I asked, unable to keep from giggling at the sight of writing on Sophie's arm.

"That's no scribble," said Shula. "Can't you see that it's numbers?"

My curiosity aroused, I took my teacher's arm and examined it. Yes, there were numbers printed in blue-green ink on her arm.

"Why did you ever do such a thing to yourself?" I asked again.

Sophie turned her head away strangely and looked out the window. No one spoke. What had I done? I didn't dare move a hand or a foot. Finally, Sophie turned back to us, a strange, faraway look in her eyes.

Sophie didn't come to teach us two days later, nor did she come at the end of the week. Shula, however, came by the very next morning.

"I know! I know what she has written on her arm!" she said, a bit arrogantly. "My mother told me."

"Big deal!" I said. "I also know. A number. She has a number on her arm, several numbers."

"That's right. But what does the number mean?"

"What?"

"It's the work of the Germans. Hitler's Germans. The Nazis. They did it to her."

"Why?"

"It's a concentration camp number. Sophie was in one."

"Then why doesn't she wash it off or erase it with an eraser?"

"Because ... my mother told me that that number is not just written in pen."

"Then how?"

"It's a tattoo. It will remain on Sophie's arm forever. The Nazis tattooed it under her skin with a hot needle."

"What?" I cried in alarm.

"Don't worry. There are no Nazis left today, only Arabs. My mother said we were very bad girls and that we are not allowed to ask Sophie questions like that. Now she won't come anymore because of you."

A week later, our good-hearted teacher did come back, despite everything. She came and taught us regularly, three times a week, not expecting any pay, for a long time, until finally a school opened in our neighborhood. Sophie kept her promise. She repaid Abba's kindness many times over.

66 Holidays without Abba

Abba's letters were brief, but oh, so full of yearning for us. He always assured us that he had everything he needed, as if he were at some resort. But was everything he wrote true? We knew that every word had to pass the censor.

Later on, it was permissible to write more than twenty words, but only once a week. Abba asked us to try and post our letters to him from different parts of the city in an attempt to get more letters to him. Didn't he realize that we were only allowed to write once a week too? Besides, had he forgotten that it was still dangerous to travel around town? Officially, there was a cease-fire, but in practice, it all depended on the mood of the Arabs.

Sometimes there were long intervals between one letter and the next, despite Abba's assurances that he took advantage of every opportunity to write. Abba, too, complained. In one of his letters he wrote that he hadn't heard a word from us for two months and he was terribly worried. That was too much for us! That meant that all those letters that we had taken such trouble to write each week were being detained somewhere and might not ever reach their destination! Imma sent a telegram through the Red Cross, and as a result, we received a note from Abba that he had received several letters at once.

Once Abba noticed that a letter received by one of his relatives in the camp was written in Imma's handwriting. It didn't take long for him to realize that Imma was writing the letters for our friends and relatives. It was as if he had discovered a treasure. From then on he tried to read all the letters he could find in Imma's handwriting, no matter whether they were written to him or to someone else. He was so anxious to receive mail from each of us that Imma taught us to write a few words in English and he was overjoyed to read the sentence or two which Naomi and I had written ourselves. He even asked for fingerprints from our little sisters.

* * *

Summer passed, and Tishrei, the month of the High Holidays, drew near. The government did all it could to help us. The Zeltzers opened a grocery store in a room on the ground floor of a house down the street. We were all very happy about this. It was as if they had transferred their store from the Jewish Quarter to Katamon.

Yehuda, too, opened a fruit and vegetable store nearby. There was no more distribution of food at the Park Lane Hotel, and now we had a place to buy our food.

Food supplies all over the country, especially in Jerusalem, were strictly rationed by the government: one ration of sugar per week per person; one ration of oil or margarine; one of oatmeal; etc. No one was permitted to buy more than his quota. Each member of the family received a coupon book, and the girl in the grocery store would cut out the appropriate number of points from the book for the products sold, for which of course we also had to pay. Women learned to bake cakes and cookies from oatmeal with no eggs or flour, to prepare many different dishes from small fish, to substitute cabbage for onions in cooking. It was hard to get along for months with no eggs, poultry or meat. It was hard to be satisfied with a tasteless coffee substitute in place of real cocoa and coffee and to drink milk powder instead of milk. But Imma and Savta taught us to thank God for what we had and to be happy when our rations were slightly enlarged for the holidays.

Unfortunately, just as the holidays were approaching, the Teachers Union stopped paying Abba's salary, for his name no longer appeared on the list of those employed for the new school year. Until then, his salary had been paid regularly every month, even though he was in Trans-Jordan.

Uncle Shimon, Imma's brother, was a school principal, and he had seen to it that Imma received Abba's money. Now, besides her anxiety over Abba's welfare, Imma had to deal with financial difficulties as well. That year I prayed with all my heart for the holidays to come a little later, but of course my prayers were in vain.

Two days before Rosh Hashana, Savta went to Aunt Rivka's, and our Bobba and Zeideh took her place. Imma and Bobba worked hard preparing for the holiday. Bobba had brought some small fish in her shopping basket, and she set about cleaning them.

"Even if we don't have gefilte fish this year," she said, "we do have these fish, thank God, and we will be able to recite the traditional prayer 'May it be Thy will that we be a head and not a tail.'"

I couldn't look at Imma's face. I knew that it was neither the fish, whose sharp odor filled the house as they cooked in the pan, nor the lack of the other holiday foods that saddened her. She must have been wondering whether the High Holiday *machzor* that we sent to Abba would reach him. And the *shofar* which the Chief Rabbinate had sent — would the P.O.W.s be allowed to blow it?

On *erev Rosh Hashana* I couldn't help remembering the new dress Imma had sewed for me last year for the holidays: a white silk dress with red dots like pomegranate seeds. Where was it now?

"You'll wear what you have," Imma said, as if reading my thoughts.

In the street beneath our window, I heard people returning home from the synagogue. If Abba were here now, he would wish us all, "May you be inscribed for a good year."

Zeideh recited *kiddush*. We washed our hands, and each of us received a piece of bread dipped in honey. "May it be Thy will

to grant us a New Year as sweet as honey," we recited with all
our hearts as we ate the apple dipped in honey. Then we ate
some beets (*selek*) and prayed, "May it be Thy will for all our
enemies to depart (*l'histalek*)." Finally, we added a special
prayer, "May it be Thy will to bring Abba back from captivity
soon."

Between Yom Kippur and Succot, Uncle Yitzchak came to
visit us several times. He was Imma's younger brother and the
head of a boys' institution which had recently moved to
Katamon from Sanhedria. Downstairs in our garden was a
lovely, paved patio with grapevines growing along a wooden
trellis overhead. Uncle Yitzchak used the wooden framework
supporting the grapevines to build us a *succa*. He pushed the
grapevines to the sides and tied blankets around the framework
to make walls. We cut *s'chach* from the trees lining the street.

Zeideh bought a set of the four species, but the *lulav* and
etrog he bought were not as nice as what he usually had. The
Chief Rabbinate assured us that before Rosh Hashana they had
sent a set of the four species to the P.O.W.s, but our neighbor,
who also sold *etrogim*, sent a set to her son nevertheless.
(Much later, we learned that the hundreds of prisoners had to
share two sets of the four species.) On the afternoon just before
Succot began, we helped Imma move our black table and all
our chairs downstairs to the *succa*.

The holiday eve arrived. We heard *kiddush* and then sat in
our *succa* in silence, eating our meal of hot soup. The aged
faces of our sages peered out at me from the one lone picture
that Zeideh had hung to decorate the *succa*. A few pomegran-
ates hung from the *s'chach* together with one very plain paper
chain that Sophie had helped us make from some lackluster
paper, which was all we could find that year.

Zeideh talked to us about the *mitzva* of rejoicing on the
holiday, and he began to sing "*Vesamachta bechagecha*." We
joined in the singing very unenthusiastically. After our short

dinner, we recited Grace and went into the house.

"Aren't you going to sleep in the *succa*?" I asked Zeideh, as we walked up the stairs.

"It's too dangerous this year," he answered curtly.

"Do you think Abba is sleeping in the *succa*?" I asked.

"Who knows?" answered Zeideh, but Naomi said, "Abba? Abba has been sleeping in a tent for five months already."

57 A Real School

Fall winds were blowing the yellowed leaves onto the sidewalks, and again we were on our way to school, real school! It was amazing how much even the worst of students longed for school after such a long vacation. From all over the neighborhood, girls of all ages streamed to the new school opened on Halamed Hey Street.

It was due to no small effort on Imma's part that our new school was opened. For a few days, we and many other girls had attended the first public school for girls to be opened in Katamon, but it soon became clear that we didn't fit in there, despite the warm welcome we received from the principal and teachers. A few mothers decided to ask Rabbi Liberman, the principal of our old school, to open a religious school in our neighborhood.

At that time there was a cease-fire, but the Arabs did not observe it very strictly. There was as yet no bus to Katamon, and so Imma and thirteen-year-old Chaya had to walk all the way to Rabbi Liberman's home on the other side of the town. The gunfire in the streets forced them to stop and seek shelter in the stairways several times as they walked.

Weeks passed, and finally their long and dangerous venture bore fruit. A youth club was opened by a few young women in a small, one-story house at the eastern end of Katamon. A few weeks later, a real school opened there.

Words cannot describe our happiness, as we finally got ready for our new school. I was not yet reconciled to the loss of my beautiful, black school bag at Zion Gate together with everything that was in it. The new school bag which Imma sewed for me from a yellowish, woven fabric made me feel even worse.

Naomi, who, as usual, behaved so maturely, put on *her* cloth school bag and declared that the shoulder straps were really very comfortable, and so were the big buttons and crocheted buttonholes. It took quite a bit of persuasion on the part of Imma, Savta, and Naomi to convince me to wear my unusual school bag to school, but once on the way, I saw other children with similar bags.

"That is one of the results of the war," Naomi commented, glancing at me out of the corner of her eye, as if she were several years older than I.

No words can describe how wonderful it felt to sit in a real classroom and study together with the many old and new friends who had moved to Katamon from all over the city. Our school building had a balcony and a yard, but, best of all, there was a spacious empty lot opposite where we could again play the wonderful games of our childhood.

68 No Winter Clothes

The leaves of the plum tree, whose fruit we had eaten while it was still green, now began to yellow and drop from the tree, one after the other. The pomegranate trees were stooped over, and the grapevine shed its leaves onto the smooth patio floor, from which they were blown all over the yard. The rosebushes were already bare. Winter was on its way.

In the afternoon, as we worked on our homework, Imma and Savta were busy knitting sweaters. Yudale, who had already stopped crawling, took great pleasure in pushing our big chair from one room to the other. We had to force ourselves to ignore the tremendous noise he made.

"He won't even recognize Abba," Imma would say.

"Ab-ba, Ab-ba," he would repeat, not understanding what the word meant.

"Abba, Abba," Ruthie and Yehudit would stop playing and call out. Naomi and I would choke back the tears welling up in our throats. Savta would remain silent. Only the increased speed of her knitting disclosed the deep emotion she was feeling.

"How will we get through the winter?" Imma worried out loud. I couldn't decide what it was she was most worried about — our family, totally unprepared for the cold weather, or Abba, so very far away from us.

The season's first rain caught me on my way home from school. It beat fiercely on my bare head, on my thin dress, and on the cloth school bag on my back. By the time I got home, I was soaked to the skin. My school bag was also wet through and through.

"See," I remarked reprovingly to Imma, when I saw that all my books and notebooks were soaked, "this bag is no good!"

Imma helped me spread the books out on the table to dry. A few days later, Savta brought us our cousins' old leather school bags. I received a worn, old, brown school bag, which I wouldn't have glanced at twice in normal times. Now, however, after my unfortunate experience, I preferred it to the cloth bag.

Imma and Savta had finished knitting three sweaters for the youngest children, but they had only begun to work on the sweaters for Naomi and me when the nurse brought some sweaters to school. They had been donated to the needy by the

United Nations Works and Relief Agency. After a lengthy discussion, the nurse and the teacher decided who would get the sweaters. I did not want to be one of the recipients.

"We aren't poor," I protested. "We don't need charity!"

The teacher explained to me that the sweaters were not necessarily for poor people but for the war refugees. "And that's exactly what you are!" she ended her explanation, and directed the nurse to write my name on the list in her hand. A few girls looked at me in envy, but later, when the nurse opened the package and began to distribute the sweaters, no one envied me anymore. Never in all our lives had we set eyes on such ugly sweaters!

Almost all the girls rejected the present in disgust. The first to recover from the shock was Chana, who was now in fifth grade.

"Who cares how they look, as long as they're warm," she said, trying on her sweater.

The others all turned up their noses. I adamantly refused to accept the dark brown sweater allotted to me, but the nurse and teacher forced me to at least take it home. "Imma will decide what to do," they said. I cried so bitterly that Imma postponed her decision until the pouring rain three days later decided for me.

* * *

Two weeks had passed since our last letter from Abba, but we heard that in a letter to Uncle Avraham, Abba had complained of inadequate clothing. Apparently, Imma's anxiety was justified.

For a few days I was unable to picture anymore exactly how Abba looked. Could it be that I was forgetting my father? Then, one night he appeared very clearly in one of my dreams, lying on the ground in the darkened tent, his big, green eyes

244

gleaming. It was raining outside, and large drops of rain penetrated the yellow woven fabric of which the tent was made. Abba sat and gathered the rain water in a cup he was holding.

I looked at Abba and saw that he was still wearing the same thin white shirt he had worn the day the Old City fell, and he was shaking with cold. Just then a Legionnaire walked in and handed Abba a sweater.

"This is from the Red Cross," he said, "a present for the prisoners." Abba put on the dark brown sweater.

"But it's so ugly," said a friend in the tent.

"I have no choice," answered Abba. "The main thing is that it's warm."

Then the tent disappeared, and I saw Imma standing beside me.

"Get up, get up," she urged. "It's seven o'clock already."

Shivering with cold, I left the warmth of my blanket and hurriedly dressed myself. As I washed up, Imma poured boiling water on tiny lumps of chicory in our glasses, to which she added a bit of brown sugar and milk powder. This "coffee" was our only drink for many long months.

Without a word, I put on the brown sweater, my gift from U.N.W.R.A., and took the old leather school bag. Naomi and I set out for school, despite the thunderstorm raging outside. It was a long walk, and the pouring rain had made small rivers along the sidewalks. We shivered with cold and our teeth chattered.

Our hands turned first red, then purple and blue, until they could hardly hold the school bags. We alternately stuck one hand after the other under our sweaters. The exposed hand, carrying the school bag, would freeze. A bombardment of hail began to hit us mercilessly on our heads, forcing us to seek shelter in one of the entrance halls.

"Never mind," Naomi comforted me. "Better to seek shelter from hail than from shells."

"It must be hailing on Abba's head, too," I said. Naomi

245

looked straight at me, wordlessly.

We waited until the storm had let up. Then we left our shelter and ran to school as fast as we could.

That winter was exceptionally cold and rainy, as though the heavens were trying to wash away all the filth that had clung to the earth during those long months of fighting. Almost every day, bountiful rains fell on our heads as we walked to school. Imma bought us wool head-scarves and long training pants (which we loathed) to wear under our skirts. Almost every day, while helping us take off our wet clothing after school, she would mourn the loss of the coats we had refused to wear when we left the Old City. Could she have forgotten the terrible heat spell on that fateful day, the flames on Jewish Quarter Road, the difficulty we had getting out through Zion Gate?

Our house was as cold as ice, and we had no means of heating it. Our fingers grew red and swollen and sore to the touch. The skin cracked and oozed yellow pus which itched unbearably. Our toes were so swollen that we had difficulty putting our shoes on. We did our homework sitting in the big turquoise bed, our frozen legs covered with a feather quilt. Hard as it was to hold a pen, we didn't stop writing to Abba, and we were never free of anxiety over the hard winter we were sure he was having.

A full two weeks of waiting passed until the postman finally brought us a letter from Abba. Despite the heavy rains, strong winds and cruel cold, he began as always, "I feel fine and lack nothing but the sight of your dear faces."

69 Homecoming

In Rhodes, the cease-fire talks were already in full swing, but we missed Abba even more than ever. Would he really be freed soon? It seemed as if the talks were dragging out interminably. The longer they continued, the more impatient we became. At times it seemed as if the negotiations would continue forever and that there would never be an exchange of prisoners.

Letters arrived from the captives asking that *matzot* be sent to them for Pesach. It seemed as if they too had lost all hope and no longer believed they would be freed.

By the beginning of the Hebrew month of Tevet, it seemed even less likely than before that they would be released, but then suddenly we received news that the first group of prisoners were on their way home! Our hearts overflowed. We couldn't concentrate on our lessons at school, nor could we play afterwards.

In the afternoon we gathered in groups along the stone hedges lining the streets, jump ropes and balls set aside. We talked and argued loudly.

"The wounded who were taken captive will be the first to be released," said Chana, our information supplier.

"Also the aged and the infirm," added her sister Rachel.

"How do you know?" Frieda and Yaffale asked.

"From an authoritative source!" Chana replied, and of course no one challenged her or asked for her "authoritative source."

We were all disappointed. Most of our fathers were neither wounded, sick, nor aged. Then Chana turned to me and said, "Actually, your father just might come, too. After all, he has connections!"

I wanted to slap her face. My father had "connections"? How ridiculous! Stunned, I stood there speechless, but Naomi, boiling in anger, retorted,

"Your nonsense is really too much! What 'connections' could my father have with the Arabs?"

"Sure he has," Chana insisted. "Your father was in charge of all the residents. The Arabs must certainly honor him for that.

Maybe they will send him home with the first group."

Angrily, we left the group and walked upstairs. Just that morning I had told myself that if Abba didn't come in the first group I would be unable to continue living; I would simply be unable! But after the incident with Chana I changed my mind. Why, if Abba came home now, it would prove that Chana and her stupid talk was correct.

"Don't worry about what she said," Naomi told me. "Abba would never accept any special treatment." Her eyes met mine in complete agreement.

A few days later, two army trucks stopped, one after the other, at the end of the street. The back door opened, and a few men in uniform jumped out. Others got down more slowly and began to limp down the street.

"The captives!" passers-by called out.

Within minutes a large crowd had gathered around them. Women ran out of the houses, wiping their wet hands hastily on their aprons, to join the crowd in the street. Abba was not among those released.

Towards evening, one of the released men brought us a letter, a letter written in Hebrew! It was from Abba. In the kitchen, by the light of the kerosene lamp, Imma spread out the two sheets of paper, covered with clear, neat, Hebrew letters crowded together — the first Hebrew letters in Abba's handwriting we had seen in the eight months of separation.

Imma began to read out loud:

"To my beloved ones, my precious wife, together with our lovely children...

"Over eighty men are going home now, but I am not among them, for I am neither a boy nor an old man, neither ill nor wounded nor mentally unwell..."

The sheet of paper trembled in Imma's hand, and tears covered her eyes. And then, all the promises to be strong that we, the "big girls," had made, evaporated into thin air.

70 Abba

It seemed that only yesterday the plum tree was dry and bare. Now, overnight, it had turned completely white. How beautiful it was that morning, and how surprised we were by the white blossoms which covered it. We could hardly recognize it.

"Oh, the plum tree! How beautiful!" we called out in admiration.

How could it be that we hadn't noticed the branches coming back to life, or the appearance of the buds? It must have been because we were so involved in other things. Recently, additional groups of prisoners had been released, bringing with them stories and messages from those they left behind.

That morning a clear, blue, cloudless sky greeted us, and the warm sunshine infused us with energy. We ran the whole way to school. About two hours before class was over, Nachum, one of Abba's many cousins, appeared. What was he doing in our school?

His eyes shining, Nachum called to us to come outside.

"Abba's here!" he said. "I saw him in Sarafend." (Sarafend had been the name of a British army camp near Rishon Letzion. Now it is an Israeli camp renamed Tzrifin).

Although years have passed since that joyous day, I'll never forget Nachum's shining eyes as he uttered those two simple words, "Abba's here!" Hearing them, I felt the blood rise to my face and my temples throbbed.

"Abba!"

I ran like a whirlwind into the classroom and grabbed my school bag. Naomi ran too. Nachum called something to us, but we could no longer hear what he said. He ran to catch up with us, and as we walked beside him on the way home, he tried over and over again to explain to us that Abba would be in Sarafend for a while and that we would have to wait patiently, but we were too excited to listen.

Was it a mere coincidence that after so many dark rainy days, the sun had just begun to shine? Was it just my imagination that the whole world was celebrating? I couldn't wait to get home. Time after time, Naomi, a severe look on her face, had to pull me out of the street and back onto the sidewalk as I ran and skipped. Why didn't all traffic stop on a day like this? The street had been washed clean, the houses shone; it was as if the whole world had woken up to a new life. In my excitement I imagined that all the people in the street were looking at me.

At home, Imma already knew. Nachum had notified her too. We will always be indebted to him for hurrying to bring us our good news. Now, Nachum left us alone with Imma and went home.

What could they be doing there in Sarafend for such a long time? Night fell. The little ones went to sleep, and we went downstairs to wait. It was cold outside, but who cared? One lone street lamp lit up the street. Imma, Naomi and I sat on the fence, and Savta and Uncle Yerachmiel, who had just arrived from Tiberias, stood beside us. A few other families were also waiting in the street, along with ours. Light streamed out through the windows of the houses, for we had recently begun to use electricity again. We waited.

Suddenly the rattle of a command car broke the quiet. It stopped several yards away and a few men got out. Who was that, walking towards us, wearing a heavy army coat, its shiny metal buttons jingling as he walked? He wore a khaki beret on his head, and the big green eyes looking out from the thin, drawn face were searching.

Could it be? It was! Abba!

* * *

That wasn't how I had remembered him. It seemed to me that he had been taller. Maybe it was his beret. His face had been full when we parted, and now, his cheeks were sunken. He had changed. Nine months was such a long time.

Everyone crowded around him. I barely managed to hug his big hand before I felt a choking feeling in my throat. Hastily I pulled my hand away from his and I fled. Again those stupid tears! They always came when they were least wanted! Now Abba would think that I wasn't happy to see him.

I ran down the concrete path and skipped past the staircase leading upstairs. Suddenly, two big hands grabbed me from behind and hid my sobbing face in the heavy coat with the shiny metal buttons.

After everyone had gone upstairs, our family remained in the garden. The long white branches of the plum tree were lifted towards the heavens, silhouetted against the black sky, as if the tree were standing in prayer. Was this its prayer of thanksgiving?

71 View from Mount Zion

Years passed. King David's Tomb, on top of Mount Zion, served as a substitute for the Kotel which was still in enemy hands. Every Shabbat, Jews from all over Jerusalem would stream to Mount Zion. It was difficult to climb the steep mountain, and difficult to walk back down. Nevertheless, for years, every Shabbat after dinner we walked from Katamon up to the top of Mount Zion.

We would stand besides David's Tomb, surrounded by our fellow Jews, and pour out our hearts before the Holy One. Like David, we prayed, "When will we be able to come before the Divine Presence?" Standing there, we felt as David must have felt when he was exiled from his city. "My soul yearns deeply for the courtyards of God's House." We would recite the *mincha*

251

service and Tehillim together with the congregation at David's Tomb.

Then we would leave the synagogue and climb up to the lookout tower on the roof. There, up above, we would stand and look at the Old City. The Mount Zion lookout was always crowded. Those who knew, would explain to others where the Temple Mount and the Western Wall stood, and where the Old City wall, the Jewish Quarter and Batei Machse were, even though not all of these could be seen from where we were standing.

We would stand there silently, for a long time, straining our eyes. Would we be able to catch sight of the house, our house? There on the right was the Shiloach (Silwan) valley, covered with tiny houses. To its left was the wall, the Old City wall. Behind it, a street going down.

"That's the stepped street down to the Kotel," Imma would say.

Beside the street was a long, large building with a domed roof.

"There it is! That's our house, Batei Machse!" we would cry, excited anew each time. "Batei Machse! The building is still standing!"

Then we would try to find our apartment. Straining our eyes again, we would count the windows: One, two three ... There it was ... The fourth one, our window! There could be no doubt that that was our wide window, the window where we had spent so much time in our childhood, where we used to sit and watch the people going down the steps to the Kotel.

We could also see the burnt, soot marks on both sides of the window. Was the apartment behind the window also burnt? Or had it survived, like the stone wall, the window, and the dome?

Countless times I would look hard, searching for a face in the window: a man, a woman, or perhaps a child, an Arab child. But no, it was impossible to see a little girl from such a distance.

Again I would strain my eyes, searching for signs of life: perhaps laundry being blown in the wind, blankets hung out to air . . . But I always saw an empty window. And the black soot on the wall strengthened our assumption that no one was living in the house.

"Our house is waiting for us," Naomi would say.

Neither did we ever discern any movement along the narrow street, which had always been filled with throngs of people going down to the Kotel on Shabbat. What interest could the Arabs possibly take in the Kotel?

The Churva could not be seen at all. Why couldn't we see the high, domed roof of the Churva rising above the other buildings? I knew why, but my heart refused to believe it. I knew what had happened. With my own eyes I had seen the furious rabble behind the Legionnaires, the red sky and the sparks flying in all directions. The memory alone made me smell smoke and fire.

Then I would move away from the railing of the lookout tower. Standing to one side, uninterrupted, I would reconstruct the Churva of my childhood in my mind's eye. I had no need even to close my eyes to do so. No. It was so simple to picture Naomi and myself in the synagogue on Friday night, happily singing *Lecha Dodi* along with the congregation, looking up in wonder at the deep, blue ceiling strewn with stars and at the chandeliers with their transparent glass pendants. Yes, it was better to remember it that way.

The years passed and we grew up. No longer did we go for walks with our parents, sisters, and little brother. Now friends took their place. Together we walked, summer or winter, rain or shine, to David's Tomb to pray on Shabbat. The newly paved road to Mount Zion was always crowded.

After services, we still climbed up to the lookout on the roof. Moshe Rabbeinu had ascended to the top of Mount Nevo, hoping and praying that the decree be rescinded, and that he be allowed to enter the Land of Israel.

"From afar you shall see the Land, but you may not enter." Thus spoke the Lord to Moses, and so Moshe Rabbeinu ascended Har Ha'avarim and looked out. From afar, he gazed at the Promised Land, at the Temple Mount.

Mount Zion was our Har Ha'avarim. And we, too, could only look.

72 The Way Back

Long years, nineteen of them, passed. Had time succeeded in lessening the pain?

* * *

It was Monday morning, the 26th of Iyar 5727 (June 5, 1967). We listened to the eight o'clock news:

"Egyptian planes have appeared on the radar screens in the south... they have opened fire... our forces are firing back..."

Before we could digest the news, the sirens began to wail. Again we were down in the bomb shelters, listening to the echoes of the explosions all around and reciting Tehillim.

There was war again, and all at once, the recollections returned. The musty storeroom, the mighty explosions, the terrible destruction. It was happening all over again. At one and the same time, we were being attacked in the south, the north, and the center of the country. Once again our enemies rose up to destroy us.

Twenty-four hours of tension and fear passed before the wonderful news was announced. Hundreds of enemy planes had been destroyed! Our mood improved, but still, we were worried about our soldiers. In the shelters of Jerusalem the sounds of babies crying mixed with those of voices in prayer. Another difficult, fateful day passed. Wednesday afternoon, an excited voice suddenly interrupted the radio program.

"The Western Wall is in our hands! I repeat, The Kotel Hamaaravi is in our hands!"

Was it possible?

We all burst into tears.

The war was over much sooner than we had thought possible, and the results were far beyond our wildest expectations. Huge areas of the Promised Land were restored to us: Hevron, Beit Lechem, Shechem, the Old City of Jerusalem and the Temple Mount. The inheritance of our forefathers was miraculously returned to the Jewish people, and esteem for Israel soared throughout the world.

It was some time before I was capable of going to the Kotel again, even though it was now in our hands. The war was over, but the price we had paid was so very high. So deep and painful was the wound, that at first, I could not fully rejoice at our victory.

Time had to pass before I realized that I must not let the pain and mourning over those who had fallen in any way diminish the magnitude of our gratitude for our miraculous victory. Along with the pain, I began to comprehend that the Six Day War was one more step in the redemption of the Jewish people — a process which was gathering impetus and growing stronger before our very eyes.

Only then was I able to feel joy and give thanks for all that Heaven had granted us. Only then did the desire to visit the liberated Old City and the Kotel overwhelm me.

Together with my husband, Chaim, I got off the bus at the central post office, the closest bus stop to the Old City. Now Jaffa Road was open to its very end. The walls which had blocked the street and separated new and Old Jerusalem were gone.

We walked down Jaffa Road towards an area where Jews had not been allowed to set foot for nineteen years. Before us, we saw the wall of the Old City. How strange it was to be able to come close and touch it! I looked to my right. There were the skeletons of burnt out buildings. Like ghosts, they gazed at me. Some of the doors were sealed with iron; others had wide vacant spaces where doors had once been. They were the remains of the looted stores...

"It's the old shopping center!" I exclaimed.

We walked down a wide street. There, below, was a gate in the wall. My heart began to pound. Jaffa Gate! Could it be? To the right of the gate loomed a fortress and tower — the Tower of David! With great emotion we walked in through the ancient gate. The square between the gate and the *shuk* was teeming with people — just like then, only the human scenery had changed a bit.

We made our way through the crowd. With each step I took, my wonder grew: It was really true — the road was open. We turned right towards the Armenian Quarter and then stopped beside a high wall with sharp pieces of broken glass cemented onto its top ledge. It was still a frightening building, with all those barred windows.

"The Kishle!" I cried, all excited.

"Yes, it's the Kishle. Do you remember it too?" Chaim was surprised.

"Remember? Of course I remember. This was the infamous British prison. How frightened we all were of this place, especially our 'boys' with their illegal weapons."

Soldiers stood at the gate of the terrible jail, but now we approached them fearlessly. No longer were they scowling British soldiers. Now they were *our* soldiers, Israeli soldiers. We walked past the building. Here, where the passageway was narrow, the British used to put up a blockade during the curfew. Again, I felt like a prisoner who had just been freed — believing yet not believing that he could really go wherever he wanted, with no restrictions.

"Savta," I wanted to call out, "come and see! We can simply walk by, on the main road, without showing identity cards or sneaking through side streets!"

But Savta was no longer in this world to hear me, and we continued to walk.

The vaulted road shut out the sunlight. The sudden darkness caused my heart to beat faster, just as it had when I was a little girl taking the 2/a bus home from school. The street gradually widened and opened up to the sun again. The further we walked, the more excited I became. Soon we would reach the turn in the road. Here the old bus used to slow down, scraping the wall of the narrow street as it squeezed through.

A few more steps and there it was — Zion Gate. The gate was now wide open. Trembling, I walked up to it and leaned my head on the stones. I saw a newly scrawled inscription "Shema Yisrael . . . Hear O Israel, the Lord our God, the Lord is one!"

"We left the Old City from here," I whispered hoarsely, seeing in my mind's eye the throngs of people pushing and pulling as they all tried to squeeze through the narrow opening in the blockade. It was a miracle that we had managed to escape with our lives. I stood still and recited the blessing aloud:

"Blessed art Thou . . . Who performed a miracle for me on this spot!"

And Chaim answered, "Amen."

Suddenly, I felt I had to hurry. For such a long time we had had to content ourselves with a view from afar.

"Let's go home," I said, and began to run.

I passed the large Armenian housing complex, and then the Sephardi housing complex and school.

"Here it is! This is the house!" I exclaimed.

"We're here!"

Chaim stood beside me. On our right lay the quiet, peaceful Silwan valley, its small houses surrounded by cacti.

"What an innocent-looking landscape," I said. "The Silwan valley. It's hard to imagine that mortars could ever have been fired from there."

"Let's go inside," Chaim finally said.

There was no longer an iron gate at the entrance to the Deutsche Platz. We walked through the broad, stone archway and turned right, up to the courtyard on the middle story.

"Who lives here?" I asked, noting the brand new pavement in the courtyard. Young voices echoed from the room, the voices of boys learning Torah.

"What is this?" I asked in surprise, "A *beit midrash*?"

"A yeshiva. Yeshivat Hakotel. The rest of the Jewish Quarter is still in ruins. These boys are the *chalutzim*, the first settlers. Rabbi Binah brought them here immediately after the war. They have established a yeshiva here."

We walked down towards the main courtyard. Three square protrusions could still be seen in the ground, reminding me of something. Yes, these were the cisterns, the water cisterns. Down there, at the bottom of those cisterns, were the guns, the last weapons of our fighters. Weren't they rusty by now? I looked for the storeroom at the side of the courtyard which had served as our last shelter. We stood at the entrance to its dark corridor.

"This is where we sat and waited for death," I whispered.

Opposite us, the voices of the boys studying Gemara grew louder. Again I thought of Savta. "Do you hear, Savta?" I wanted to ask her. "Here, in your house, they're learning Gemara again! *Am Yisrael Chai* — The Jewish people lives on!"

My own house had been on the top floor. We went out to look for the stairway, but it was still covered with debris, making it impossible to walk up.

We went out to what had once been our lot. I was stunned at

the sight of the debris and rubble.

"Why, this can't be!" I exclaimed. "We all stood here in the open lot on the day we surrendered. Why is it so full of ruins now?"

The answer, of course, was that the Arabs had continued their destruction even *after* the Quarter fell. They never rebuilt or resettled it. And the few Arab refugee families who moved into the ruins did nothing to improve the site or rebuild.

The whole place looked desolate and lifeless. How cruelly the Arabs vented their anger on the trees and stones! Except for our house, which was virtually undamaged, I could identify nothing. I couldn't tell what had been where, and I had to leave the directing to Chaim. We came to a place that had once been part of a street.

"This is Jewish Quarter Road," Chaim announced, but to me it bore no resemblance to the busy street that I recalled from my childhood.

"Here is the entrance to the Churva," he said, pointing to an opening in a wall. We walked in and found ourselves standing in a courtyard on the side of which were some small buildings. Walking down two large, ancient-looking stone stairs, we came into a wide, empty, open space.

"We are 'inside' the Churva!" Chaim announced, beaming with joy.

But I collapsed on the stairway, too stunned to speak. I looked all around me, but could find no sign of the magnificent synagogue of my childhood. Finally, I replied, "I'm afraid that you're mistaken."

"Not at all. I'm not mistaken. Look, over there is the eastern wall with its niche for the *aron*, and this is the *bima*. The debris covering the floor has already been cleared away and the floor uncovered. Look at it."

I bent down to the ground. Under the dust, the white marble flooring shone out.

"Yes, this really is the floor of the Churva," I answered sadly.

I gazed at the stump of the shattered *bima* — the marble *bima* — and hid my face in my hands. This, then, was indeed the Churva. This was all that was left of that grand synagogue: the magnificent Holy Ark, the decorated walls, the stained-glass windows, the star-shaped dome, the chandeliers — all, all in ruins!

I don't recall how long I sat there. Suddenly I heard the sound of a donkey braying from the building in the courtyard. Startled, I stood up and looked inside. Two donkeys were there, chewing on straw, heaps of dung strewn all over. The sight of them released the tears that had been choking me all this time. And once released, they poured down my cheeks in a torrent.

Chaim stood beside me, his face still radiant with joy.

"How can you smile so?" I accused him.

"How can you cry?"

"Our magnificent synagogue, our holy house of prayer, has been turned into a stable! How can I not cry?"

"Have you forgotten the story from the Gemara?" he asked. "After the destruction of the Holy Temple, Rabbi Akiva and his colleagues went up to Jerusalem. When they reached the Temple Mount, they saw a fox walking out of the site of the Holy of Holies. All the other Sages began to cry, but Rabbi Akiva began to laugh. The Sages asked him, 'Why are you laughing?' and he asked them, 'And why are you crying?' They answered, 'In the Torah it is written regarding the Holy of Holies — If anyone who is not a priest enters, he shall die! But now foxes frequent the site! How can we not cry?'

"Rabbi Akiva answered, 'And that is precisely why I laugh! Now I am sure that just as the prophecy of destruction has been fulfilled, so shall the prophecy of redemption and the rebuilding of Jerusalem and of our Holy Temple be fulfilled.'

"You cry, but I am happy. I am happy that the Churva was not turned into a church or a mosque. I'm happy that, aside from a few refugee families, the Arabs did not resettle or rebuild the Jewish Quarter. They must have known in their hearts that we would come back."

"Yes," I agreed, a bit encouraged, "now we can rebuild the Churva undisturbed."

"Now we shall rebuild the entire Jewish Quarter, including the Churva. Just as the prophecies of destruction were fulfilled, so shall all the prophecies of rebuilding Jerusalem come true."

Slowly I stood up and went over to kiss the marble stones of the *bima*. Then we made our way towards the Kotel. Again we walked out towards the road going downhill. Only then did I notice that the stepped street had disappeared, and a steep, narrow asphalt road had taken its place. With light steps we walked down the road. I felt as if all this were happening in a dream. Soon I would see the Wall again. "Shir Hamaalot... when God will return the remnant of Zion, we will be as in a dream..." The psalm of King David seemed to sing itself.

Finally, I was standing before the Kotel. How very different it was now from the Wall I remembered! I was standing in a spacious open plaza, comfortably paved with stone. The Wall before my eyes was much, much wider than that tall, narrow section of the Wall which had formerly been exposed to our eyes, squeezed in between Arab houses. All those houses, which had been built onto both sides of the Wall and had always seemed to threaten to suffocate us, had disappeared.

A large crowd of men, women, and children filled the plaza. The great variety amazed me. Religious and non-religious, Sephardi and Ashkenazi, new immigrants and old-timers. The entire Jewish people!

Chaim went to the men's half while I went towards the women's section. I walked up close to the Kotel, laid my arm on the stones and kissed them. I closed my eyes.

There are those who cry at such a meeting with the Kotel, but I did not. Instead, I experienced a feeling I had never known before, a spiritual joy, a closeness to God. It filled me and permeated my whole being. I felt that the joy within me was flowing over and out, from me to the others, and from them back to me.

I did not cry, for I knew that this was no longer the Wailing Wall. The Wailing Wall — remnant of the destruction of our Beit Hamikdash — had become a place of joy and of redemption.

I opened my eyes and stood looking at the women nearby. Some were praying out loud, their bodies swaying; others prayed so quietly that only their lips moved, but no sound could be heard.

Those who were familiar with the prayers recited long passages from their *siddur*, while others simply whispered a request. Some had never in their lives uttered a formal prayer, but their hearts, their hearts spoke wordlessly. Still others did not pray at all; they simply walked up to the Wall and silently put a small note into one of the cracks in the ancient stones.

From all directions came the sound of prayer — prayers in all versions, uttered in countless accents, sung to different tunes. Here at the Wall, the Jewish people were one, united, whole. Here all were equal.

Then I looked at the Wall itself. I looked down at the bottom layers, at the huge, ancient, cracked stones, and then up at the stones above. The higher the stones, the smaller and denser they became, until finally, they merged with the blue domed sky. There, up above, was the gateway to Heaven through which all our prayers could once more ascend.

I stood there for a long time, one small piece of that great whole — part of a holy people. My lips whispered a prayer, the same prayer we had recited at home during the war and when in danger, "And to Jerusalem, Your city, return in compassion..."

And then another prayer, one of my own making, found its way to my lips:

"Please God, may it be Thy will to rebuild our ancient city from these heaps of dust; to rebuild the Churva and the other houses of learning and prayer from these charred stones; to rebuild the third and final Temple from this lone Wall. And may this new and perfect structure, be ours eternally, an everlasting home for *Am Yisrael.*"

The Author's Father:
Harav Shlomo Min Hahar (Bergman)

Harav Shlomo Min Hahar, father of the author and one of the leading figures in *Forever My Jerusalem*, is a beloved and familiar figure in Yerushalayim.

A fifth-generation Jerusalemite, he is a descendant of Rabbi Eliezer Bergman of blessed memory, the first German Jew to actually make his home in the Holy City together with his wife and children, in 1835. (Until then, most Ashkenazi Jews came to Jerusalem only towards the end of their lives.)

The name Min Hahar is a translation into Hebrew of the German name Bergman — man from the mountain.

Rabbi Bergman was a *talmid chacham*, a businessman, and a public figure who contributed greatly to the flowering of the Ashkenazi Jewish community in Jerusalem in the nineteenth century. He was one of the founders of the Holland Deutschland Kollel and of Batei Machse, one of the first "modern" housing projects in the Old City.

His descendants followed in his footsteps — both as *talmidei chachamim* and as men of action. Reb Nachum, his grandson, was one of the founders of Me'ah She'arim. A true pioneering effort of that time, Me'ah She'arim was the largest of the first suburbs built outside of the Old City walls.

Harav Min Hahar was born in the Old City of Jerusalem in 1911. Because of the extremely difficult economic conditions prevalent at that time, his father, Rav Chaim Yehuda Bergman, went abroad temporarily, leaving his family — including little Shlomo — behind in Jerusalem. When World War I suddenly broke out, he found himself stranded in Germany, unable to return home. He was appointed to the post of *dayan* (rabbinical court judge) in Nuremberg, and after the war ended, his family joined him.

The young Shlomo studied in a German elementary school and then went on to Lithuania to further his Torah studies. He studied in Kelm, Ponievezh, Telshe and Mir for ten years, and received his *semicha* at Mir from Harav Eliezer Yehuda Finkel. Just before World War II broke out, the Bergman family managed to return to Eretz Yisrael. They settled first in the village of Neve Yaakov just north of Jerusalem, and then returned to Batei Machse in the Old City, where Shlomo studied in a teachers' seminary for a year and then joined the Hagana.

He married Matilda Agasi and began his teaching career in Yesod Hamaaleh, a small village in the Hula valley. A year later, he and his family moved to Sedei Yaakov, a settlement in the Jezreel valley, where he served both as rabbi and teacher. In 1945, after his father's death, he returned to Jerusalem with his wife and three daughters. Another daughter and a son were born in the Old City, and the youngest daughter was born in Katamon, after the war.

During the difficult years of 1945-1948, when the Min Hahar family lived in the Old City, Harav Min Hahar worked as a teacher. Appointed a member of the committee in charge of the Jewish Quarter, he acted as intermediary between the residents and the military establishment. When the head of the committee, Rabbi Orenstein, was killed, Harav Min Hahar took his place.

After the surrender, he was taken to Trans-Jordan with the other Old City captives as a prisoner of war. He served as the *muchtar* (community head), representing the Jewish prisoners of the Old City to the Arab Legion until his release over nine months later. Meanwhile, his family, together with the other refugees from the Old City, had moved to Katamon, where they were to live for the next twelve years.

Once home, Harav Min Hahar continued teaching until 1960, when he was appointed by the Jerusalem Religious Council to the position of *rav* in the neighborhood of Bayit Vegan. For over twenty years he faithfully served the people of Bayit Vegan through peace and war, through good times and bad. Today he remains active in the field of education as well as in his community, teaching young and old alike, and answering dozens of halachic queries daily. With hundreds of former students and disciples, Harav Min Hahar is known and respected as an authoritative *posek* and *talmid chacham*, and is a source of comfort, strength and wisdom to those who seek him. May God grant him and his wife many more long and fruitful years.

GLOSSARY

*(The terms that follow are defined as they are used in this book.
Plural forms appear in parentheses.)*

ABBA: father

AFIKOMEN: the middle of the three *matzot* used during the Passover
seder, half of which is hidden, then eaten at the conclusion of the
meal

AM YISRAEL: the Jewish people

ARON KODESH: the Holy Ark used to house the Torah scrolls

BARUCH DAYAN HA'EMET: "Blessed is the true Judge": said upon hearing
tragic news

BARUCH HASHEM: thank God

BEIT HAMIKDASH: the Holy Temple in Jerusalem

BEIT KNESSET: synagogue

BEIT MIDRASH: Torah study room in a yeshiva or synagogue

BEREISHIT: Book of Genesis

BIMA: platform in a synagogue, from which the Torah scroll is read

BIRKAT HAMAZON: grace after meals

BOBBA: (Yiddish) grandmother

BRACHA: blessing

BRIT MILA: circumcision, performed on a male Jewish child on the
eighth day after birth

CHALLA (CHALLOT): special white bread for the Sabbath

CHALUTZ (CHALUTZIM): pioneer

CHAMSIN: a period of unusually high temperatures in the Middle East,
caused by a hot, dry air mass

CHANUKA: the holiday commemorating the rededication of the Second
Temple

CHEDER: school for young boys

CHUMASH: the Five Books of Moses

CHUTZPA: nerve; audacity

ERETZ YISRAEL: the land of Israel

EREV ROSH HASHANA: the day before the Jewish New Year

EREV SHABBAT: the day before the Sabbath

ETROG (ETROGIM): citron, one of the four species used on Succot

GABBAI: official in charge of supervisory duties in the synagogue

GEMARA: the Talmud

GERRER CHASSIDIM: followers of the dynasty of rabbis originating in Gur, Poland

HAGGADA (HAGGADOT): the story of the Jews' redemption from Egypt, read on Passover during the *seder*

HALLEL: a prayer of praise to God

HASHEM: God

HATOV VEHAMEITIV: "God is good and does good": blessing recited on joyful occasions that are shared by two or more people

IMMA, IMMALE: mother

IYAR: the eighth month of the Jewish year

KAPPARA: atonement

KASHER: to make kitchen utensils suitable for the preparation of kosher food, either by immersing them in boiling water or heating them to high temperatures

KISLEV: the third month of the Jewish year

KOTEL HAMAARAVI: the Western Wall

LAG BA'OMER: the holiday of the 33rd day of the Omer; bonfires customarily are lit at night

LULAV: palm branch, one of the four species used on Succot

MAAPILIM: illegal Jewish immigrants

MACHZOR: a special prayer book for the holidays

MASHIACH: the Messiah

MATZA (MATZOT): unleavened bread, eaten during Passover

MAZAL TOV: congratulations

MECHITZA: partition dividing the men's and women's sections of the synagogue

MEZUZA (MEZUZOT): a handwritten parchment containing special sections of the Torah and placed, rolled up, on the doorposts of Jewish homes

MINCHA: the afternoon prayer

MITZVA: commandment

NISSAN: the seventh month of the Jewish year

OMER: an offering of barley from the spring harvest, brought to the Holy Temple in Jerusalem on the second day of Passover; the period of counting between the Festival of Passover and the Festival of Weeks

PAROCHET: the curtain covering the ark where the Torah scrolls are kept

PESACH: Passover, the festival of freedom from slavery in Egypt

PEYOT: earlocks worn by some Orthodox Jews for ritual reasons

PITTA (PITTOT): a round, flat bread that can be opened and filled with salad, meat, or other foods

RAV: rabbi

ROSH HASHANA: the Jewish New Year

S'CHACH: branches and leaves that form the roof of the *succa*

SEDER: reading the *haggada* and eating the ceremonial meal on the first night of Passover in Israel (the first two nights in countries outside Israel)

SHABBAT: the Sabbath

SHEHECHEYANU: blessing recited for new things and special occasions

SHEKET: quiet

SHEMA: the declaration of Jewish faith said twice daily and before going to sleep

SHOFAR: ram's horn, sounded on the Jewish New Year and special occasions

SHTIBEL: (Yiddish) small synagogue

SHUK: marketplace

SHUL: (Yiddish) synagogue

SIDDUR (SIDDURIM): prayer book

SIMCHAT TORAH: the Festival of Rejoicing over the Torah

SUCCA: the temporary hut lived in during the Festival of Succot

SUCCOT: the Festival of Tabernacles

TALLIT: prayer shawl

TALMID CHACHAM (TALMIDEI CHACHAMIM): Torah scholar

TALMUD TORAH: school for children

TANACH: the Holy Scriptures

TEFILLIN: two small leather boxes with straps, containing passages from the Torah, worn on the head and on the arm during the morning prayers

TEHILLIM: Psalms

TISHREI: the first month of the Jewish year

YAMIM NORAIM: the ten days between Rosh Hashana and Yom Kippur, devoted to prayer and repentance

YESHIVA: academy for Torah study

YOM KIPPUR: the Day of Repentance

ZEIDEH: (Yiddish) grandfather

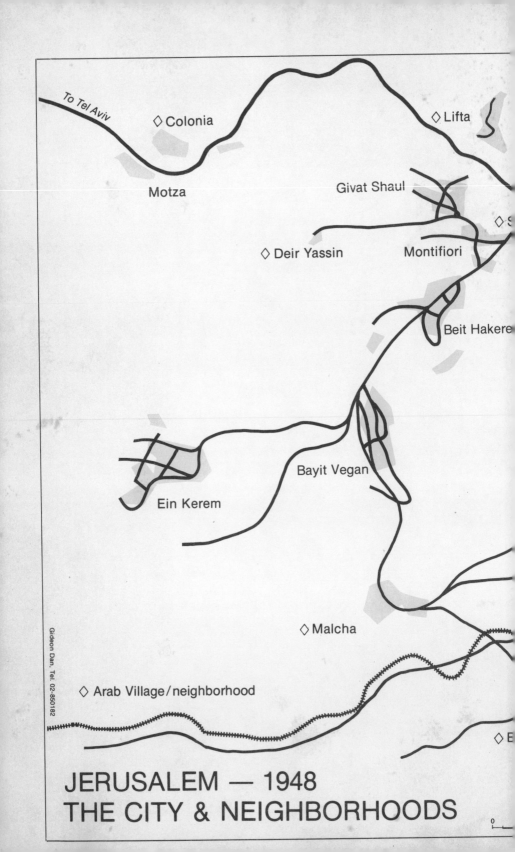

To Tel Aviv

◇ Colonia

◇ Lifta

Motza

Givat Shaul

◇ Deir Yassin

Montifiori

◇ S

Beit Hakere

Bayit Vegan

Ein Kerem

Malcha

◇ Arab Village/neighborhood

◇ E

Gideon Dan. Tel. 02-850182

0

JERUSALEM — 1948
THE CITY & NEIGHBORHOODS

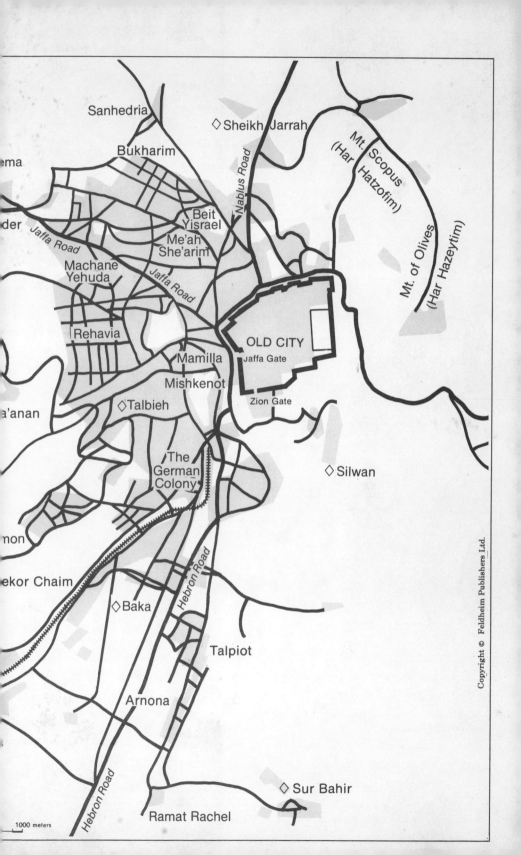

Sanhedria

◇ Sheikh Jarrah

Mt. Scopus
(Har Hatzofim)

Bukharim

ema

Nablus Road

der

Jaffa Road

Beit
Yisrael

Mt. of Olives
(Har Hazeytim)

Me'ah
She'arim

Machane
Yehuda

Jaffa Road

Rehavia

OLD CITY

Jaffa Gate

Mamilla

Mishkenot

a'anan

◇Talbieh

Zion Gate

◇ Silwan

The
German
Colony

non

Hebron Road

ekor Chaim

◇ Baka

Talpiot

Arnona

Hebron Road

◇ Sur Bahir

1000 meters

Ramat Rachel